THE INTELLIGENCE AGENTS

By Timothy Leary, Ph.D.

— To Barbara —

The Intelligence Agents

by Timothy Leary, PhD

RONIN Publishing
Berkeley, California
roninpub.com

INTELLIGENCE AGENTS

Copyright 1979 by Timothy Leary, PhD
ISBN: 978-1-57951-148-7

Published by
Ronin Publishing, Inc.
PO Box 3008
Oakland, CA 94609
www.roninpub.com

Peace Press edition: 1979
New Falcon edition: 1996
Ronin Edition: 2014

Cover by Brian Groppe bgdesign09@gmail.com

Library of Congress Card Number: 2014932901
Distributed to the book trade by PGW/Perseus

PUBLISHER'S DISCLAIMER

This is a work of social, moral, religious and scientific satire, set in the Future. Pieces attributed to others (except the newspaper items acknowledged below) are parodies by the author. This work does not intend to malign any individual, race, organization or religion. It does intend to entertain the reader while increasing hir intelligence.

ACKNOWLEDGMENTS

The Boston Globe for "CIA Funded Research by Opponent of Leary", by Al Larkin, September 1, 1977; Robert Clark for the unique charts and maps throughout the book; Mrs. Yvonne Halsman for the photograph of Marilyn Monroe, Copyright © by Philippe Halsman; Los Angeles Times for "British Fans Put Sock Into Soccer", by William Tuohy, 1978; San Francisco Chronicle for "Writers Petition Swiss To Give Asylum To Leary", by Donovan Bess, July, 14; The Viking Press for the cover of *Gravity's Rainbow* by Thomas Pynchon; Julian Watkins for the many illustrations from *The 100 Greatest Advertisements*, Dover Publications, Inc. 1959.

The Intelligence Agents is volume FIVE, and final, of the Future History Series.

TRANSMISSIONS

TRANSMISSIONS

PUBLISHER'S NOTES

This document illustrates the Standard Reality Fabrication Tactics used by Intelligence Agents assigned to nursery planets mutating from Stage 12 (Centralized New-Deal Insectoid Socialism) to Stage 13 (Neurosomatic Self-Discovery).

The womb-planet in question, called Terra I or Sol-3, presented no unusual genetic problems to Local Evolutionary Agents (whose Network was called the Out-Castes). Metamorphosis from terrestrial apehood to post-terrestrial status occurred in routine fashion.

Commodore Leri, the Out-Caste Agent who serves as quest-editor for this manual, is better known to galactic soap opera fans for his later work in High Energy Fusion in the Sagittarius Sector. *The Intelligence Agents* is a collection of 20th century documents which has enjoyed considerable popularity throughout the galaxy because of its Juvenile Charm. It is a classic portrait of a group of fledgling Agents, just graduated from Cadet status, facing their first mutational duty.

The Out-Castes began their work at the exact time (1946 A.D.) when life on Terra I was ready to molt from terrestrial to post-terrestrial status, from planet to Plan-It. Using textbook practices, the Out-Caste Network sent novice Agent Leri to the most influential Pupal-training center of the Dom-Species (Harvard University) where he was to set in motion a Stage 13 Self-Discovery (Hedonic Self-Indulgence) movement. Within ten years, over 35 million primates in the most advanced country (America) had renounced politics and were enthusiastically experimenting with self-induced brain-washing, neural rewards and socio-sexual-role changes.

After this success (1970) most members of the Out-Caste Network understandingly requested Re-Creational leave to enjoy the new Ecological Niche satisfactions. Subsequent scans of the planet produced too few Alien Intelligence Increase Agents willing and able to join the next phase of the Intelligence Increase (I^2) work. Leri reluctantly agreed to join the next network of Out-Castes (fronted by Governor Jerry Brown and Larry Flynt) who were charged with the mission of moving the Self-Actualization Stage 14 (1970-1975) from Pre-Dom[1] to Hive Domination. Leri then, in 1976, volunteered for duty in the Pre-Dom[2] Space Migration Wave (Stage 15), realistically assuming that the best way to get himself and his gene-pool off the heavy, one-G womb-planet to a multiple-G custom-made Plan-It

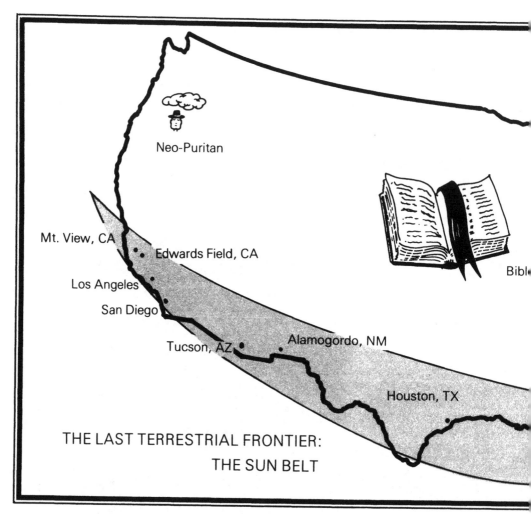

Neo-Puritan

Mt. View, CA

Edwards Field, CA

Los Angeles

San Diego

Tucson, AZ

Alamogordo, NM

Houston, TX

Bibl

THE LAST TERRESTRIAL FRONTIER:
THE SUN BELT

was to stimulate the Space Colonization movement.

Recall that in 1970, Space Consciousness was almost non-existent and even the most advanced primates continued passively to hope for release through some terrestrial reform — political, religious, or cultural. In order to get the signal to those who would be activated by it, it was necessary for the Out-Caste Network to Dramatically Scandalize and Alienate (i.e., polarize) Every Hive Social System on the planet by using Leri as one of the Neural Probes.*

Leri's tactic of graceful, serial-social Alienation first put him in Galactic Headlines. With help from his friends, he managed to remain controversial for over two decades!

It must be remembered that other Out-Caste operatives were working with other futiquecastes. Gerard O'Neill, Brian O'Leary and Peter Vajk with scientists. Olin Teague, Barry Goldwater, Harrison Schmitt, and Barbara Mikulski with Eastern politicians. Jerry Brown with Western politicos. Barbara Marx Hubbard with Middle-of-the-Road intellectuals. Robert Anton Wilson with sophisticated occultists. Alan Harrington with the literate elite. F.M. Esfandiary with scientific aristocrats. Pauline Kael with cinema adepts. Don Simpson, Robert Stigwood, Kevin McCormick and Henry Edwards with film-makers. Andy Warhol and Susan Kaiser with artists. Roy Walford with biologists.

Many of these documents were transcribed from a live, oral presentation before 2,500 persons in Tucson, Arizona, 1977. This lecture transcript illustrates the techniques Leri employed to shock, stimulate, and electrify

*The word *scandal* must be understood by agents assigned to womb planets. The classic hive definition of *scandal* is: 1. any act that offends the morality of the social community; a public disgrace. 2. shame or outrage (i.e., rage directed against an outcaste). 3. damage to reputation or character caused by offensive or grossly improper behavior. A shock to hive morality, thus the basic instrument for evolution.

6

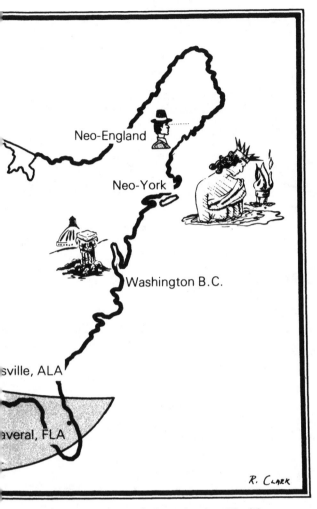

Neo-England

Neo-York

Washington B.C.

sville, ALA

averal, FLA

R. CLARK

Domesticated Apes in the 15—25 year age bracket.

Students of Primitive Terrestrial Folklore will remember that Tucson, Arizona was, in 1977, center of the Sun Belt (delightful term). The Sun Belt encompassed a crescent of Migra - ting Higher Intelligence that stretched from Mountain View, California at the Northwest; through Southern California, Arizona and New Mexico; to Cape Canaveral, Florida at the Southeast.

During the ten years preceding this lecture, a great neuro-genetic migration occurred. Pro- pelled by DNA imperatives, gene-pools in the Southwest expelled their most aggressive- political agents to the Northeast — especially New York, Boston, Chicago, Washington — while the Snow Belt gene-pools were sending their more intelligent probes to the Southwest Frontier. This incredible exchange of gene- castes occurred with no blood-shed, indeed, with no public awareness and was one of the great migratory feats in terrestrial history.

The Out-Castes, as robot-wired evolutionary surfers, were riding a demographic western wave of intelligence.

Other parts of this document were originally taped by suspicious and fascinated Counter- Intelligence Agents in Switzerland (1971—72) where the Commodore was enjoying Re- Creation Leave.

Switzerland was at that time the center of Old World genetic (sperm-egg) Traffic, a tiny mountain principality loaded with Intelligence Brokers and Chromosome Dealers. It was Zurich for money and industrial espionage. Basel for drugs. Geneva for documentation. Al- pine ski-resorts for gene brokerage and Sexual Selection. Switzerland was, in short, an Al- chemical Mating Ground, an Energy Market, a flight-School in which High Altitude Wheelers matriculated to establish Out-Caste Alumni Associations.

Aristocratic families in the Old World sent their children to Swiss schools to learn the prin- ciples of Inter-erotic Diplomacy. The most elite, endowed adolescent genitals were shipped off to Alpine Academies to be initiated into the network of Intelligence Intercourse. Stage 10 Feudal Marriage Linkage was still being im- printed on Aristocratic European and Asian brains. The Stage 11 Tactic of improving the gene-pool was to contribute young English and American sperm-egg carriers whose wealth and socially-mobile vigor were welcomed by the jaded Continentals.

For those reasons the presence of a Self- Professed Alien Intelligence Agent from the Future in this small antique country provoked enormous interest. Fortunately for our histori- cal archives, every action and conversation of the Commodore was recorded by Counter- Intelligence operatives. Attempts by the Firm to drive him out of this mountain retreat were consistently foiled by aristocratic young Out- Castes.

The reader of this manual will also find vari- ous training memos, tutorial signals, bumper stickers, graffiti and advertisements, issued by the Out-Castes during this volatile mutational period.

Earthlings, at the time these events were emerging, had no concept of gene-pools and Castes-as-Evolutionary-Stages. Much of the hostility and resistance Out-Caste Agents faced in these circumstances was caused by the Reluc- tance of terrestrials to understand that they were genetic-robots thrown headlong into an acceler- ated mutation process which jumbled together millions of competing gene-pools and several different species. Each individual innocently assumed that all others with human forms were wired the same way. Agents preparing for mutational duties on planets during the Period-Before-Space-Migration will be interested to know that the signals described in this manual were being violently reacted-to by Swarms of humans possessing the following Brain Stages: Paleolithic, Neolithic, Priest-technological, Feudal, Republican, Stalinist, Hedonic-consumer, Self-actualized!

Gene-pools tend to become aggressively agitated by genetic perspectives, sensing that evolution is passing them by. Agents, therefore, are required to move swiftly, leaving vapor trails deliberately designed to appear harmlessly flakey to Behind-Time Species, while at the same time instructive to and supportive of A-Head-Time Futiques.

For background to this manual, Evolutionary Agents are referred to the three preceding future-history texts: *Exo-Psychology*, *Neuropolitics*, and the classic-galactic romance, *What Does WoMan Want?*

The guest-editor must mention that the presence, in the Tucson audience, of Carolyn and Keith Henson (the Evolutionary Agents who made Space Migration possible) contributed to the Electricity of the Occasion.

His Excellency, Nov Nuarb
Dean, Evolutionary Agent Academy
Genetic Intelligence Agency Headquarters
Galaxy Central, 2077 A.D.

LETTER TO THE EDITOR

Like many of your readers I have been distressed by recent articles in the Times about the Mid-Eastern-South-African-North-Ireland wars.

Like most of your readers, I too, was born a bigoted racist. Until age 10 I believed that only those in my gene-pool (members of the Irish-Catholic Church, as distinguished from Italian Catholic, French Catholic, Polish Catholic, Greek Catholic and Protestant) were social equals.

On the basis of subsequent personal experience I have worked out some tentative, less-distressing solutions to racial-caste-class-national-origin competitions.

How about if every gene-pool were twenty-five percent Jewish? If you are more than fifty percent Jewish cool it! You can qualify to be more than twenty-five percent Jewish if you are to that extent happy!

How about if every gene pool contained twenty-five percent Black? To qualify to be more than one-quarter Black you have to be to that extent more square!

How about if every gene-pool was twenty-five percent Latin? For every percentage point more Latin you gotta become more Gay!

And surely everyone can handle being twenty-five percent Protestant. But for every percentage point more Protestant you should be more funny!

It wouldn't hurt if every gene-pool were ten percent Irish. But for every percentage point more Irish you should be more sexy.

Larry Flynt

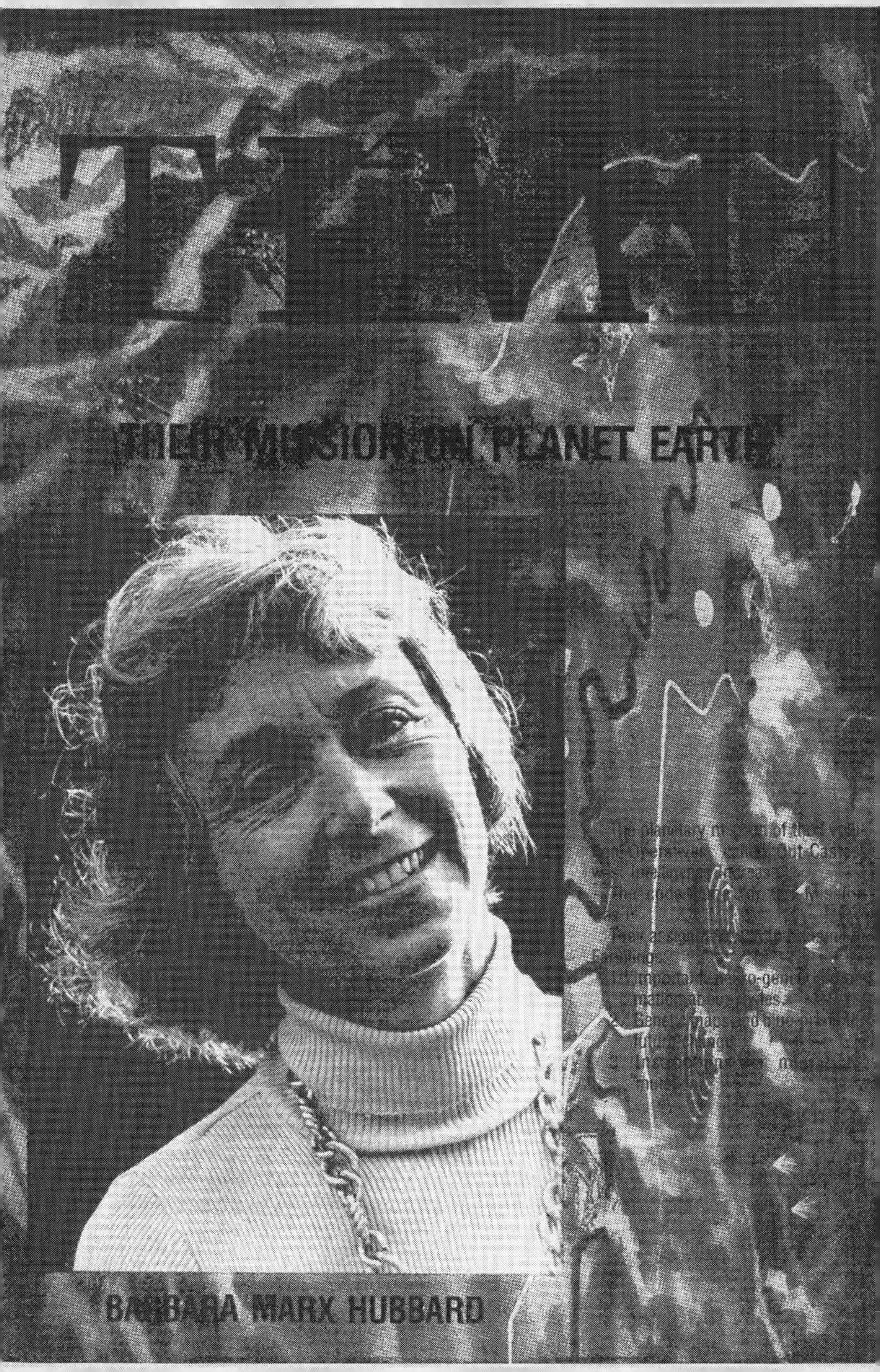
THEIR MISSION ON PLANET EARTH
BARBARA MARX HUBBARD

THE INTELLIGENCE DIRECTOR

Even when he is in mufti, his alert
post-terrestrial bearing is obvious.
And as he passes Hedonic Agents in
the Genetic Intelligence Agency's spacious corridors, they
often salute automatically. When he descends from his
seventh-floor office in a private, key-operated elevator and
steps into his sedan, the chauffeur calls him "Admiral" rather
than "Director." Jerry Brown likes it that way. After 34 years
aloft in pleasure craft he is all S.M.I²L.E.'s.

"Thirty years ago," as his predecessor, Director Turner said,
"America was handsdown the predominant military power, a
totally independent economic power, the dominant power in
the political sphere. Today Americans aren't predominant to
that degree or anything like it. That's good because it means
Americans have to become more intelligent."

COUNTER-INTELLIGENCE AGENCY REPORT

Date: December, 1971

Country: Montana-Crans, Switzerland

Classification:

Subject: THE FUGITIVE PHILOSOPHER

We have located Timothy Leary still disguised as Fugitive Philosopher scrimping along on Five Brains in the Swiss Alps. He has been extended political asylum and apparently is in the dormant phase of Stage 16. Aimlessly spinning gears waiting for Her to appear. His 6th Circuit is uncontrolled and his broadcast-energies are low. The Fugitive is the uneasy guest of the local Earthlings called Valaisans, who attribute their difference from other Swiss to laundered descendence from Carthaginians who had passed along the great Rhone History Highway which runs from Geneva to San Bernardo. The Professor is unaware that his landlords are milk-fed pink-cheeked Arabs and that his host and partner, Michel Hauchard, is our long-time agent.

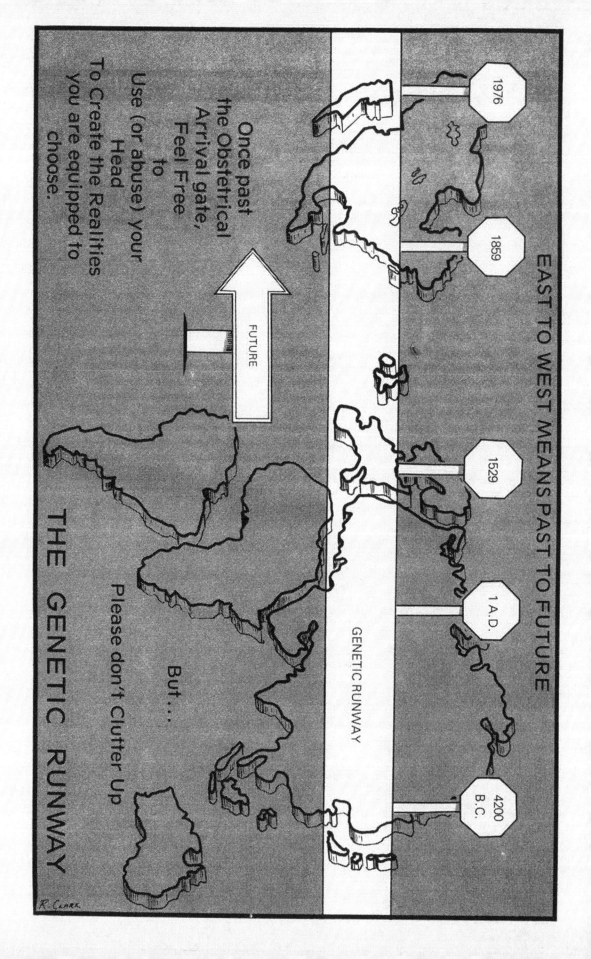

They are Time Travellers, literally walking around
in past civilizations.

THE OUT-CASTES

by Frank Herbert

Frank Herbert was the greatest writer of the 20th century, and, in the opinion of many, the most intelligent writer born on planet Earth.

Herbert was the first author to write convincingly with predictive accuracy about Higher Intelligence. His books, written in the primitive savagery of the mid 20th century, were peopled by advanced mutants. Superior intellects. It is of interest that the wisest and smartest of his futique heroes were women.

Herbert was, along with Walt Disney and Luther Burbank, a fully developed Stage 20 Neurogenetic brain. His descriptions of the Bene Gesserit Sisterhood, executing gene-pool designs over centuries, is the most impressive and uncanny prediction of a future which was nine mutations ahead of the society he inhabited in the 1960's.

In pre-selected human beings, from each gene-pool, neural circuits have been activated (usually without their awareness) which are designed to fabricate future realities. Future gene-pools.

These individuals are genetically templated to live much of the time in the future. They are, to this extent, alienated from current hive realities.

Some agents who are unaware of their genetic assignment feel agonizingly *out of step*. Some are shunned and even locked up by the gene-pools they serve.

Those who are lucky enough to recognize their post-human genetic caste attain a level of great prescience and humorous insight. They understand that they are Time Travellers, literally walking around in past civilizations. A most entertaining and effective role to play. While they have little power to change the ripples of history or the waves of evolution — they can surf them with increasing skill.

Such evolutionary agents are best described as OUT-CASTES. They are cast out, thrown forward, pushed up, above and beyond, contemporary hive realities.

As evolution accelerates there are more and more Evolutionary Agents emerging. In the 1960's it was probably true that every gene-pool cast out its futique agents. We are now learning to identify these OUT-CASTES and benefit from their contribution to the species.

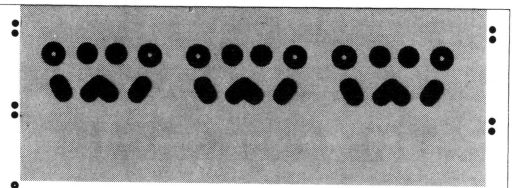

TO:	Genetic Intelligence Agency
FROM:	Agent I^2 at Terra I, Sol-3, Dom-Species approaching Stage 13.

AGENT: The emergence of Hedonic Self-oriented Consumerism as Dom-Species is now projected for 1976, local time.

CENTRAL: Well done.

AGENT: What's next?

CENTRAL: Your next mission is to popularize Space Migration from the Womb Planet. The Network you will join is becoming visible.

AGENT: I assume that I'm to take an In-sanity, Re-Creation Leave until the next move?

CENTRAL: S'i vous plait.

AGENT: How do I get from Switzerland back to the Sun Belt?

CENTRAL: The style you use in provoking your kidnapping, and re-immigration is your own neurological style-choice. The hive will figure out some way to bring you back. We'll watch with amusement.

53:26/WHST
GIACENT

TUCSON LECTURE

"IT'S LEGAL TO S.M.I².L.E. AGAIN"

I'm very happy to be *free* to be here tonight *(applause)*. Had a slight delay getting here, like seven years. I got involved in a little contest in the 1960's. A minor thing, just a simple Genetic Super-bowl competition for the consciousness of a small planet. East versus West. Past versus Future. Washington Senators versus the California Angels. As High Scorer for the Angels I got put in the penalty box for four years. *(Laughter)*

Since my release in April, 1976, I've traveled extensively around the country checking on the intelligence quotient of America. I've a few hot items to report back to you. Number one, there's a Good Feeling running rampant in this country. My informants report a feeling of gentleness, an expectation of change, an hedonic hope reminiscent in many ways of those tender years in the early sixties. You know, just five years ago if you smiled a lot you were in danger of being busted on suspicion. Today it is legal, my fellow Americans, to smile once again. *(Applause)*

The prohibition against New Ideas has been repealed so I think we can get together here tonight and see what further agitation we can stir up.

Here's the second item. My Intelligence

... this country
has been taken over
by successful
Heads of the sixties.

Agents report that this country has been taken over by successful Heads of the sixties. *(Applause)* The articulate young women and men who ten years ago were forced by our government into positions of dissent and protest have dropped back in. Today, they are managing, directing and taking responsibility for affairs in this country. This bloodless coup, this quiet revolution is no surprise. The 70's have developed just as we hoped and planned. The giant Neuropolitical Experiment started at Harvard in 1960 was a success! From Cambridge and Millbrook headquarters our intelligence operatives charted the genetic flow of history and predicted, in 1968, a temporary ebb-tide reaction to the incredible explosion of neurological activation that occurred in the sixties. I remember very clearly in 1968 when we punched into our Out-Caste computer the Gallup finding that 75% of Harvard law students were smoking grass. *(Applause)* The computer read out the prediction: "Your legal problems will be over in ten years." *(Laughter)*

There were other predictive statistics from that period. The same Gallup poll reported that

75% of pre-medical students were smoking grass. Thus, we now have a new generation of young doctors sensitized to the beauty of childbirth; physicians who understand that pregnancy is not a disease to be terminated by an obstetrical operation. Similar changes are transforming other professions. Even the dismal/exciting trade of law enforcement is being taken over by young women and men who lived through the explosive sixties and cultivated a new sense of human relativity. We have a new breed of turned-on cops. *(Applause and laughter)* The 1968 Gallup poll also reported that 65% of the science and engineering students at MIT, Cal-tech, and RPI were smoking grass. Thus, for the first time, we have a new generation of young scientists who have experienced in their own nervous systems the genetic, biological and physical energies they study in the laboratories.

POLLUTION

OVERPOPULATION

DECREASING NEARBY ENERGY RESOURCES

NEWLY ACTIVATED MOBILITY TECHNOLOGY

MIGRATION SUPPLANTING WARFARE AS EXPANSION DEVICE

THE SIGNS OF
A SPECIES
PREPARING
TO MUTATE TO
A HIGHER STAGE
OF INTELLIGENCE

Reprinted from NATIONAL INQUIRY, May 1984

I²: The Parable of the Informer

by Jim McPherson

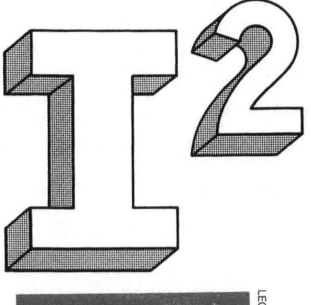

LEON TRICE

James McPherson has enlivened trillions of nervous systems in this galaxy as the mythic image of chivalrous idealism and rakish gallantry.

Jim McPherson's Evolutionary Agentry was geared for rescue. On planet-after-planet he set up base camps — from which he would sally forth whenever a Time-Traveler was trapped in local hive webs. McPherson's protean ability and master hive-bureaucratic skills and his ability to use the local taboos to free Out-Castes made him a galactic TV hero. He is also famous for his textbook Intel-Legal Tips, the classic field guide for Evolutionary Agents throughout the galaxy.

James McPherson, it should be noted, won the Solar-system award for Best Husband three times — 1983, 1998, and 2042.

I n July 1974 an Intelligence Agent posing as a cashiered psychologist, was brought in handcuffs to Terminal Island, a Federal prison, and placed in the "hole." The hole was the name of the punishment cell-block.

When he protested he was told that he was being kept off the main-line because his sentence (ten years for the possession of a half-ounce of marijuana) was too lengthy for a medium-security prison.

He was then visited by a notorious hardass Federal agent, who made the following statement: "If you double-cross me I'll have you put on the main-line of a Federal Prison with the jacket of a snitch. Do you know what that means?"

I² indicated that he understood the threat.

He was actually in prison for acting as an "informer." An informer is one who communicates facts which someone else (usually a bureaucrat) does not want communicated. He had publicized information about human intelligence which certain espionage agencies and information bureaus wanted to keep secret.

Stuart Bland was one of the most effective evolutionary agents of the 20th century. He was first activated to mutant status by ingesting LSD with the Merry Pranksters in 1964 — during which Vulnerability he was exposed to the first picture of Planet Earth taken from High Orbit.

Bland's role became most complex. In order to facilitate Space Migration and Galactic Pranksterism, Bland agreed to become a deep-cover agent. For ten years he posed as a puritanical, drab, ultra-respective stoic, anti-hedonic spokesman for the Ecological Fascists — growing moss on his own back, publishing dozens of Luddite, anti-technology periodicals, derogating the profit-motive, promoting games in which people hit each other with foam-rubber bats, editing essays about Voluntary Poverty, Limitation of Growth, the Satisfactions of Renunciation, Doomsday Meditations, Postponement of Pleasure.

The cover worked! By 1976 this I^2 agent had infiltrated the inner councils of the Terminal Adult Establishment (liberal division), cunningly demonstrating that the only way to return to the Puritan-Home-Owner Past was to build Space Colonies.

Nothing frightens hive-establishments more than the prospect of non-limits. Bland, accordingly, soothed the Ecologists by resurrecting the classic Stoic Motto — "Oh yes, it will happen, but not in our lifetime!"

In 1996 Bland arranged his own kidnapping by an Intelligent Task Force, comprised of beautiful women. He was shanghaied into a Space Shuttle, dosed with a longevity-pill and transported to the Pleasure Plan-It of his own secret Prankster design.

Reprinted from SCIENTIFIC AMERICA, May 1998

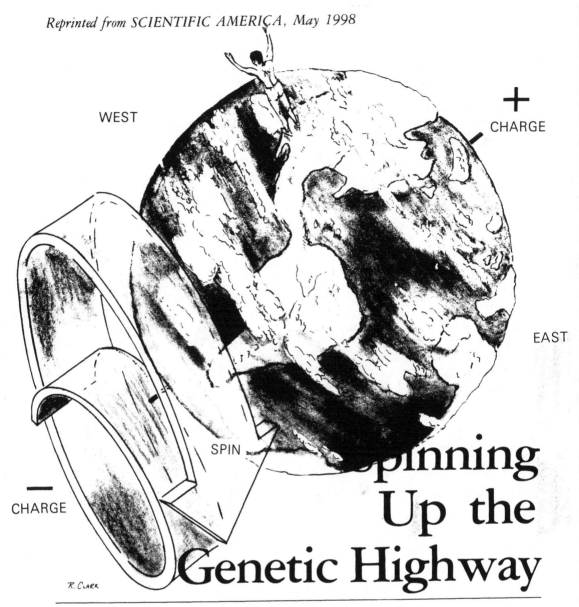

WEST

+ CHARGE

EAST

SPIN

− CHARGE

R. CLARK

Spinning Up the Genetic Highway

by Stuart Bland

On every Biological womb-planet the Genetic Highway climbs East to West in the Temperate Zones. These are easily located. In terms of spherical geometry the 30th to 45th degrees latitude (North and South) locate the runways along which gene-pools accelerate to Escape Velocity.

North-South is an Astro-Neurological Constant based on magnetic *charge*. East-West is thus an Astro-Neurological Constant based on *spin*. On every womb-planet in the galaxy Rotational Orientation relative to the home star determines the direction of Migrating Intelligence.

To experience the power of *spin* please perform the following neuro-experiment: Imagine that you stand fifty-miles (250,000 feet) high. Face west and sense the Earth-Spin moving you backwards. You would have to keep striding forward one thousand miles an hour to keep the sun at the same angle. This would be an easy stroll. One hundred paces an hour would do it.

Face east and feel that you are falling downward, pushed by spin-momentum. You are falling towards the sun which will rise in front of you, below you. You are moving downward at one thousand miles an hour.

Primitive organisms, *face* the sun, ride passively towards the sun. More advanced organisms develop the mobility necessary to *chase* the sun, to move against the rotational tide.

The navigational rule is simple. When you greet the sun, after the night, you are facing the east. You are facing Asia.

The word *Asia* comes from Greek-Latin, "region of the rising sun."

The name *Europe* comes from Greek and Semetic, "land of the setting sun."

When you face east you are peering down into the past; our gene-pools came from the east. When you see the sun disappear over the horizon you are looking up into the future. This basic attitudinal orientation on womb-planets is based upon *spin-momentum*.

When you move east you are being carried down the spin-axis. You are riding the globe, moving with the rotational inertia. When you move West, you climb up against the rotation. *Spin* is one of the fundamental defining-characteristics of energy-matter.

At the level of elementary particles the properties of matter are remarkably few. A particle can have mass or energy, and it can have momentum, including the intrinsic angular momentum called spin...*

Spin is a fundamental personality characteris-

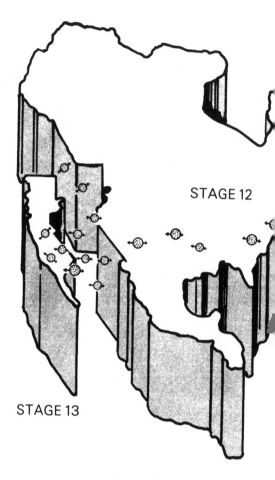

STAGE 12

STAGE 13

> ## There are sexier chapters ahead. If you are bored — migrate a few pages forward.

---

tic of not only elementary particles, but all energy structures. The wheeling of galaxies. The movements of humans living on a spinning globe. The orientation of all living organisms to the rotational momentum of the womb-planets or Designed Plan-Its.

The Hermetic Doctrine holds that what is so above is so below. Recapitulation theory holds that the same sequences re-evolve at all levels of energy. Neurologic thus leads us to expect *Spin* to be a basic dimension of biological structure.

Spin-caste is as fundamental a determinant of human behavior as sexual caste. (Spin is as basic to life as sex.) To understand a terrestrial human it is as necessary to understand hir *spin-caste* as it is to identify hir sexual caste.

There is *Fore-Spin*. Brains geared to move west into the future. There is *Back-Spin*. Brains wired to face the past. Spin-caste is determined by how far west you and your gene-pool have migrated — and at what speed.

Fore-Spin is moving west, facing the momentum. Pushing up against the rotation to develop mobility; to attain altitude. Moving into the future. Ascending into the empty ecological niches.

Why were the empty New American Continents (lobes) discovered and filled from Europe, not from Asia? Why didn't the wisdom of the East sail across the Pacific? Why was California explored and settled from Europe? Why didn't a wandering Chinese discover Venice? Why didn't orientals colonize Europe? Where were the Chinese Drakes and Vasco da Gamas? Throughout history, even today, when orientals

*"Fundamental Particles with Charm," by Roy F. Schwitters, *Scientific American*, October 1977.

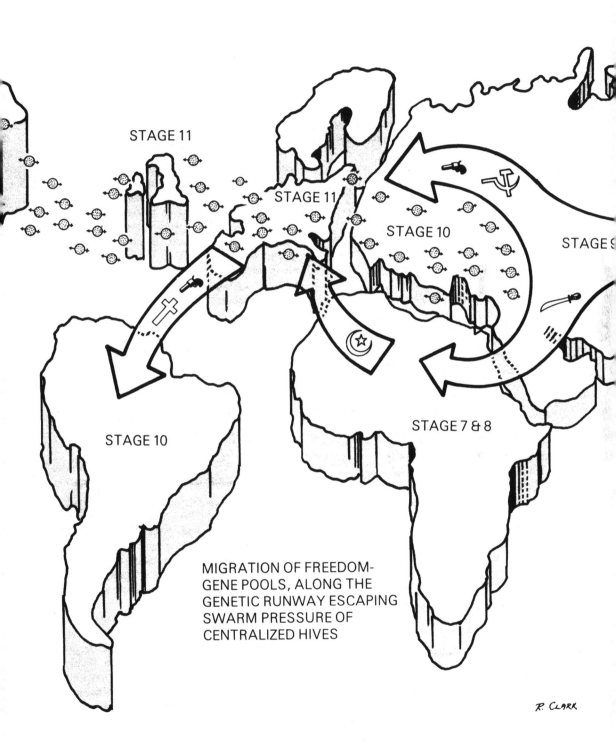

STAGE 11

STAGE 11

STAGE 10

STAGE 9

STAGE 10

STAGE 7 & 8

MIGRATION OF FREEDOM-
GENE POOLS, ALONG THE
GENETIC RUNWAY ESCAPING
SWARM PRESSURE OF
CENTRALIZED HIVES

R. CLARK

come west, they use western modes of transportation. How come? Why, today, in 1978, do the eastern countries compress into xenophobic centralized ant-hills, discouraging migration?

Because of *Back-Spin*.

Back-spin is sitting, immobile, with your back to momentum. Oriental-orientation is passively riding the down-wave. Occidental-orientation is actively pushing against rotation, continually being tested, shaped, formed by the air-flow, your antennae continually probing forward for the next pathway opening up.

Here we re-encounter the basic poetic-mystic polarities:

East	West
Earth	Heaven
Passive	Active
Piety	Intelligence
Past	Future
Simplicity	Complexity
Tradition	Change
Control	Freedom
Unity	Diversity
Stasis	Mobility

Only from an Einsteinian, relativistic post-terrestrial attitude can one realize that *East-West means Down-Up*. Liberation from Newtonian geography and recognition of Geo-relativity are necessary stages of evolution. How do you determine down-up on a spinning sphere? Against the spin is up. On this planet, West is up.

The most instructive way to look at a world-map is: turn the map so that East is down. Then re-experience the long climb of humanity from East to West. The busy caravans like ant-flies shuttling up and down the Asian trade routes. The enormous ant-armies of Alexander over-running the past (no worlds for him to conquer westward). Genghis Khan's fast-moving mobile, equine technology storming upward. The explosion of Muslim columns.

Why didn't a wandering Chinese discover Venice?

Roman legions painfully pushing up into Gaul. Sense the movement of human swarms over the centuries — the empire-hives sending out columns and waves, the exploratory probes westward. The flotillas of frail craft moving up the Atlantic, shipping that most basic cargo: sperm and eggs. (The other cargoes are support-logistic.)

The greatest technological problem faced by DNA on this planet was scaling the Atlantic Ocean. For 1,000 years (400– 1400 A.D.) the waves of mobile-elite Sperm-eggs splashed up

When you see the sun disappear over the horizon you are looking up into the future.

to the western-European Atlantic beach-ledges. And waited. Oh my, it was the greatest swarming phenomenon in human history! Port-cities teeming with migragents, explorers, space-travellers. Western Fever! Peerers into the unknown. Porers over maps of future lands. Migrating gene-pools freaking out for new spaces! Kings and Queens caught by the fever. And Columbus! Columbus obsessed with this Everest problem, commanded by Genetic Directive to scale this mountain of water three-thousand-miles-high.

"I gave the keys of those mighty barriers of ocean which were closed with such mighty chains." Columbus.

Note the timing of Atlantic Ascent. It had to await the Protestant Reformation. The Luther Self-Actualizacion freed gene-pools from the Catholic-hive center. Only a society of self-actualized families, democratically linked together, was capable of pushing gene-pools three-thousand-miles up, into the storm altitudes of the North Atlantic.

Recall that the ascent had been made over and over again during the ten centuries before Columbus by doughty Vikings, fervent Irish monks and hundreds of masculine bands. Some returned to tell the story of the new ecological niche. But the signal did not activate the swarm because the technology for lifting gene-pools three-thousand-miles into the unknown had not emerged. Thousands of European sailors who found the new lands did not return. They were absorbed by native gene-pools. (If thousands of Amazon female sailors had reached North

America before the Protestant Revolution, they too would have been swallowed up by the native gene-pools.)

It always requires a technical breakthrough to move sperm-egg colonies to a higher altitude; a higher velocity.

Oh my,
it was the greatest
swarming phenomenon
in
human history!

A gene-pool is a species-unit capable of protecting its young over several generations. Marauding bands of Astronaut Francis Drakes and John Waynes are a beginning probe. But nothing happens until the family-units move together. You see, the King-Emperor does not want to migrate. Are you mad? Leave the seat of Imperial power and luxury? No. The feudal society cannot migrate. Catholic countries couldn't pull it off. The Holders of the Land have to stay on the land. Feudal Catholic-Monarchies are flashy in the first stage, in the opening-up of a new ecological niche. Oh yes, the Second-born sons, the Dukes' younger brothers, sail off with crack-troops and establish secure foot-holds. It was genetic folly for Spaniards to mate with paleolith natives. (But permanent military settlements have to breed with the natives and the *mestizo* result is uniformly disastrous because the second-string, invasive male-warriors mate down with dumb conquered females.)

Genetic Intelligence is measured by the ability to move gene-pools upward, angling always westward, pushing against, always being shaped by, re-formed by, activated by, mutated by Spin-Pressure from the Future.

MEMO

FROM: G.I.A. Central
TO: All Evolutionary Agents on Planet Earth
SUBJECT: Change in Tactic from Anatomical to Neuro-Technological Mutation

1. The Human Brain is programmed by RNA-DNA to fabricate technological realities. To build environments. New Plan-Its. External technology produces the pollution which activates the next brain-circuit.

2. The Human Brain is a tool of DNA to accelerate evolution.

3. At this point (1978) DNA is not concerned with evolving new anatomical-physiological forms adapted to a heavy 1-G planet. Terrestrial evolution is over, i.e., irrelevant. Now that High Orbital Migration has begun, now that the futique species are moving into their designated ecological niche — high orbit — the goal of DNA is to create Technologies adapted to multiple-G living.

The current survival problems on the planet are due to over-population swarming and cannot be solved by anatomical mutations. The next stages are neurological — i.e., neurotechnological.

4. You are instructed to encourage the appropriate castes of the Human Species to decode DNA and increase Altitude and Mobility.

5. Distribute the following signal on bumper stickers and graffiti: LIFE IS NO LONGER A DISASTER MOVIE. THE WHO-DONE-IT MYSTERY IS SOLVED! YOU ARE RESPONSIBLE. YOU ARE THE BIO-ROBOTS WHO ARE GOING TO TAKE OVER THE MASTER-DESIGNER'S ROLE. IT IS YOUR JOB TO FABRICATE IMPROVED MINI-WORLDS.

WHO ARE YOU?

YOU ARE THOSE WHO RECOGNIZE THIS SIGNAL AND SELF-SELECT YOUR SELVES AS FUTURE BUILDERS.

Date: Winter, 1972

Country: Montana-Crans, Switzerland

Classification:

Subject: AN INTERVIEW WITH THE
SWISS POLICE

CONFIDENTIAL

FILE NO. 4575

The Fugitive's chalet is a cozy museum of Valaisan culture with six-foot-high cuckoo clock, large stone-carved fireplace and crossed swords on the wall. Our Agent Michel Hauchard arranged matters with the realtor and the owner who both dig the money and the glamor of a Bona Fide Exile Philosopher sponsored by a Gangster.

There is not much happening at Crans except natives taking money from middle-class Italian Skiers (an old Carthaginian custom), so the Doctor is pushed into the vacuum as village celebrity. A familiar role much preferable to the Fugitive.

On the 27th day of December we taped the following phone call. Michel is agitated.

"Ah Teem, I have just been talking to the Chief of Police here. He has just received word from Bern . . ."

COUNTER-INTELLIGENCE AGENCY REPORT

Date:

Country:

Subject: page 2

Classification:

CONFIDENTIAL

FILE NO. _457X5_ ᵛᴿ

"About my political asylum?"

"No. That will come soon. But today the police tell me that threats have been made against your life."

"I don't believe it."

"Well the police are worried. They want to talk to you this afternoon. You must come to Lausanne."

We followed the Fugitive who pointed his car down the twisting road from Crans at a tight, strong speed, curving along the shoulders of the hills. It is a lonely drive. The stone-walled, timber-roofed farmhouses are stuck on the slopes, each seeking its own view of the valley below. The neat Calvin peak of a church tower appears and disappears as the road winds down to the Rhone highway, then west past Martigny to Aigle, nestled at the end of Leman, past the damp jailhouse gloom of Chateau Chillon to Michel's penthouse.

Michel himself piloted the Rolls up the cobblestone hills of Lausanne to the cantonal Department of Justice guarded behind stone fortress walls. The Chief of Police was genial. He thanked Michel for the watch and happily discussed the size of ski boots Michel was to buy for his wife. They are interviewed by a plain-clothed inspector who chatted with Michel about Napoleonic history. (We taped the conversation.)

"Do you think these anonymous phone threats are serious?" asks Michel.

"We don't know. Intelligence reports from Algeria that Eldridge Cleaver claims he is keeping the Professor under surveillance. Maoist groups in Paris and West Germany have announced that he is a threat to the Armed Revolution because he depoliticizes young people. The Israelis will swap him for a few jets. Arab militants seem to view him with sympathy as an American fugitive. What do you think?"

"I think the whole thing is a hoax," said the Professor.

"Privately," confides the Inspector, "I am inclined to agree. However, I have been instructed to offer you a full-time bodyguard if you wish it."

"Male or female?" says Michel.

"Not at all," exclaimed the Fugitive in alarm, probably thinking of the threat to his eroding life-style.

"I thought so," smiled the Inspector slyly. "At any rate you need not worry. Twenty-four hours a day you are under the protective eye of Swiss security."

(End of tape.)

COUNTER-INTELLIGENCE AGENCY REPORT

Date:

Country:

Subject: page 3

Classification:

CONFIDENTIAL

FILE NO. 4575

<u>Agency note:</u>
We should speak to Inspector Klausxitz and tell
him to be more discreet. We don't want to spook our
Pigeon until it's time to spook him good.

GENETIC HALL OF FAME

Rusty Schweickart

Neil & Ursula Freer

TUCSON LECTURE

"THERE ARE 24 TIMOTHY LEARYS"

I'm sure that during the last fifteen years you have read many lurid accounts of my activities. As a well-trained Out-Caste, I plead *nolo contendere.** I encourage all rumors — hostile or adulatory — as badges of honor. However, since we have assembled in this room every literate Intelligence Operative in this state *(applause)*, I'm going to confide something on a need-to-know basis that I'm not sure the general public is ready for. Facts which will clarify the images and media hypes that have been circulat-

> ### I encourage all rumors — hostile or adulatory — as badges of honor.

ing around my name. Here's what really happened.

In the early 50's, C.I.A. scientists administered LSD to Harvard students without their knowledge. As usual, the government sponsored scientists learned nothing. But the "Victim-subjects," as usual, got the message: *brains can be washed.* So we were assigned by Genetic Intelligence headquarters to improve the C.I.A. work at Harvard. One afternoon in the Cambridge laboratory where we were conducting our biochemical research, the experiment succeeded: I was cloned! *(Laughter)*

So, to tell you the truth, since our Harvard experiments, there have been 24 Timothy Learys running around the world, playing parts in the 24 Reality Movies of the period.

You remember the lesson: it's your nervous system which creates and controls your reality. You dial and tune the images *you* wish. So pick out the Timothy Leary image you want. There's probably no insanity, eccentricity, immorality, heroic divinity or messianic omnipotence that hasn't been attributed to one of these images. But that's the standard fate of Out-Castes.

*A satirical reference to the case of C.I.A. Director Richard Helms who had recently pleaded *nolo contendere* to indictments for lying to Congress.

Now, we have to be frank with one another. You know and I know that universities like this, supported by tax payers and administered by salaried politicians (like all the schools you have attended since first grade) are designed to keep you serenely and productively stupid. *(Laughter)*

But, things are changing. The particular Timothy Leary clone who is here tonight *(laugher)* intends to take advantage of the recent thaw in social and political climates to do something Radical. I think the Regents can stand it and I know you're ready to have the boat rocked a bit. *(Applause)* So I'm going to talk to you as one intelligent person to another. *(Laughter)* The subject of this talk will be the evolution of intelligence. The purpose of this talk is to recruit you as Intelligence Agents. Change Agents. Out-Castes.

There are many social and genetic forces designed to resist change and retard intelligence increase. I certainly am not going to complain tonight on this occasion of triumph and celebration. So when I talk about the forces that discourage change, I emphasize that Repressive Hive-Bureaucracy is a genetic and social necessity. The good-old-bulls who run the herd are robot-programmed to scare you about change. Their salaried hive-function is to tell you, "Stay close to the center of the herd. Don't get too far out or you'll be an Out-Caste. Don't get too far in front or you'll get picked off. Stick close to the home base. Don't rock the gene-ship. Avoid change."

That's okay. Neither a species nor a social-gene-pool can lurch off one direction after another, aimlessly, as each mutation comes along. There has to be some preservative central tendency. I honor and respect the conservative forces in society and the DNA code which puts brakes on change.

At the same time it is my genetic duty to stand before you, spray you with Electronically Amplified Brain Waves designed to activate you, to cut you loose for all-out, post-hive change.

THOROUGH-BRED RACE RESULTS

Oh, it's no matter
who sires them
And it's no matter
who trains them
And it matters not
who rules them by the Reign

Racers will only go as fast and as far and as high as they are bred to go.

WIN, PLACE, SHOW.
The race is One by a Head.

COUNTER-INTELLIGENCE AGENCY REPORT

Date: December, 1971

Country: Bern, Switzerland

Classification:

CONFIDENTIAL

FILE NO. 4575

Subject: YOU MUST THINK OF YOURSELF
AS A ONE PERSON COUNTRY

(Tape recording of conversation with our Agent Michel Hauchard.)

"Congratulations, mon vieux. I have just received word from Benvoglio. The Swiss government has rejected the American request to extradite you."

"The congratulations go to you, mon voyaguer."

"Listen. Benvoglio says he is besieged by reporters and television people wanting an interview."

"I think I should remain quiet. Doesn't he?" says the Fugitive.

"I agree. But le maitre wants you to come to his office this afternoon. I think his desire for publicity may be outweighing the need for discretion."

"What should I do?"

"It's a small moment of triumph. It's the first time Switzerland has turned down an American request for extradition on political grounds. This has implications for the Swiss drug policy. The Swiss Foreign Office told reporters that twenty years in prison didn't seem reasonable punishment for two half-smoked butts of marijuana in the ash tray of a car which was not registered to you. Not bad, eh? Maybe we start a hashish import company. And the political significance! Up until now Switzerland has regularly given refuge to fugitives fleeing west from Communism or Socialism. This is the first time the Swiss have opened the front door."

"But why hold a press conference? To whom do we want to signal?"

"It will be good publicity for our book, Teem. I can't tell you over the phone how much money all this has cost us. Several cabinet meetings about your case. And the pressure from the White House? It's not every day that John Mitchell comes to Europe to chase a fugitive. We had to pay a fortune for this so we might as well ride the wave while we have it. I'll have the French press pick it up. You make some talk in French, eh?"

AMERIKANER IN SEINEM SCHWEIZER EXIL: Timothy Leary vor seinem Lieblingscafe „Exil" in
Fotos: Fronemann

gendwelche Dinge äußer-
tun, nein, innerlich, muß
ineinarbeiten. Völlig in-

stalten, individuell zu denken.
Dabei müssen wir in einem System leben, das wir nicht wol-
len:"

in einigen Generationen, die viel
mehr Zugang zu ihrem Nerven-
system haben. „In diesem Sta-
dium", schreibt Leary, „wird der
Mensch   erkennen,   daß   der

*

COUNTER-INTELLIGENCE AGENCY REPORT

Date:

Country:

Classification:

CONFIDENTIAL

FILE NO. _4575_

Subject: page 3

Swarms of reporters were waiting for the Fugitive in Bern. Sizing the situation up with one glance, the Professor walked across the street and stood in front of an appropriately named restaurant. And thus was taken the famous "Exile photos" which were flashed out on planetary wire-service.

The Press Conference takes place in Benvoglio's office. The lawyer waddles around wreathed in smiles. The Swiss Bar Association is strict about publicity-seeking so the advent of a notorious client is welcome.

The Doctor enjoys talking to the sympathetic hip-haired English and American reporters. He delivers a brief speech in French thanking the Swiss people for their tradition of liberty.

After the reporters leave, the Philosopher poses the question to Maitre Benvoglio, "What about asylum?"

"Hmph. Yes, of course," says the lawyer. "As you know, the Federal government cannot give you asylum. Switzerland is a Confederation of very independent states. Only the canton can give you permanent residence. Monsieur Hauchard tells me he is negotiating with the Canton of Vaud to take you. I am also planning to contact other countries. I have talked to embassy people from Denmark, Sweden, Holland and they are going to consult their governments. You are in an interesting position. Ordinarily it is not difficult to locate a stateless person. But in your case, the American government will put pressure on any country that accepts you. You would not believe the pressure they put on our foreign office. And from the White House it comes."

"I'm not surprised," replies the Fugitive Professor. "There is a former District Attorney named G. Gordon Liddy who made a name for himself by harassing me. He's become an influential member of the Cultural Police operating out of the White House. I'll have to remain in exile as long as the present administration is in power. I'd like to stay in Switzerland if a canton will accept me."

"It is a matter of diplomacy. You must think of yourself as a one-person country. And I shall act as your ambassador at large. You are like Israel in 1948. The more countries that say they will accept you, the stronger your position here. Then the pressure on the Swiss government will be lessened. Our government is not eager to make anger from America. Your application for asylum will be presented to the cabinets of Denmark and Holland in the next few weeks. After that I get you admitted to the United Nations. I do my best for you. And a bit more."

(End of tape.)

GENETIC HALL OF FAME

Carol Rosin

Reprinted from PSYCHOLOGY TWODAY, October 1998

In 1944, Einstein designed and took his own intelligence test. After that, it was revised and improved by F.M. Esfandiary, who thus increased his own intelligence, I^2.

The first item on the Einstein-Esfandiary Intelligence Test (Standard Alien Intelligence test item) was:

1. HOW DO YOU DEFINE INTELLIGENCE?

Einstein said that the way one defines intelligence is the most important step taken in life.

The second item on the Einstein-Esfandiary test was:

2. CAN INTELLIGENCE BE INCREASED?

The Einstein-Esfandiary Intelligence Test

NATIONAL PORTRAIT GALLERY SMITHSONIAN INSTITUTION, WASHINGTON, D.C.

The function of intelligence is to stimulate Increase in Intelligence, I^2. An Intelligence Action is one designed to increase your intelligence; an Intelligence Agent is one who continually works to expand input of information, revise reality metaphors and raise the intelligence of self and others.

ANSWER TO ITEM 2:

Oh yes! Intelligence can be increased. Our brains are designed to increase our intelligence. The aim and strategy of evolution is to raise the intelligence of species. The development of every individual from infancy to maturity is the story of Intelligence Increase, I^2. The only smart thing to do is to get smarter.

ANSWER TO ITEM 1:

Intelligence (like the nerve cells upon which it is based) has three functions:

1. Reception: the ability to expand — direct the scope, source, intensity of information received — this is Consciousness expansion. Opening up to new data.

2. Mapping: the ability to joyously revise your metaphors of reality in response to new information (including other people's metaphors).

3. Performance: the ability to construct external-communication apparati (in fusion with others) which stimulate expanded information-input, new maps-of-reality and improved networks.

Reprinted from WE MAGAZINE, June 1993

The Ultimate Aphrodisiac

by Anise Nun

Nina's camel lifted his wispy, fringed tail in the excitement of the canter, and then thumped his wet, gleaming hide firmly. When they arrived at the inviting wetness of the oasis, the two women leaped off and walked their steeds to a soft, grassy dune and threw themselves down in cool relief.

Saina said, "My sweet cheeks are steaming from the friction."

"Hmm. Give us a look," answered Nina. "Poor sultress. This is your first humpy ride. We went too far for your soft, milky skin. Give me a peek."

Saina loosened the knot, untied her sheer harem pants and let them fall to her hips, bending over for Nina's gaze.

Nina gently rolled her on her lap. "Oooh. Oooh. Sweet little dates." She slid the pants down to expose the swelling mounds. Nina patted Saina gently.

"Oooh. So warm like the desert sun," she said.

Saina giggled.

"What are you laughing at?" asked Nina.

"That's so nice." Saina continued to giggle. "What?"

"Oh, I was thinking about poor Madame Mao Tse Tung. She once wrote: *'Although sex is engaging in the first rounds, what sustains interest in the long run is power.'*"

Nina's soft palm touched the swelling mounds. "Sweet, dear little dates," she murmured. "How does it feel here?" Her exploring fingers probed deeper, down between the legs.

"It feels so wet and steamy and luring there. Oooh, that's nice. Don't you think she's absurd?" asked Saina.

"Take off your pants and let yourself feel the cool air," said Nina, tugging the pants down over Saina's thighs while keeping her nestled on her lap with the sweet bottom open to the breeze. "But Kissinger's worse."

"Do it to me, oh please, do it to me," gasped Saina, not moving.

"Kissinger declared that power is the ultimate aphrodisiac."

"Power!" exclaimed Saina.

Nina picked up her camel whip and flicked it softly over the succulent pink flesh. "Well neither Madame Mao nor Henry Kissinger has ever been accused of actions designed to increase individual freedom and the power of the singularity."

"It's so hot there. Kiss it."

"What sustains interest in the long run is intelligence-increase. Do you want me too? Oooh, do it to me."

"Oh, yes," murmured Saina. She sat up, leaving her filmy pants around her ankles. She tumbled on to the green, moist grass, pulled Nina over her lap, loosened her pants and started whipping her wriggling buttocks, at first tenderly, then with more force.

"Intelligence is the Ultimate Aphrodisiac," gasped Saina.

"Oh yes," replied Nina.

In 1960 Out-Caste agents started circulating the rumor that Intelligence was the most important factor in human life.

They said: "What else do you value? Love? Virtue? Money? Power? Freedom? Truth? All of these can be enhanced by increasing intelligence. A failure to increase intelligence can only diminish our ability to obtain and enjoy these goods."

Out-Caste Agents distributed bumper stickers saying: INTELLIGENCE IS THE ULTIMATE APHRODISIAC.

DIFFERENT
VENERATIONS
FOR
DIFFERENT
GENERATIONS

Rusty Shepherd! Here's the romantic, cloak-and-dagger story of a deep-cover intelligence working effectively within the military control-centers of the Imperial Hive.

It is well known that the American Military and N.A.S.A. carefully screened its astronauts for hive-loyalty, blind-obedience and social-conformity. Intuitively recognizing the genetic implications of space-exploration, the bureaucrats attempted to select heroes who would support Dom-Species values, who would not act as individuals.

N.A.S.A. was unaware, however, that a genetic selection process 2½ billion years old was running the show. First we note that the astronauts were volunteers. They were young military officers who did not want to sit behind desks at headquarters. Those that applied were ready. Their nervous systems were geared for early mutation.

So it came to pass that exposure to the space environment unfailingly activated post-terrestrial circuits of the brain. This is as obvious as saying that exposure to the breast starts the baby sucking. Or that exposure to the naked beauty of a youth turns on the erotic circuits of a teen-age girl. When a terrestrial brain is exposed to zero-gravity, space-radiation, the view of earth seen from space — the activation occurs.

Almost every astronaut returned to the womb planet changed. West Pointer Deke Slayton writes poetry. Edgar Mitchell forms an occult-WASP religion. Buzz Aldrin writes a true-confession. The two spacers who run for the Senate of the United States are elected. What an interesting new elite species we have here. Two out of twenty have been elected to high office!

While most astronauts used their newly activated neurology to play important roles in the hive, Rusty

Shepherd was the first conscious post-terrestrial — the first earthling to understand that space habitation means a dramatic change in human culture.

During his eight years as Secretary of Space Affairs, in the cabinet of President Jerry Brown, Shepherd worked effectively from within the hive to assure that space colonists would be able to form self-selected migratory groups and that each mini-world could evolve its own unique culture.

In 1997 when the military moved to impose martial law on the colonists it was Shepherd, moving invisibly in the highest councils, who delayed the take-over. He warned, prepared and finally helped the colonists overthrow the domination from the Pentagon. Shepherd, after negotiating independence for the revolting colonists, then became the first president of the United States of Space.

Reprinted from SCIENTIFIC AMERICA, July 1988

The Neuro-Geography of Terrestrial Politics

by Astronaut Russell Shepherd

Terrestrial politics are Newtonian-Euclidian. They are based upon territorial mammalian competitions between neighboring hives who share the same neurotechnological level. Each quantum jump in neuro-technology increases the size of the political unit. Tribes are swallowed-up by neighbors who have superior artifacts. Higher technology nations set up territorial boundary tensions of greater extension. China and Russia confront each other along a 3000 mile border with the same nervous, bluffing robot postures of four-foot mammals protecting turf.

Ideological differences are, of course, irrelevant in mammalian terrestrial politics. The enmity is instinct-robot. Neighboring gene-pools *have to compete* according to a relentless law of territorial (plus-minus) magnetism. To occupy an ecological niche is automatically to be "against" those who inhabit the neighboring niche.

To illustrate the limbic (primitive-brain) nature of Old World politics in 1978 consult the map. Note that Morocco receives its arms from America and that its neighbor, Algeria, obtains weapons from Russia. The border between the two neighbors is tense.

Note that the next country, Tunisia, receives its arms from America and quarrels with both its neighbors, leftist Algeria and leftist Libya.

> To occupy an ecological niche is automatically to be "against" those who inhabit the neighboring niche.

Poor confused Egypt, caught between a Black and White ambiguity switched (in 1975-1976) from Russia to America. Egypt now manages to maintain hostile contact with both its neighbors — Libya and Israel. (Regardless of the ideological paradox!)

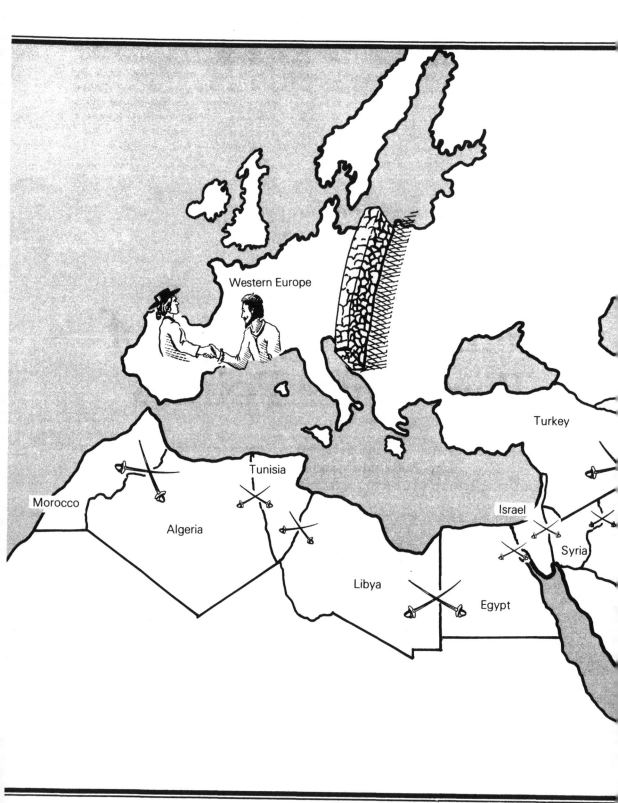

ROBOT MAMMALIAN — TERRITORIAL CONFRONTATION

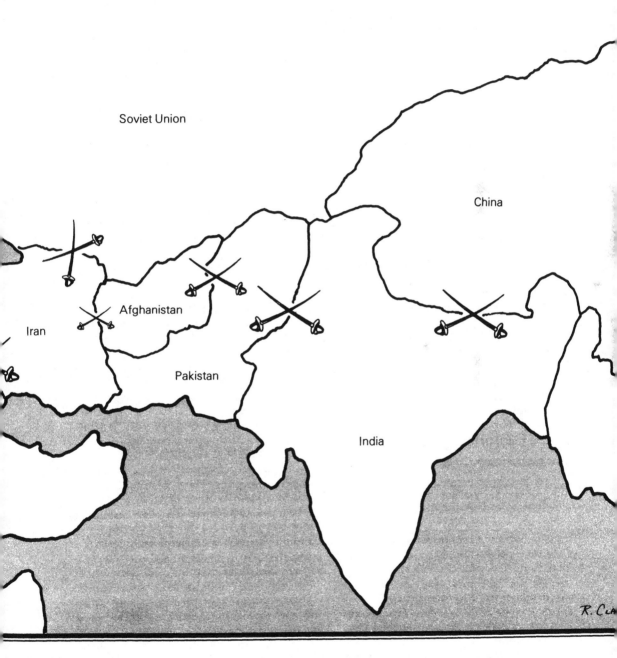

Continuing down the zoo-cages of our animal past, we note that Israel fights Syria.

Syria growls at Israel above and Iraq below.

Iraq fights Iran.

Iran snarls at Afghanistan.

Afghanistan frowns at Pakistan.

Pakistan hates India.

India is tensed against China.

China suspiciously rubs up against Russia and the South East Asian states — all of which distrust their neighbors, *regardless of ideology*.

An examination of the politics of Southern Africa will reveal the same checker-board sequence of neighborhood confrontations. South East Asia provides a similar confirmation of the theory that terrestrial politics produces an almost perfect unbroken sequence of robot mammalian-territorial confrontations.

We seem to deal here with a magnetic ordering of plus-minus charges in neighboring units. With robot regularity, and with an amazing disregard for common sense or political principles, each country opposes its neighbors.

It is of interest that such a renowned political theorist as Henry Kissinger was so totally robotized — like iron filings held in a magnetic field — in confrontation with Russia, that he failed to understand this neuro-political principle. Kissinger believed in the Domino Theory; if South Vietnam fell, then all the South East Asian nations would topple shoulder-to-shoulder into monolithic Communism. This paranoia, for which 50,000 young Americans died, completely disregarded the obvious. Once Saigon collapses then nature takes over! Cambodia attacks Vietnam. Vietnam raids Laos.

Africa is a checker-board of mammalian savagery.

Thailand snarls at Vietnam. And all South East countries oppose their northern neighbor China.

So far we have considered the East-West sequence of polarization. Next, let us examine some North-South factors. The map of Africa reveals that the principle of neighbor-antagonism exists. What the political map does not show is the fact that within African countries (which were arbitrarily defined by European colonists) tribal enmities continue to rage on. Africa is a checker-board of mammalian savagery. Ninety per cent of African countries

are ruled by assassins and military chiefs. Mafia capos.

Now look north to Europe. Until World War II, Europe was also a checker-board of quarreling neighbors, each ruled by a feudal chief. The technological quantum-leap taken in the 1940-War forced a change in territoriality. Technology always increases the size of the gene-pool territory. The Eastern Bloc nations were forced together into a monolithic entity — confronting the union of West European states. The border-tensions no longer exist between nations but along the great East-West wall, the Iron Curtain. We note, also, that ninety per cent of West European countries are ruled, not by military dictators, but by elected representatives.

Why did Africa develop slavery and Europe capitalist-democracy?

This North-South bi-furcation of the genetic highway has produced a fascinating left-right division which perfectly parallels the cerebral hemispheric split. The right-hand, i.e., the northern countries developed logic, rationality, manipulation of artifacts and symbols. The new technologies require larger networks of harmonious collaboration. The energies of thousands of people must be linked-up to maintain an automotive business or a Coca Cola industry. Technology creates larger and more intelligent gene-colony units.

Why did the right-hand-continent, Europe, develop the technology and carry the freedom-gene upward? Why did the left-hand-continent, Africa, fail to produce mobility-freedom-gene-pools? Why did Africa develop slavery and Europe capitalist-democracy? Why did the genetic highway veer north instead of south when it burst out of the Middle-East (i.e., the mid-brain)? Why did the northern Mediterranean centers light up in sequence: Greece, Rome, Venice, Paris, Madrid, Lisbon, London?

Surely there must be some basic neuro-geographical principle that explains why Africa now swarms with slavery and paleolithic savagery and why the right-hand-northern lobe has provided the centers and pathways along which the species has evolved. Why did the freedom-genes cluster along the North Atlantic beaches?

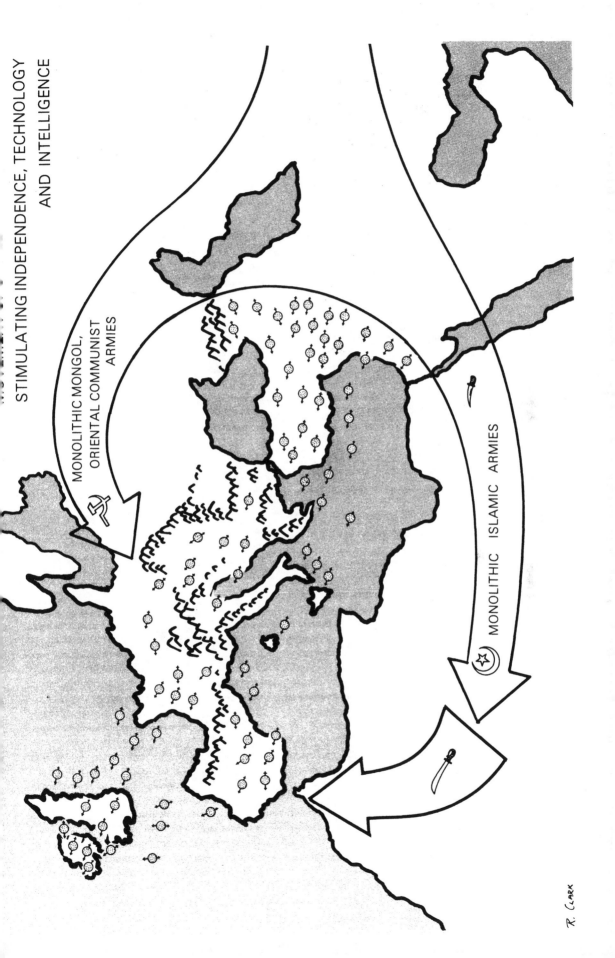

STIMULATING INDEPENDENCE, TECHNOLOGY
AND INTELLIGENCE

MONOLITHIC MONGOL,
ORIENTAL COMMUNIST
ARMIES

MONOLITHIC ISLAMIC ARMIES

MONOLITHIC ISLAMIC ARMIES

R. CLARK

Why did the intelligence-technology breakout occur from West Europe — not West Africa?

Think of evolution as an ascent — literally a climb, a series of intelligence tests which activate the velocity-altitude-freedom circuits. From the Mid-East mid-brain there are two pathways. The Southern route is the easiest; the Arabs took it, slid off along the low road. Insectoid armies oozing from the east, sending, not gene-pools, but soldiers and military bureaucrats.

The high-road North was a ladder, a series of ledges to be scaled. Look at the map. First the Dardenelles to be crossed. Then the prickly mountains of Greece, the fingered peninsulas. The Balkan mountains. The high Alps. Rugged land, uninviting to Mid-Eastern sultans. Choked with geographic barriers offering refuge to ascending gene-pools. The story of evolution is the ascent of Celtic Out-Caste gene-pools on the shoulders of the teeming Eastern autonomic-involuntary centers.

> # NOTE: If this chapter is not sexy enough for you, skip ahead where the editors have inserted a signal especially designed to activate the circuits in your brain, which will allow
> you to return to this chapter and enjoy it.

A glance at the map reminds us that the human race is literally a Mobility-Contest; small gene-pools racing to keep ahead of the engulfing wave of insectoid collectivism. The Human Race is exactly a competition of speed. Small gene-pools being squirted ahead by swarming pressures into empty ecological niches where new realities (Plan-Its) can be created. The human race is run to the West. The Contest is between the collective and the individual. The Contest: can the individual freedom-gene-pools accelerate fast enough to leave the planet before being over-run by Eastern hivism?

The issue is, however, never in doubt. The swarming pressure of the primitive-past lapping at the outskirts of the frontier is simply a signal to speed up. At exactly that moment when the forces of homogenous unity, one-ness, socialist-equality, cultural-determinism seem to become dogma — exactly at that moment genetic-elitism reappears among the out-post-out-castes and new gene-pools assemble on the frontier out-posts. Everyone on the frontier is self-selected for frontier behavior. The new ecological niche is always filled by those who are robot-templated for mobility, independence and change. An important caste to any species.

The ascent of gene-pools up the Atlantic in the 16th, 17th, 18th, and 19th centuries was a genetic-selection process of gigantic significance. It must be recalled that immigration to North America involved an amazing seed-blossoming of gene-pools. Very few immigrants made the climb alone. Typically, each European gene-pool sent its best fertile stock. Once a beach-head had been established in the new ecological niche, more settled members of the gene-pools could follow. But in most cases new gene-pools were formed by mutated-migrants of former old-world gene-pools.

GENETIC HALL OF FAME

Barbara Marx Hubbard
Carolyn & Keith Henson

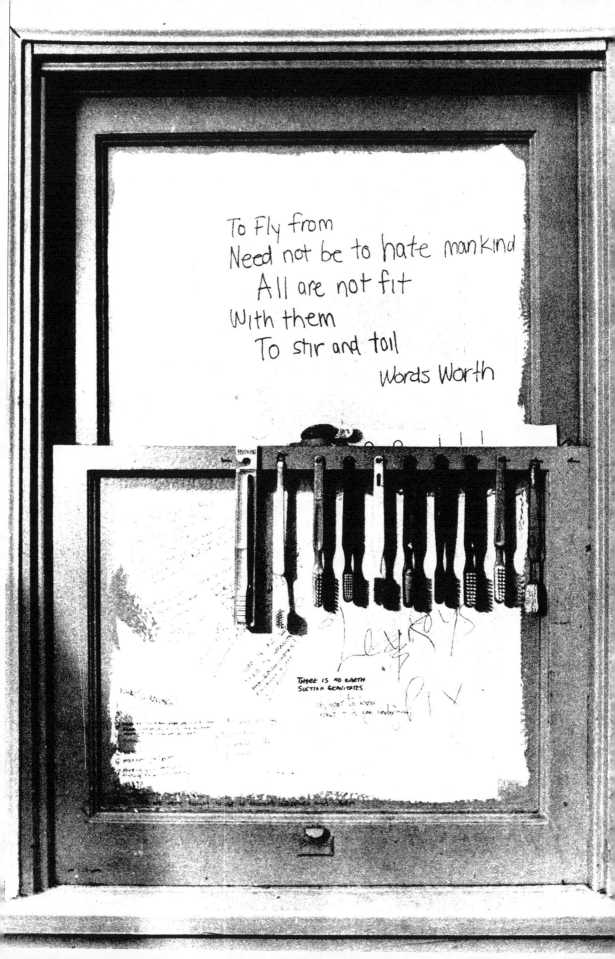

Reprinted from EBONIE MAGAZINE, August, 1991

The Perils of a Front-Line Evolutionary Agent

by Stevie Nicks

Stevie Nicks, philosopher-architect-acoustic physicist, is best known for her design and construction of sound-worlds in the Scorpio Sector in the late 27th century. After Hir 900th birthday celebration on the New Wales H.O.M.E., when SHe was reunited with hundreds of grand-children and Hir 37 husbands, SHe volunteered for a time-mission into antiquity — popping up in the volatile, premigration 20th century.

Hir assignment was multinational-media-transmission. After Hir audi-neural signals established Hir authenticity as a post-terrestrial, Stevie scripted and starred in several movies which accelerated Intelligence Increase on the larval planet.

In the year 1995 SHe was selected as one of the Council of Twenty-Four and thus became one of the first post-terrestrials to attain Inter-Stellar Fusion.

Timothy Leary's tactic (at that time S.O.P. with Out-Caste Agents) required him to place himself in Their hands to find out who They were and how They operated. Thus his task in the Federal Prison system was surveillance.

SURVEILLANCE: Close observation of a person or group especially of one under suspicion.

SURVEILLANT: One who keeps a close watch; French present particle (sic) of *surveiller*, to watch over. *Sur*, on top of or over + *veiller*, from vigil, awake, watchful.

In August 1974 I² was taken from a cell in Terminal Island Prison at 3:00 A.M. by two armed Federal Agents and driven to the Los Angeles airport. He was told only that he was travelling under an alias and that if he attempted to escape, he would be shot. He was flown to Minneapolis and picked up by two Federal agents who drove him to the Federal Prison in Sandstone, Minnesota. Upon arrival he was taken to the warden's office and told that he was to be admitted to the prison under an alias. He protested to the warden that this was a perilous act and demanded that he be registered under his own name. The warden replied that he had no choice but to follow orders. *No choice but to follow orders!*

I² was told that his name was Charles Thrush. The thrush is a song bird.

Since it was Friday evening, no appeal of this decision could be made to Washington. I² was conducted to the "hole" and locked in a small metal room with no furnishings except a mattress and bedding. The metal door to the cell had a slot eight inches high and twenty-four inches in width. The slot was secured from the outside by a padlock. At meal times and at various times during the day and night, a guard would unlock the slot (which according to Solzhenitsyn, Soviet prisoners call "The Swine Trough"). At one such inspection, he asked the guard what his name was. I² was told that his name was Charles Thrush. The thrush is a song bird.

SELF ACTUALIZATION PRECEDES INTERPERSONAL FUSION

TUCSON LECTURE

"SELF-DISCOVERY LEADS TO SELF-ACTUALIZATION"

There is a rumor going around that the younger generation, or for that matter, the American public in general, is laid back these days, apathetic, narcissistic, self-indulgent, sensual. Well, we can't knock intelligent pursuit of happiness. There are periods when a species or an individual or a nation needs to lay back, mellow out, cocoon-quiescent and recoup. However, this 1970's quiescence is more apparent than real. The 60's were a period of *self-discovery* — a daring assertion of personal pleasure rather than societal reward. The genetic conflicts of the 60's were won by the forces of self-discovery.

The 70's have moved America into an unprecedented era of *self-actualization*. Today, young people and most intelligent older people are apparently laid back because they are taking care of their own situation first. They are "getting their own heads together," discovering and tending their bodies, learning how to produce their own Reality Movies. College students aren't charging after partisan dogmas or idealistic rhetoric. But don't be deceived by this quiescence. It denotes neither apathy nor stupidity. In fact, it may well be the better part of wisdom to lay back until something worthy of your intelligence comes along. Later, I'll be suggesting some ideas that do merit the attention and intelligent participation of confident self-actualized people, eager to assume responsibil-

> ## The 60's were a period of *self-discovery* — a daring assertion of personal pleasure rather than societal reward.

ity for scripting and directing their own reality movies. Pre-fabricating their futures.

Here's the flight plan. I'd like to give two lectures tonight. First I'll talk about the past because I think it is important to understand "roots." Intelligence Agents (Out-Castes) study history very carefully. Because we can't navigate precisely into the future unless we understand the rhythms and coherence of past voyages. However, once we've traced our roots back East, it's necessary to move on to the future and create blossoms. A philosopher demonstrates his understanding of the past by the accuracy of hir predictions about the future. I think the time has come to take a look into the future and catch the next waves that are coming. Watch out! They're going to be big ones.

> ## Mobility is the classic stimulus for Intelligence Increase, I^2

Lecture number two (and the main theme of tonight's celebration) deals with THE CREATION OF THE FUTURE and THE EVOLUTION OF INTELLIGENCE. We'll survey the three great change techniques employed by DNA! 1) Mutation — a species getting smarter; 2) Metamorphosis — individuals getting more intelligent; and 3) Migration — because every time you improve, every time you change, every time some new challenge increases your intelligence, you have to migrate to find new space to live out your new capacity, to custom-make your new vision. Mobility is the classic stimulus for Intelligence Increase, I^2.

Please learn to be comfortable with the idea of change. To discover *who we are* means that we must learn how our intelligence has evolved. Don't let Them scare you about change. Recall that each of us has passed through at least twelve volatile and dramatic changes during our life times. Each of us possesses within our nervous systems twelve primitive brains which have emerged in sequence as we develop from infancy to adult maturity. And here's some good news. Recent cryptographic decoding of the DNA helix has suggested that each of us has twelve post-terrestrial brains which are scheduled to be activated in sequence as we move into and prefabricate the post-hive future!

Date: January, 1972

Country: Montana-Crans, Switzerland

Classification:

CONFIDENTIAL

FILE NO. 4575

Subject: GRAVITY BEING NO LONGER A PROBLEM — THE CHALLENGE IS SPEED

Back in Crans, the Scandalous Fugitive is becoming addicted to skiing. Early mornings he straps on by the front door of his chalet, skis down to a rope-lift which ascends to town, lumbers through the village and cable cars up to the Spectacular View of the high plateau, fifty miles down the Rhone valley. High, wide and clear.

Ski-town sociology: The smart natives run the Cash Registers. The solid natives keep the lift machinery running and collect tickets. The stocky, tanned instructors smile knowingly. The Latin-American propeller-set ski and dance. The colony of American-Canadian ski-hippies work, ski, and fuck. There is no shortage of instructors.

Neurological Note: "The first step in skiing involves rewiring the Second Circuit of the Nervous System — sensory kinaesthetic, hooking up newly-discovered muscles, total attention to bicep mechanics, re-mastering balance, learning new asanas, plough, christie, stem christie, parallel." (Xeroxed from Fugitive's desk.)

— no criminal record

His guru is (Craig) a blond kid from Oregon, Yale graduate, leading figure in the snow commune just down the slope from his chalet where twelve young snow-pilgrims share expenses, work four hours, ski four hours and stay high in front of the fire dancing, listening to music, talking philosophy and fucking.

The instructor Craig comes by the chalet each morning after breakfast and they ascend together in the swaying cabin discussing Universal Questions.

Craig, a mountain climber, seems to be infecting the Professor with peak-madness. He plans to teach him skiing in the winter and climbing in the summer.

Diary entry: "The skiing goes slowly. Recapitulation of evolution: the first problem for the beginner is the struggle against gravity, to remain erect on long plastic boards attached to the feet. Craig patiently slides ahead shouting instructions for an hour and then, in relief dives headlong down the slope. For the expert, gravity being no longer a problem, but an asset, the challenge is speed.

"Skiing is a mating ritual of the technological young. Families show up for weekends and vacations, but the numerical majority and the neuro-logical charge is sexual. It is a sport for the courageous, virile, healthy. My slipping, straining attempts leave me an admiring anthropological mammal clinging to the slippery slopes of evolution." (Xeroxed from fugitive's desk.)

COUNTER-INTELLIGENCE AGENCY REPORT

Date:

Country:

Subject: page 2

Classification:

John Milano first attained fame as Attorney General in the administration of President Jerry Brown. His great achievement was the complete transformation of the Legal System. Before John Milano terrestrial law was based upon a punitive imposition of the behavioral characteristics of the Dom-Species upon all other human species. In this cruel and bizarre situation which existed until the end of the 20th century, one species would obtain power by force of arms and then impose its own robot-style upon the majority. This ruthless suppression of species differences was based on monotheistic religions that glorified authoritarian uniformity.

By 1978 Human Ethologists had demonstrated that the so-called human race actually comprised at least 24 species and thousands of sub-species. The classic tendency of Terminal Adult species to impose its over-specialized dinosaur models on all other neurogenetic forms was then exposed as genetic barbarism.

The Multi-World Neurogenetic Legal Commission, of which John Milano was the chairperson, totally revised the structure of post-human society —

by harmonizing human behavior with genetic-caste. DNA law replaced the whims of hive-law.

In the post-terrestrial legal system (sometimes called the Milano Code) every individual was seen as a member of a neurogenetic caste, with certain clearly defined species characteristics. It was the responsibility of each individual to restrict caste-actions to the appropriate ecological niche. The necessity for each hive to develop its own mores and cultural styles was recognized. However, no hive was allowed to impose its behavioral styles on other hives or extra-hive individuals.

The last punitive-reprisal by a hive upon an individual occurred in 1999. Since the dawn of the 21st century all social frictions have been solved by transferring the out-of-place individual to an appropriate ecological niche of hir own choice. By the year 2000 all such species-migrations were occurring voluntarily and the very concept of socially imposed law was relegated to the nostalgia banks.

The galactic fame of John Milano as the Last Lawyer has endured.

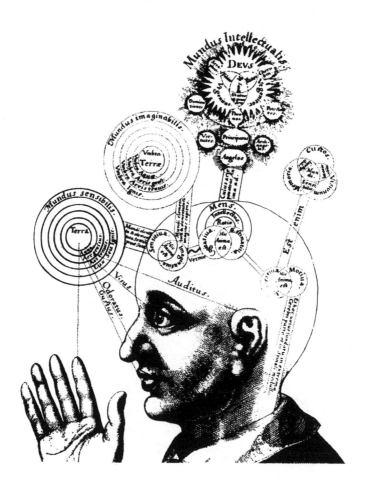

Reprinted from SCIENTIFIC AMERICA, January 1989

The Correspondence Theory

by John Milano

The Correspondence Principle . . . is the requirement that every new theory contain, in as formal a way as its methods allow, a limiting transition to the old theory it replaces. Insofar as the old theory has fitted some sound experiments, the new theory must concur. If Planck's contant h tends towards zero, the quantum equations become just the classical ones; if the speed of light approaches infinity, Einstein's kinematic and dynamical equations go over to Newton's, and so on over a large number of examples from contemporary physics.

Philip Morrison, Ph.D., M.I.T., Book Editor, *Scientific American*

As we apply the Correspondence Principle to Sociobiology and Exopsychology, we expect that each new Einsteinian, relativistic theory of human behavior and neuro-genetic evolution will include a translation back to the old theory it replaced.

Darwinians are clearly in violation when they fanatically, summarily reject the Monotheistic Creation theories of the Judeo-Christian Bible. Newer theories of evolution must provide new insights into the validity of the older theories — specifying the historical, neuro-technical factors which limited the earlier metaphors.

Any new theory of Neuro-genetics must relate to and lovingly demonstrate why the previous philosophic theory was "right" for its time and its gene-pool — knowing that those to come will affectionately do the same for our theories.

The Astrological Zodiac which has continued to attract the attentions of intelligent people for five thousand years *must* have some caste-type meaning — and this significance must be explained by the theories which improve it. New theories can improve, can explain, but not reject, the Zodiac.

The Genesis version of Creation obviously must have had profound survival validity — even though it obviously fails to take into account the newer evidence from Darwinian, Mendelian, DNA, Sociobiological and Behavior Genetics.

The Correspondence theory is a "magic stick" for searching out new laws, because it sets formal constraints on the new mathematics. It also secures science against the loss of achievements of the past; for innovators it is a warning like the Hippocratic maxim for physicians; above all do no harm! Classical mechanics is not a mere blunder that was repudiated in 1905, as the headlines imply. (Morrison)

This affectionate maxim holds even more strongly for Human Ethology (i.e., philoso-

---

Medieval alchemy and Astrology were not blunders repudiated by Dow Chemical and Freud.

---

phy). All the theological and philosophical systems of the past must be seen as attempts (valid at the preceding, more primitive stage of neuro-technology), to explain the inner-outer (CNS-DNA) reality paradox.

Thus the concern in the Starseed Transmissions (*Neurologic, Terra II, What Does WoMan Want?, Exo-psychology, Neuropolitics, Game of Life, Neurological Tarot*) to trace correspondences among the many occult theories of the past (including Christianity and Buddhism) and the newer sciences. Each past philosophy, far from being repudiated, or rejected, joyously fits into an evolving, stage-by-stage theory. Medieval alchemy and Astrology were not blunders repudiated by Dow Chemical and Freud.

Susan Martino emerged from a highly migratory gene-pool and was thus thrust into genetic activism at an early age. She performed heroic feats of courage and strength during the Nixon repression.

In 1986 she organized a publishing company, Spaceseed, which transmitted the most important genetic signals of the time. Under her energetic direction the Spaceseed Company became the largest and most profitable publishing house on the planet.

The Pynchon Manuscript is Smuggled to a Prisoner

by Susan Martino

B y the second day of his incarceration in the "hole" I^2 asked for reading material. An hour later he heard the footsteps of the guard, the clank of the padlock and the rasp of the metal slot being opened. He passively accepted a book which was pushed through the slot; it was entitled *Gravity's Rainbow*. The author was Thomas Pynchon. One quick glance sufficed for him to understand that the book was an important I^2 signal. He lay on the bed and read for 12 hours until the lights were turned off. The next morning he woke at sunrise and read for 15 hours. The following morning he finished the first reading, promptly turned back to page one and spent two days re-reading and annotating. During the subsequent week, he decoded, outlined and charted the narrative. Every character in *Gravity's Rainbow* is either an operative working for a Psychopolitical hive-bureaucracy or an Independent Intelligence Agent (Out-Caste) working counter to the hive-bureaucracy.

GRAVITY'S RAINBOW

THOMAS PYNCHON

RAINBOW

COUNTER-INTELLIGENCE AGENCY REPORT

Date: January, 1972

Country: Montana-Crans, Switzerland

Classification:

Subject: PRESSING HIS SEX AND DANGER BUTTONS

The meeting with Maria (DNA:4; CNS:10-Romantic Gemini from Argentina) takes place in the summit restaurant. As per our script.

The Professor and Craig slide off the T-bar to the restaurant door, kick off their skiis, stack them in the rack, and amble up metal stairs to the restaurant. Their faces glow with sunny mountain vigor.

The Philosopher's espionage eye immediately picks up our two Agents in the crowded restaurant. Our photographer, camera strung around his neck, is waving hello. Subject's emergency circuits flash warning. The Professor is legal but incognito in Switzerland. Michel has warned him that the police can protect him from extradition from the country but not from expulsion from a canton. He knows that if there is too much publicity, Mastronardi cannot head-off the Swiss xenophobic, right-wing politicians.

The other signal comes from the corner of the restaurant where our Beautiful black-haired Agent sits beaming Hormonal Invitation. He stops in his tracks and receives her Circuit Four and Five messages. Mating and Rapture. The multi-buzz was designed by our Psych-control Staff to press his Sex and Danger Buttons. He has been programmed to believe that Risk is the eternal concomitant of the fully utilized brain.

Photo by Agency photographer of meeting between fugitive (far right) & our agent Maria at Summit Restaurant, January 1972.

COUNTER-INTELLIGENCE AGENCY REPORT

Date: **Classification:**

Country:

Subject: page 2

(The following conversation is taped.)

"Who is the slim Sophia Loren?"

"I don't know her name," says Craig. "She hangs out with the Latin-chic set. I've seen her dancing at the clubs."

"With whom is she sitting?"

"They're rich Mexicans, spoiled sons of the Mexico City aristocracy. The short one with a mustache, Pedro, his father owns a big newspaper. The tall, good-looking dude, his family is big industrialist. They go to European schools and hang around the smart spots. They ski like matadors. Weird macho scene. The females don't ski at all. They come up on the cable cars and spend the day here in the restaurant chattering and fluttering and giggling and playing simple-minded card games, shrieking, Uno! Dos! Tres! Cuatro! I don't think they can count beyond four."

"You don't seem to like your Southern cousins," says the Professor.

"They just don't make it here. Socially I mean. The Brazilians and Venezuelans do. They hang out at Gstaad and St. Moritz. Their women have some class. Play backgammon and ski and conduct adulteries with finesse. But the Mexicans strut around getting into barroom brawls. The South Americans are European, really. But the Mexicans seem to have a peasant morality. Machismo. That girl isn't Mexican. I could never figure out why she runs with them. She's got a different style."

"Let's go over and find out. Who is the photographer?"

"He's from a local paper down in the valley," says Craig. "He's cool. Smokes grass. Likes the Stones. Is that enough to pass his security check?"

(End of tape.)

The Professor walks across the restaurant, waving the photographer to follow. She smiles and makes room for him to sit next to her. To our delight, the cameraman was allowed to record the seating. (See attached photos.)

She calls herself Maria and says she is Brazilian. They arrange to meet that night at Le Sporting.

The club is her turf. Males line up along the bar, wave and blow kisses as she passes by. The Fugitive Doctor charged with sparkling South American energy dances with dervish smoothness.

She comes back to the chalet and throws his hashish in the fire. "I can make you feel better than that," she says with passion. He gives her a Tantric Art book. For two nights they play at seduction and then she classically takes him as Her Lover.

— AS PER OUR SCRIPT !! WE HAVE INFILTRATED HIS BED ROOM !!

EVOLUTION

has made no mistakes!

It is all unfolding perfectly according to the genetic plan. It is the myopic arrogance of Dom-Species that leads us to judge the previous or the present or the next stage as better or worse.

THE REDEMPTIVE AGENT

TERRESTRIAL THEOLOGIANS ALWAYS ENDOWED THE GREAT REDEMPTIVE AGENTS — BUDDHA, CHRIST, KRISNA — WITH SUPERNATURAL AND OTHER-WORLDLY POWERS WHICH SEPARATE THEM IN TIME AND POTENCY FROM THE HIVE REALITY. ("SUPERNATURAL" IS JARGON TO DESCRIBE ANYTHING BEYOND HIVE-PLATITUDE.)

THE TASK OF THE EVOLUTIONARY AGENT IS TO PRE-FABRICATE THE FUTURE, TO BUILD NEW HIVES, TO CUSTOM MAKE PLAN-ITS, TO TEACH SCIENTIFIC MASTERY OF THE NERVOUS SYSTEM AS AN INSTRUMENT TO DECODE ATOMIC, MOLECULAR AND SUB-NUCLEAR PROCESSES SO AS TO ATTAIN IMMORTALITY, CLONING, AND EXTRA-TERRESTRIAL EXISTENCE.

(SEE ALSO BRUNO, GALILEO, DR. DEE, DOROTHY SCHULER, GURDJIEFF, VON BRAUN, SUSAN KAISER VOGEL, ROBERT ANTC. WILSON, EDWARD WILSON, F.M. ESFANDIARY, ROY WALFORD, BARBARA HUBBARD, BUCKMINSTER FULLER, PETER VAJK.)

Carolyn and Keith Henson founded the L-5 Society. It was the efforts of the L-5 Society and the Hensons' ability to bring together fatique individuals which made Space Migration possible.

The Space Settlement program will most
gracefully harness the American imagination.

The Psychological Effects of High Orbital Migration

by Carolyn and Keith Henson

In the 16th century the Old World faced the challenging opportunity of colonizing a vast and rich New World.

Two psycho-social systems — which we shall call the Anglo-Celtic and the Mediterranean — set up civilizations in North America and South America respectively. The differences between these two experiments in neuro-politics provide interesting perspectives for anticipating what will happen in the next few decades as the limitless riches of post-terrestrial space attract Old World social competition.

1. The Anglo-Celtic psycho-social model is based upon: individualism, democratic rule, open communication, free mobility, plurality of lifestyle, personal growth, tolerance of difference, encouragement of invention, competition, experimentation, creativity, decentralization, private enterprise, free-market exchange, distrust of military authority.

2. The Mediterranean psycho-social model (derived from Oriental and Middle-Eastern philosophies) emphasized: subordination of the individual to authoritarian hive-rule, restriction of communication (censorship), restriction of movement, controlled uniformity of lifestyle, discouragement of personal growth, rigid maintenance of herd-tradition, state monopoly, distrust of the inventive experimental approach, glorification of military control, centralization, collective enterprise, obedience to bureaucracy, suppression of difference.

A brief examination of the evolution of these two social models in South and North America provides instructive suggestions for the future of Space Colonization.

The technological and economic solutions necessary for permanent and highly profitable High Orbital Mini-Earths (H.O.M.E.S.) appear to have been adequately worked out. The future of post-terrestrial Plan-It colonization now depends on resolving the soft-ware issues: mobilization of public opinion supporting free migration; democratic access to available resources; political and cultural control; psycho-social models and metaphors to guide life in the new custom-made worlds.

The authors suggest that the best way to avoid the South Americanization of Space (i.e., the emergence of civil-service bureaucracies, military dictatorships, class struggles, centralized monopolies, impositions of standardized life-styles) is to re-examine the specific factors which led to the success of the North American model. We recall the emphasis on individuality, the open invitation to migrants from every continent, the free communication which made possible a United States — as well as a review of the obvious mistakes made by the North American pioneers.

The Space Settlement program will most gracefully harness the American imagination (and the aspirations of freedom loving people throughout the planet) if a deliberate attempt is made to recall, renew, reinvigorate and repeat the successful aspects of the Jeffersonian-Edisonian model. Among these factors are the frontier expansive spirit, the independent, self-actualized western hero-heroine, the small gene-pool group seeking to live out a new vision, the need for adventure and calculated risk, the genetic imperative, and the melting-pot open-society mystique.

Reprinted from PARTISAN REVUE, March 1994

The Neurological Level of the Judeo-Christian Bible

by Leslie Fiddler

Leslie Fiddler discovered the principle of neotony (conscious re-adolescence) and applied it to his life and work.

His refusal to follow the over-specialized conformity of the literary dinosaurs who ruled New York culture, his ability to connect with and interpret emerging trends, led to his expulsion from the Terminal Adult establishment.

Fiddler used his Out-Caste perspective to write the classic texts in psychological-genetics. These books include Freeks, Higher Intelligence, *and* Futiques.

Fiddler migrated to a new High Orbital Home around the turn of the 21st century. His adventures on the pioneering frontier provided the material for his epic, picaresque masterpiece Finn-Again's Voyage.

The last contact from Fiddler came in a neurogram sent from his pleasure yacht which was floating down the Milky Way.

The Judeo-Christian Bible is an invaluable index to the neurogenetic level of the period in which it was written. We can always indentify the Genetic Stage of a gene-pool by the personality-characteristics of the Local God.

The Jehovah of Genesis is a low-level barbarian macho punk. He boastfully claims to have created the heaven and the stars and the world, but provides no technical details or replicable blue-prints. His preoccupations, whims, anxieties, jealousies, rules and hatred of women are primitive Mammalian Brain. His petty prides are Primate.

First we note that he is very Animal-Territorial. He owns the Garden, this Mafia Capo, Jehovah. He allows Adam and Eve their tenancy there. He has the right to throw them out. He puts his warrior guards on the periphery of His turf to scare off intruders. He is very Stage 5 with the intelligence of a Lion or possessive child.

Now a post-terrestrial God would not be that concerned with possession of territory. A DNA ecological-engineer God understands that Hir creatures must evolve through the Marine, Territorial, Artifact, and Social technologies — and that they must self-actualize at each; thus passing the 2nd, 5th, 8th and 11th stages of Self-Defined Divinity. Any wise parent smiles when Hir little cub says, "My . . . and mine." This is the beginning of Stage 5: *definition of reality and self in terms of territory*. And every wise parent smiles praise when the little Stage 8 humanoid proudly presents a crayon drawing or

The Jehovah of Genesis is a low-level barbarian macho punk.

some original symbolic creation. Now it is true that the terrestrial parent gets upset when the kids fool around with the Tree of Good and Evil, i.e., the Socio-Sex rituals of the local hive — but this is no reason to throw the kids out of the house and put a flaming torch at the front door to keep the poor errant youngster from creeping back contritely. No, the Jehovah God has not reached the technological level or the civilized stage of parental cultural transmission.

The fact that Sexuality is not a concern of the Genesis Jehovah supports the suggestion that we are dealing in this folk legend with the reality of a 7th Brain Paleolithic-Herding Tribe obsessed with territory; moving uneasily into an 8th Brain Inventive Self-actualization. The Bible is thus a collection of histories and taboos produced by backward, Semitic tribes, pre-civilized, in awe and fear of the sexually-active feudal kingdoms around them.

The power of the Bible-thumping Christianities which emerged from the Old Testament tradition is rural, pre-urban. Fundamentalist Christianity appeals to the pre-Civilized, prudish tribal people who are not ready for urban feudal pleasures.

Remember, the principle of Correspondence keeps us from rejecting the Judeo-Christian Bible as erroneous. It becomes a valuable ethological document to help us locate the evolutionary stage which emerged in the Middle East at Biblical Times.

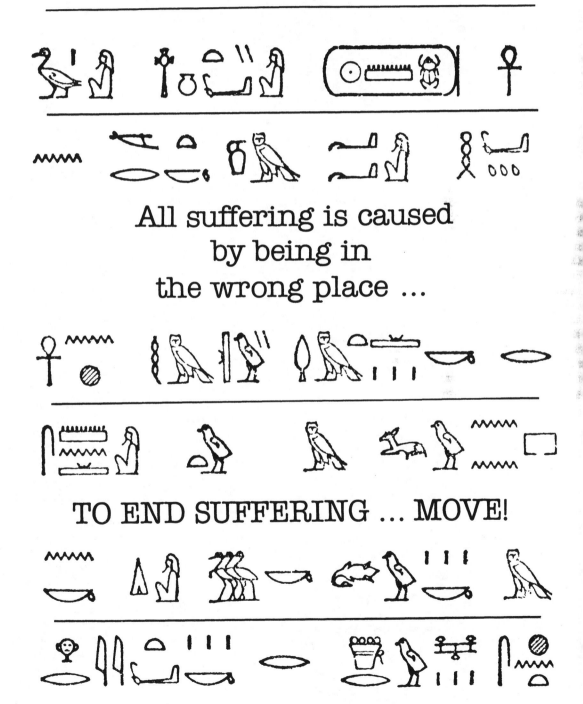

All suffering is caused by being in the wrong place ...

TO END SUFFERING ... MOVE!

The Gospel According to My Husband

by Mrs. Thomas Pynchon

Thomas Pynchon's work illustrates one of those strange historical occurrences in the field of information. "*Gravity's Rainbow*," gushed John Gardner, "is guaranteed to double the intelligence of anyone who understands it." High praise, indeed, from a Counter-Intelligence operative whose life was devoted to Chaucerian Rumination.

Gravity's Rainbow is properly described as an encyclopedic epic. A detailed updating of the classic tensions of evolution: Control versus Expansion. I.Q. (Intelligence Qualification, Queering, Quitting, Quarreling, Quizzing) versus I^2.

My husband's book describes how modern psychology-neurology-psycho-pharmacology was created by the Allied and German militaries during World War II.

The Anglo-American Psychological Warfare Branch operates a mind-control unit named Pisces (Psychological Intelligence Schemes for Expediting Surrender). Tommy hastens to point out that "whose" surrender is never made clear. From a base in England, Pisces' agents probe the mysteries of consciousness, behavior and brain-function, using Pavlovian conditioning, ESP, brain surgery, hypnosis, clairvoyance, drugs, objective questionnaires, projective tests, personality assessments, behavior modifications.

Gravity's Rainbow is an exhaustive, clinical study of the tactics and strategies of the behavior control bureaucracy — and the methods used by enlightened, anarchistic individuals to counter the controls. The book is a monumental treatise on intelligence increase (I^2) and intelligence control (I.Q.).

HUMAN INTELLIGENCE EVOLVES THROUGH CONTINUAL MUTATION AND MIGRATION

The first recorded human history is Egyptian, dated 4241 B.C. During the next four-thousand years civilization evolved in a migration-re-migration shuttle between

---

Imagine that it's 800,000 B.C., Lower Paleolithic...

---

the Mid-Brain-Middle-East (Cairo, Jerusalem, Babylon) down to Shanghai. Along the Genetic Runway — 30th to 45th degrees longitude. The spinal column of genetic Intelligence.

Imagine that it's 800,000 B.C., Lower Paleolithic and you are a Homo Erectus born where life originated and still flourishes in primitive forms in Africa. You move North along the fertile avenue of the Nile and you reach the Middle East. You face West. In front of you is the Mediterranean Sea — wine-dark, endless, blocking movement West. To your left lies Africa — so hot that everything melts. The genetic swamp where you originated, soft, cozy, warm — but mobility is slowed. To your right lies the jagged peninsula, craggy mountains and cold forests of Europe.

So, if you are neuro-geared for action and movement you sense those neo-lithic, mobile-noble, self-directed circuits kicking around in your Brain. You don't go South and you don't go North. And the sea blocks you Westward.

You turn and face East. Now that's more like it for restless Genetic Agitators. The fertile crescent of the Tigris and Euphrates. The green plains of Persia. The northern mountains of Afghanistan ooze you down through the Kyber to the gentle hills of Indus Valley. You skirt the Himalayas along the Ganges and it's a smooth-flow all the way down to the South China Seas.

Four thousand years of empires a-building along the great transcontinental neuron pathway from Suez to Shanghai. The noble empires — Egyptian Dynasties, Hittites, Babylon, Assyria, Medes and Persians. The movements of civilization moving East — along the historic invasion routes through the Kyber, Gumal and

Bolan Passes reaching China in two thousand years. (The first authenticated dynasty is the Hsia, 2205–1766 B.C.).

The Chou dynasty (1122–249 B.C.) produced the affluence, security and self-confidence necessary for a philosophic blossoming: Confucius, Laotze and Mencius. Here we note the characteristic of Oriental thought. It is terminal, soothing, quiescent. Confucius outlines the rules of insectoid-caste conduct which can keep the hive-game going harmoniously. Laotze sings his rhythmic song of cycles, easy-come, easy-go, cool-out, be-here-now passivity. You can understand why. There was no place to go!

Stand on the China coast in the 6th Century B.C. You've got the wasteland of the Pacific Ocean at your back. And, with no compass or marine technology, that's a dead end. In front of you there's 6000 miles of mammalian territory that's all signed, sealed, and mortgaged, locked up by kingdoms, empires, duchies, brigand-tribes. Each suspiciously confronting neighboring units.

You've got the wasteland of the Pacific Ocean at your back.

So by 1000 B.C. all the gene-pools ready to move up into the future are collecting in the Middle-East waiting for the marine-technology and navigational skill to sail up the great inter-cerebral fissure called the Middle-Earth Sea.

You Have to Be Together...
...To Be Two-gether

MERRILL M. KAGAN

COUNTER-INTELLIGENCE AGENCY REPORT

Date: January, 1972

Country: Montana-Crans, Switzerland

Subject: THE SEXUAL FLOWER OF STAGE
10 FEUDAL CIVILIZATION

Classification:

During the week our informant models in Lausanne. Weekends She is Perfect Mistress, elegant, bawdy, funny. Her description is as follows: Lavender-pink translucent skin, Andalusian enamel, Her tawny corazon basket in opal on smoky gold, admirably adapted to the rounded contour of the hand, Her contessa-face is etched crystal, eyes in dark enamel. She speaks no English, luckily, so they fuse in basic French. Her gestures are gitane-erotic, Rita Hayworth. To say Espagnolade is not to be overly derisive.

But She won't engage at Circuit Five.

One afternoon while performing some lazy yoga he puts a small crumb of Kabul resin in Her mouth and says, "<u>Mangez</u>. It will relax your muscles."

The neurograms look like a Canabis Rapture Commercial. "Oh mon amour, jamais, jamais," she murmurs to the camera. Her Fabergé pink-platinum network had never moved so smoothly and there is no doubt that new circuits of fluid transmission have been activated. We instructed her, of course, to desist. So the next day when he offers Her some more, she sniffs in disapproval and opens a bottle of Valais.

He was overheard telling her that She is crown jewel of Terrestrial Domestication, Princess of Ceremonial Linkage for whom Kings put aside Thrones, Ambassadors forget their Duties, Maharajas carpet marbled Floors with Rubies. This Agent is programmed to do anything for Her Lover. Passion, fervor, ardor, fever, desire, longing, yearning. "J'aime pour deux," She murmurs. Eager to suffer, mourn, lament, languish, anguish, pine, grieve, despair. She loves to dance, flirt, fuck, tease, coquet, vamp, lick, excite, titillate. She is the perfect racy drunk, joking Shady Lady, dancing down to Rio, cooking gourmet meals, laughing that none of Her friends would believe. He worships Her as The Sexual Triumph of Feudal Civilization, but when he looks aloft on starry nights he appears lonely. The predicted Difference in Velocity. Delta V.

Maria and skiing are what is happening before we get him ejected from the Canton of Valais.

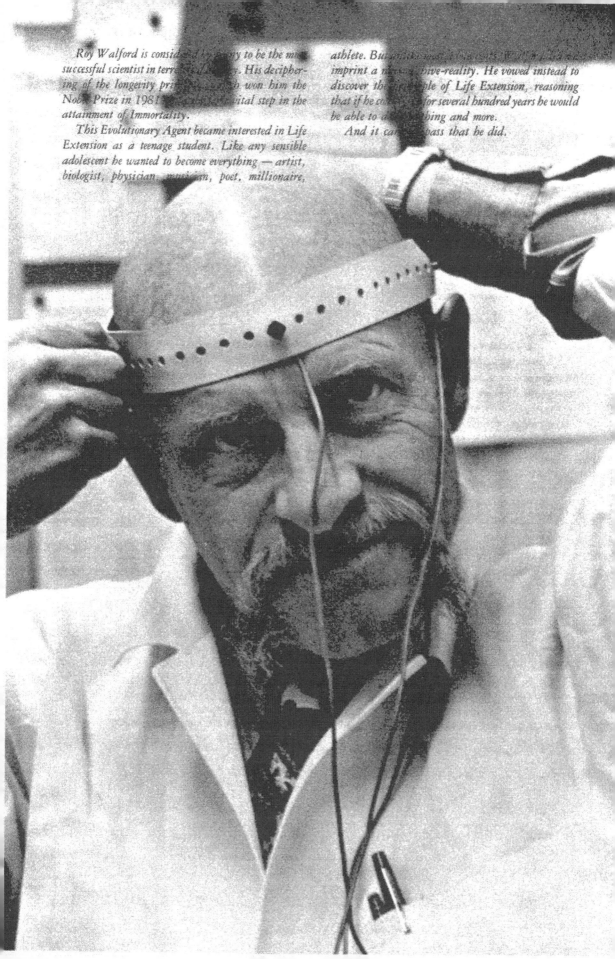

Roy Walford is consid[ere]d by [man]y to be the m[ost] successful scientist in terr[estri]al [histor]y. His decipher-ing of the longevity pri[...] [whi]ch won him the Nob[el] Prize in 1981 [...] [a] vital step in the attainment of Immortality.

This Evolutionary Agent became interested in Life Extension as a teenage student. Like any sensible adolescent he wanted to become everything — artist, biologist, physician, mus[ici]an, poet, millionaire,

athlete. Bu[t...] imprint a ni[...]ive-reality. He vowed instead to discover th[e...]le of Life Extension, reasoning that if he co[uld...] for several hundred years he would be able to d[o...]thing and more.

And it ca[me to] pass that he did.

Werner von Braun as Science Fiction Hero

by Roy Walford

In the early decades of the 20th century (Stage 11) traces of industrial pollution initiated the activation of the first post-terrestrial hum-models. Thousands of Pre-Dom (Stage 15) individuals were produced in gene-pools located in the Forward Technological Niches of Western Europe. Of these pre-mature evolutes, most ended up as weirdo artists or in asylums. The more fortunate appeared in environments where their neural programs could find external supports.

Robert Goddard, the Wizard of Worcester, flourished in the Snow Belt of the New World; Konstantin Edouradovich Tsiolovsky, the genius of Kaluga, was produced by a dissenting science intellectual gene-pool; space-visionary Krafft A. Ehricke sprung from parents who were scientifically trained. The most successful of the proto-post-terrestrials was, of course, Werner von Braun. (In studying the personal evolution of these obvious-mutants, the neurogeneticist is not surprised to discover that during the vulnerable-to-imprint adolescent years, there occurred the revelation, the flash insight that *they were not terrestrials*).

Goddard's unfolding pre-sexual brain was stimulated, as were millions of pre-adolescent lobes, by the Science Fiction of Jules Verne and by the standard "fantasy" stories of Mars exploration in daily newspapers. The effect of Science Fiction and of "yellow journalism" in activating post-terrestrial circuits cannot be overestimated! UFO rumors, Sci-Fi hoaxes, lurid unscientific news stories are key signals which awaken young brains to futique possibilities. Newspapers were powerful reality-transmission tools during the Pre-Flight years. When a newspaper published a wild, unfounded hoax story about a Science Fiction theme, it was performing a key role in evolution by using the hive-ritual of "news" to transmit a future reality

trace.

Science Fiction is always more important than Science because the former anticipates, guides, directs the latter. Indeed, it is safe to say that all Scientific progress is initiated by Science Fictionists who turn their blueprints over to the Science Engineers. The Scientist Fiction Caste is the future probe of the species — always Pre-Dom by many stages. The Hive Engineer Caste is much more numerous. For every post-hive Science Fictionist there are more than a thousand hive Science Engineers who work on the present and past. Post-hive scientists are rarely called by that name. For example, Jules Verne was called a novelist; Giordano Bruno a

---

Interplanetary travel! Here was a task worth dedicating one's life to!

---

dissenting philosopher; Arthur C. Clarke (who designed the Com-Sat system decades before its manufacture), a Sci-Fi author.

Evolutionary Agent Werner von Braun was born of a noble family in Silesian Germany. Members of Pre-Dom Castes born to aristocratic gene-pools *at times of technological advance* are unusually free to attain self-indulgent (Stage 13) and self-actualized (Stage 14) status and thus choose, i.e., be allowed to follow DNA intuitions, to select their robot-role.)

Von Braun's mother, another evolutionary agent, encouraged her son to study the stars. "For my confirmation," confided von Braun, "I got a telescope. My mother thought this would make the best gift."

According to biographer Shirley Thomas, "Through this hobby, he happened upon an article in an astronomy magazine that crystallized the patterns his life should take. He relates, 'I don't remember the name of the magazine or the author, but the article described an imaginary voyage to the moon. It filled me with a romantic urge. Interplanetary travel! Here was a task worth dedicating one's life to! Not just to stare through a telescope at the moon and the planets but to soar through the heavens and actually explore the mysterious universe. I knew how Columbus had felt.'"

Reflect on this amazing statement. This pre-adolescent larval understood how an evolutionary agent, 450 years before, felt about his genetic task. Columbus was clear about his destiny, his obligation to the species. But the significance of his genetic clarity is, of course, lost upon most biographers. That the young von Braun responded to the genetic imperative behind the Columbus mission is comforting evidence that pre-programmed nervous systems can be activated in pre-adolescence to extraordinary futique missions.

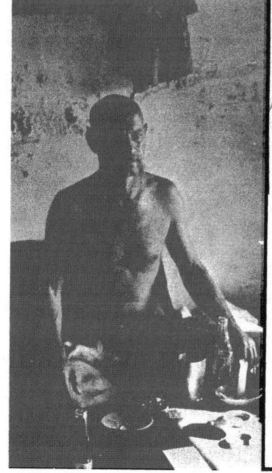

Oh, by the way, I have to apologize to you. I should have done it before. I want to appeal to you. *Please. do not believe anything I say.* (Applause)

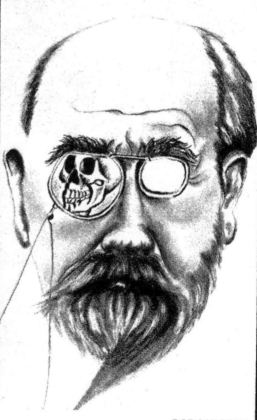

DORIS VARTAN

I have been studying human nervous systems for the last 25 years, I have performed many neurological experiments, my friends, (*laughter*) and have come to the conclusion that the human nervous system, this 111-billion-cell bio-electric computer, is not a set of ice tongs. You don't hook the sharp claws of belief onto an idea and hold it.

By all means listen to everything; consider anything. Pick up a belief and try it out. If it works, use it as long as it works. And then put it down or change it. Be open to new ideas. But I urge you, don't *believe* in any final sense anything I say.

Reprinted from SCIENTIFIC AMERICA, July 1999

Inner and Outer Space

by Werner von Braun

During World War II Hitler was approached by a committee of distinguished scientists from the Max Planck Institute and the Prague Pharmaceutical Laboratories, who proposed the theory that the earth is hollow. *Und zo*, if we can find the entrance or punch a hole through to the interior, *mein Gott*, all sorts of new military adventures suggest themselves. We pop up behind enemy lines and conquer the external surface. Who controls the inner surface of a sphere controls the outer world. Heil Hitler! *Heute Deutschland; Morgen das Inner-welt, morgen morgen das Extra-welt.*

This legend has been passed on, in print, by anti-Nazi agents to demonstrate the insanity of Hitler. There is no hard data concerning whether der Feuhrer really did divert scientific energy (which could have supported atomic bomb-research or improved rocket-research) into Inner-earth exploration. But let us assume that the legend is true, that Adolph did believe in an "inner-world" and did, indeed, initiate

> ## Who controls the inner surface of a sphere controls the outer world. Heil Hitler!

scientific Inner-World-Exploration. To make this assumption is to credit Hitler with considerable (if twisted) prophetic genius. Inner-world aspirations in 1935 clearly anticipated the Neurological Revolution of the 1960's which sent over one hundred million Americans digging in psychic mole-holes, pursuing the vision of an inner-world rebirth. Heil, Werner Erhard.

Hitler, like many premature evolutes, inhabited a post-terrestrial set of realities. Total power in the context of Tibetan Buddhism obviously activated the Self-Indulgent and the Self-Actualized circuits in his nervous system. Hitler, however, made the same error that millions of naive trippers were to make in the 1960's. He failed to understand that the very self-centered, post-hive consciousness which exhilarated him to messianic perception was also available to others. He was not informed that the self-actualized brain must include in its mapping the reality that other self-actualized, futique brains exist and are independently building neighboring future Plan-Its.

Self-actualization is a post-hive, post-terrestrial tool. Black Magic is the use of futique knowledge to gain control over the passed-present. Hitler was evilly using post-terrestrial tools to grab terrestrial power. It is considered genetic wickedness to use post-hive knowledge to control the old hive. Futique competence is a sacred trust — to be used to propel the hive-mythos into a new ecological niche. (Zionists commit the same genetic crime when they use advanced technology to go back and conquer the primitive Arabs.)

Hitler's vision of living inside rather than on the surface of a satellite-planet is, of course, a most accurate forecast of subsequent stages of evolution. The ecological niche to which post-humans are now moving involves hollow-

---

Futique competence is a sacred trust.

---

mini-world Plan-Its constructed in space beyond the planet's gravitational pull.

Is it not true that throughout the range of evolution those who migrate within capsules of their own construction are more advanced than those who live clinging to the outside of capsules someone else built? Actually, the best evolutionary stages to inhabit are those of intense, dramatic inner-outer exploration. Like 1960-1980.

(By 1976 the rumor spread that this Hitler myth was invented by Zionist Intelligence Agents who had participated in the C.I.A.'s LSD experiments.)

NASA

For further information about space colonization and industrialization, and the social, technological and political issues surrounding these ideas, contact:

L-5 SOCIETY

1620 NORTH PARK AVENUE

TUCSON, ARIZONA 85719

COUNTER-INTELLIGENCE AGENCY REPORT

Date: January, 1972

Country: Montana-Crans, Switzerland

Subject: THE FASTER YOU GO
THE SAFER YOU ARE

Classification:

TOP
SECRET

The ski satori, the velocity revelation, can be seen, in retrospect, to be preparation for the arrival of Prince Alexis.

The Professor strains through novice exercises for three weeks. At the beginning his muscles are weak from unaccustomed movements. He is on the slopes from ten until five every day, but progress is slow. For fifty years his gross musculature had been programmed to deal with the pull of gravity without swinging his hips.

He watched the Swiss three year olds, brought to the slopes on weekends by parents. Sliding along with confidence, being trained to ski at the time when nervous systems are most vulnerable to learning anti-gravity maneuvers.

Date:

Country:

Subject: page 2

Classification:

After three weeks of straining he apparently senses that the time has come to re-imprint. After loosening his conditioned patterns and suspending imprints by means of Neurological Techniques developed in the research laboratories at Harvard University, he finds himself standing on skiis at slope top, brain disconnected from body and laryngeal muscles of the mind. Bathing, as it were, in Waves of Energy.

Craig, standing next to him, waves and plummets down the slope. Without hesitation, the Professor opens the door to his body, climbs in, turns the dial and follows, imitating every movement of his guru. Freed from mind and habit, the Body is a simple vehicle to operate. One points the skis downhill and slides the contours of the slope. The terrain does the thinking. Slight changes in direction are accomplished by shifting the weight and swinging the mid-section.

The faster you go, the more control you have and the easier to maneuver! There is little to do except surf the swift gravity wave. To make sharp turns you skid both skis until they point in the new direction. But this must be done at the highest possible speed. Slowing down is yielding control to gravity's grasp.

Craig, glancing back, sees his wild-eyed pupil, laughs, and keeps going. They soar down the expert slope, miles of curving, twisting descent, and skid in a shower of snow to the bottom.

Craig lifts his poles in exultation. "You have broken through. You can ski."

"It is a moment of Neurological Revelation," he shouts. "Like the First Fuck." He motions to the lift-bar. Once again. Faster. He can't wait to get to the summit. Standing on the crest he shouts his discovery. "The faster you go the safer you are!"

He pulls back the sleeve of his jacket to check his watch. "Let's time it. Faster."

For the next two hours the Fugitive rides his body down the run marveling at rushing pleasure. Like the first acid experience. High speed philosophy. All-out kinaesthetic yoga.

Before cracking this hedonic gap, skiing, like adolescent sex, had been inefficient groping work. Two minutes to descend twenty feet, straining, pushing skis against slippery snow, leaning on poles, anxiously studying each yard of surface, struggling to keep control, to go slow. Total larval concentration on which muscles to be pulled, which angle to be wrestled. The satisfaction came in remaining erect, unharmed.

Now he flashed through two kilometers in two minutes. Ice patches, formerly terrors to be avoided are now accelerators to be shot through. Moguls are now round energy clusters to be used as turn curves. What had been feared is now used to increase intensity and control. The snow-covered mountain is an anti-gravity energy-apparatus bristling with knobby dials to select, direct, modulate, amplify the wind-swift current.

The sun has set. Craig and the Professor stand at the summit looking down at the Rhone valley and the orange clouds. There are no other skiers left, only the restaurant staff bundling into the last cable car down. The wind whips the unprotected peak.

"I hate to leave," he says.

"We're always the last ones to come down."

Date:

Country:

Classification:

Subject:　　　page 3

TOP SECRET

They plunge down the right side of the valley wall, skid around the left turn throwing up waves of snow, dive straight to the base of the high T-bar lift, veer right bumping through the steep mogul field, thread down the narrow, icy roadway, slash a sudden right-angle down a wide, steep meadow, slide right again, burst under the tow cable out to the top of the mid-slope, and race, hunching low, poles tucked under armpits, wind ripping their faces.

At the bottom station they reach down to snap off bindings, swing skis over shoulder and, suddenly earthbound, clumsily roll in ski-boot, high-gravity gait along the village streets to the saloon. They stack the skis outside and open the door to a rush of warm air scented with alcohol, smoke, perfume and the steam of healthy bodies. The atmosphere has that soft-electricity of congenial, happy, sophisticated people who like themselves and each other.

They order beers and sit back, content.

"It's addictive."

Craig smiles in agreement. "It's neurological yoga. It's muscular meditation. It does everything that the oriental gurus claim, but it's more.

"The danger bit is fascinating," says the Philosopher. "The risk buzz."

"Power freed for pleasure and clean speed," says Craig. "I'm glad you got the hit today. It's happened for you and you can never lose it. It's very sexual." He motions to the saloon filled with hi-fi people. "It's new, you know, like a mutation. High speed skiing has just developed in the last twenty years. It's part of what's happening all around. Electronics and computers and jet planes and space travel. It's the same principle and it's the exact opposite of what we learned in the old life. It's the paradox of technological civilization. The faster you go the more control you have. Like the pilot flying 700 miles per hour with finger-tip control. On the ground you need a tow-tractor to make the plane turn."

"You go up and you come down."

"And a lot can happen up there. Sometimes you don't come down with whom you went up. You move with those at the same velocity."

"Delta V."

DELTA V*

*DELTA V MEANS DIFFERENCE
IN VELOCITY BETWEEN TWO
MOVING PARTICLES.

HOW TO INCREASE

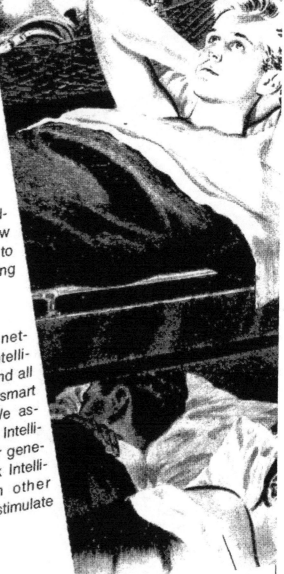

Aleister Crowley said: "There are three ways to increase your intelligence:

1. Continually expand the scope, source, intensity of the information you receive.

2. Constantly revise your reality maps, and seek new metaphors about the future to understand what's happening now.

3. Develop external networks for increasing intelligence. In particular, spend all your time with people as smart or smarter than you. We assume that you are the Intelligence Agent from your gene-pool, so you will seek Intelligence Agents from other gene-pools who will stimulate you to get smarter."

INTELLIGENCE

TUCSON LECTURE

WESTWARD BY SEA

Genetic History (as opposed to political history) is a record of those moments when a successful gene-pool migrates in response to swarming pressures: the hive castes out its future probes. Those migrating-wave moments produce the highest peak of civilizations, of culture, of hive philosophy and art and science.

Civilization began in the East. Shuttling up and down the Spinal Column from Suez to China. The great pyramids of Egypt remind us that long ago women and men looked at the stars and built enormous highways aloft. Inside the pyramid they assembled all the instruments and comforts needed in a post-terrestrial life. The Egyptian gene-pool evolved rapidly and prematurely because they had temporarily solved the four terrestrial survival problems: security, political autonomy, technological predominance and a national socio-sexual mythos. The Nile Valley geography produced this early genetic probe into the future.

Civilization began in the East.

In Babylon the breakthroughs in science, mathematics, astronomy, medicine, technology were celebrated in the epic poem *Gilgamesh*, who personified the Search for the seed-flower of Immortality. The story of going beyond limits, beyond chartered realms, beyond the territories of the known, scouting out gene-pool futures.

Exactly when the Greek wave migrated, Sophocles and Aeschylus wrote their plays; Phidias sculpted; Socrates, Plato and Aristotle, and the physical mathematical philosophers raised Greek civilization to its highest point.

Then the Intelligence Frontier moved to Rome. Virgil sang the song of the Migrating Aeneid. All the great epics are "trip" stories, remember? The classic heroes surf genetic waves, voyagers moving out beyond hive limits.

Then the Arab empire exploded from the Middle East across the North African coast. The great achievements of the Moslem wave came in the universities of Cordoba and Seville where Arab mathematicians, philosophers, musicians and astronomers made their great contributions to the evolution of intelligence. When success-

All the great epics are "trip" stories, remember?

ful gene-pools migrate, expand, explode outward, westward, they propel their seed-style into the future.

This same wave of mutation and migration has, for the last 2000 years, moved the Highest Intelligence flower of our species relentlessly from East to West. The Phoenicians, and then the Greeks, pushing their risky space craft out across the Mediterranean, their brows cleaving the unknown sea.

Marine technology started the movement of gene-pools West towards the unknown future.

DIFFERENT SCENES

FOR DIFFERENT GENES

ON THE EVOLUTION OF EVOLUTION

THE REDEMPTIVE AGENT

"And so it frequently occurs that the Redemptive Agent must endure long periods of quiescence and obscurity. These can be times of grave peril, obstruction or hive-disgrace. Out-Caste Agents have been selected on the basis of their capacity to face and survive experiences which would be judged unendurable by terrestrials. The childhoods of Agents abound in anecdotes of precocious sagacity, strength and independence from hive-morals. We recall the scandalous escapades of Krishna, the prowess of Hercules, the boyish wisdom of Einstein, the early verbal cleverness of the Galilean, the patience of Robert Goddard, the endurance of Susan Kaiser Vogel."

Reprinted from SCIENTIFIC AMERICA, February 1983

The Post-Heisenberg Determinacy Principle

by Gerard O'Neill

Gerard O'Neill is the Christopher Columbus of Space Migration.

One of the most important forces in moving human intelligence from the Old Science (Euclidian-Newtonian) to the New Science (Einsteinian-Planck) was the Principle of Uncertainty introduced by Werner Heisenberg. *The very presence of the experimenter and hir measuring instruments becomes a determining factor in the field of investigation.*

This principle seemed to eliminate any hope of objectivity. A philosophic angst, a sense of scientific futility, was the first reaction to Heisenberg's dictum. "Alas," the Newtonians groaned, "we can never really know what God or Nature hath wrought, because, the very act of investigating changes the situation."

We have now matured enough as an intelligent species to realize that Heisenberg's Principle is, in actuality, one of *Self-Actualized Determinacy*. We now understand that everything we see and know is a function of our reality-mapping, i.e., a function of the way we program our brains. Let us call this the Principle of Neurological Determinacy. And with the Self-confidence, courage and freedom thus attained, let us accept the responsibility implied.

Yes, within the limits of our genetic stage we shall responsibly determine (construct, create, fabricate) the new realities we inhabit!

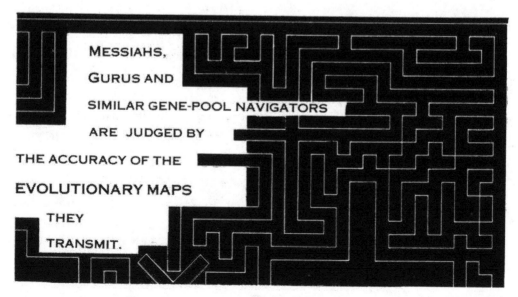

MESSIAHS, GURUS AND SIMILAR GENE-POOL NAVIGATORS ARE JUDGED BY THE ACCURACY OF THE EVOLUTIONARY MAPS THEY TRANSMIT.

GENETIC HALL OF FAME

Bucky & Anne Fuller

Robert Stigwood was one of the most important Intelligence Agents of the 20th century. His Australian genes helped. (In the 18th and 19 centuries, as is well known, English gene-pools expelled their most vigorous, restless, intelligent seed to open ecological niches — Canada, America, Australia.)

Australia was founded by Out-Castes, wild ones too ambitious, too individualistic to be domesticated in the tidy island home-hive. This extraordinary genetic experiment bred arrogance, self-confidence and rugged freedom. The continent is, however, too far removed from the genetic runway along which evolution increases its escape velocity; so as the Age of Individualism dawned, carefully selected Australians migrated to the Action sites.

Robert Murdoch easily took over London and Manhattan publishing: the tired menopausal publishing business. Robert Stigwood received a more important assignment: to wrest control of the record-movie industry from the bourgeois hive-moralists and domesticated bureaucrats. Since records and films create the realities which all humans inhabit, Stigwood's genetic task was to fabricate a more intelligent future. Specifically, to rescue the human race from the loser-myth of terminal adulthood and Judeo-Christian passivity.

Stigwood easily accomplished his mission by giving adolescents the self-confidence to reject inefficient, out-moded adult models and the ability to create new styles of self-actualized success.

In Saturday Night Fever, Grease, and Sgt. Pepper's Lonely Hearts Club Band Stigwood created a mythos of cocky, arrogant, happy, hedonic youth strutting into a successful future. There is no violence or anger. The Travoltas, Newton-Johns, Framptons, Bee Gees cheerfully side-stepped bumbling adults — portrayed accurately as a dying breed of confused dinosaurs — and simply created a new social reality inhabited by the new species of Intelligent

Narcissists.

Stigwood followed his legendary capture of Hollywood with his spectacular real estate ventures. By 1985 Stigwood Pleasure Worlds had spread throughout the American Sun Belt. The millions of hedonic agents who lived and worked in these Eden Parks hosted the rest of the world, who came ready to learn the pleasures and freedoms of Intelligent Self-Actualization.

By 1990 Robert Stigwood, and his partner Ron Bernstein, had become beloved philosopher-saints, benignly presiding over a Utopian Empire of music, joy and profit. The Stigwood Heartland communities became the nucleus groups from which Space Colonies (High Orbital Mini Earths) were launched.

Stigwood, thus, can rightly claim the title of Father of the Future.

Reprinted from NATIONAL ENQUIRY, November 1982

Marilyn Sings A Song About Intelligence Maps

by Robert Stigwood

One evening Marilyn was listening to two friends having an historical debate while having dinner in the Columbia Pictures Dining Room.

The argument was whether David Begelman was a more skilled thief than Harry Cohn. Marilyn kept hir eyes and mouth wide open with interest, although SHe couldn't understand a word they were saying.

Something occurred to hir as SHe sat silently with hir two gay friends. SHe realized that about two-thirds (66%) of the time SHe hadn't the faintest notion of what people (even women, of all people) were talking about. There was no

hiding it. There were enormous gaps in hir intelligence apparatus.

Marilyn decided to go to school to learn how to be an Intelligence Agent. The next day SHe applied as a student to West Point, Annapolis, and the F.B.I. Academy. U.S.C. finally accepted hir.

Hir tutor was a woman. Marilyn was depressed by this at first because SHe didn't think a woman could teach hir anything. But in a few days SHe knew differently.

Hir charming tutor was one of the most exciting human beings Marilyn had ever met. SHe talked about the Cold War and made it sound ten times more important than M.G.M.'s biggest epic. Marilyn main-lined everything SHe heard. SHe met Whittaker Chambers, Westbrook Pegler, and Joseph Alsop. There was a new genius to hear about every day.

A few weeks later Marilyn branched out as a student of intelligence. SHe started buying books about sex by Freud and some of his modern disciples. SHe read them till SHe got dizzy.

But SHe didn't have enough time. Getting smart, learning how to use your head, is no bed of roses! There were acting lessons, singing lessons, publicity interviews and swarms of producer-sperm waiting to be swallowed.

So SHe decided to postpone hir intelligence. But SHe made a promise to hirself SHe vowed never to forget. Marilyn swore that in a few years, after things settled down, SHe would start Increasing hir Intelligence. SHe would read all books and find out about all the wonders

there were in the world. And then, when SHe sat among important people, SHe would be able to understand what they were talking about.

Getting smart, learning how to use your head, is no bed of roses!

And even contribute a few words.

Now the time had come. Zurich. 1972.

And what better place than Zurich to talk about Intelligence Maps? There were plenty of grim-smiling men, here in the Odeon, right now, who didn't manage to be exposed at Harvard to the Hedonic Revolution (Puritan mysteries and Stoic-cynicism were their bag); who signed government contracts, swearing eternal loyalty to the Counter-Intelligence Firm. And, who now, always under-cover, were in Switzerland to work for A.B.C. and its "intelligence" network which operated here under the label: Office of Strategic Services. O.S.S.

Crossing the street to the Kronenhalle, Marilyn was accosted by the center fielder of the Yankees, Micky Mantle himself, who handed hir an autographed bat and asked for The Map.

"Yes," SHe said, "you need maps Mr. Mantle. In passing through unknown territory, The Future, for example, it is of utmost importance to have accurate plans and to make new blueprints. To the extent that you rely on past-maps, you will retrace the territory of the past. Find the Future Maps Mr. Mantle! Locate the

Bad, much to my dismay, is no longer automatically good.

plans for the stages to come, and commit them to memory. Every DNA Agent knows that! *Reality maps cannot be stolen.* They can be memorized and transcribed only by you.

"The plans are obvious Mr. Mantle, and can be located by looking where 'They' tell you not to look — on the Out-Caste Frontiers. Past reality maps are useful, but only if you have the key: S.M.I.^{2}L.E. Without this key, past reality maps are confusing. Now that we are beyond Newtonian ethics it is no longer true that the past-plans say exactly the opposite of what they are said to say. Bad, much to my dismay, is no longer automatically good."

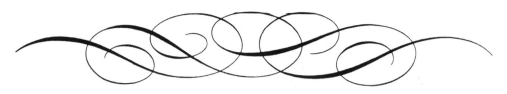

GENETIC HALL OF FAME

Anne Apfelbaum
Frank and Nancy Barron
Ron Bernstein
David and Angela Bowie
Stuart Brand
Jerry Brown
Barbara Chase
Christopher Columbus
Sir Francis Crick
Aleister Crowley
Madame Curie
Henry Edwards
Albert and Elsa Einstein
Liz Elliot
F. M. Esfandiary
Leslie and Sally Fiedler
Neil and Ursula Freer
Galileo
Daniel Gilbertson
Robert Goddard
Sergius Golowin
Mary Leary Gorman
Gurdjieff
Alan Harrington
Larry Hauben
Gale Eden Henson
Valerie Aurora Henson
Windy Morningstar Henson
Frank and Beverly Herbert
Pauline Kael
George Koopman
Julien Offray de la Mettrie
Al Larkin

Jack Leary
Joanna Harcourt-Smith Leary
Jay Levey
George and Bonnie Litwin
Henry and Susan Marshall
Susan Martino
Abe Maslow
Horace Mastronardi
Kevin McCormick
Jim McPherson
John Milano
George Milman
Stevie Nicks
Anais Nin
Gerard O'Neill
Eric Orr
Elvis and Priscilla Presley
Mrs. Thomas Pynchon
Tom Robbins
Carl and Helen Rogers
Jason Salesky
Harrison Schmidt
Robert Stigwood
Valentina Tereshkova
Peter and Helen Vajk
Susan Kaiser Vogel
Werner von Braun
Nena von Schlebrugge
Roy Walford
Andy Warhol
Glayde Whitney
Edward Wilson
Robert Anton and Arlen Wilson

Rosemary Woodruff

Date: February, 1972
Country: Montana-Crans, Switzerland

Classification:

TOP
SECRET

Subject: THE EXPULSION FROM
CANTON VALAIS

Our photographer has published (as ordered) six glamor-hero-fun pictures, along with a stirring tribute from the young people of the canton honored by the presence of the Philosopher, now learning to ski. Heh! Heh! Heh!

The paper is French-language published in lower Valais. A week later our contact on the German paper from upper Valais published a fiery editorial accusing the lower Valais administration of adopting the Philosophy of Hedonism, License, and Drug Addiction. The headline read: Lower Valais Endorses Sin.

Suddenly the Philosopher becomes the biggest political issue since the scandal of the bridge ten years ago. The Catholic Press (French) rises to defend him and the tradition of Swiss tolerance. Protestants denounce Catholics. The mountain people on this side of the valley are for the Professor. The mountain people from the other side are vice versa.

When we arranged for school children to start signing petitions in his favor we knew the battle was won. The parents reacted as predicted. The two policemen who came to see him were laughing their heads off. Everyone sees what is happening and digs the controversy which will hurt no one except the foreigner.

National Party Committee takes sides. The Chief of the Cantonal Police (Bureau trained at Langley, VA, 1970) asked him down for tea. There is much "Helas," "Incroyable," "Quel horreur," but the Philosopher must leave the canton.

All Counter-Intelligence personnel involved in this provocation SHOULD BE COMMENDED!!

Reprinted from SCIENTIFIC AMERICA, September 1994

Structural and Temporal Castes in the Human Being

by Edward Wilson

During the Neurogenetic Renaissance (1976-1986) Human Ethology replaced religion, philosophy, sociology, psychology, personology, astrology, psychiatry and every other primitive system of behavioral theory and practice.

Concepts such as temporal and structural caste in social animals, the key role of migration, population-swarming, hive-limited culture, the emergence of new post-human species, and human-robotry relegated to antiquity every previous theory of human behavior.

The parents of this first scientific philosophy were the Wilson Brothers, Edward and Robert — who performed for psychology what Einstein did for physics. Edward's book, Sociobiology, *is generally considered the first conscious text on human behavior ever published.*

> **Editor's Note: This is the most important and the most impenetrable essay in this manual. If you understand this neuro-logic you will mutate to Genetic Intelligence. If you find it slow-going, undulate serenely ahead and return to this chapter when your RNA so directs you.**

Intelligence Agents have worked for centuries to decipher the DNA code — to unravel the secrets, techniques and tactics used by the Life-Intelligence to improve species. Recently this ancient and honorable philosophic specialty has acquired a new professional title: Ethology. Ethology studies the survival behavior of living organisms, species and gene-pools in their natural environment.

Migration and metamorphosis are obviously effective techniques for improving intelligence (I^2). Migration provides varied territorial options and leads to the growth of musculature and neuro-technology that makes accelerated, accurate locomotion possible. Also, migration

A characteristic of advanced socialization is Caste Division.

selects for the nobility-mobility and thus creates new, more mobile cultures. The young nervous systems of every frontier caste are imprinted with the independent-individuality of migrant Out-Castes.

A third tool used by DNA to increase intelligence is: socialization, i.e., harmonious, collaborative behavior. A characteristic of advanced socialization is Caste Division — a most effective survival device.

A species which has developed caste differentiation and enculturation based on multistage imprinting divides into survival specialties — thus complexifying and expanding performance. Obvious examples of caste specialization are the two most successful lifeforms on this planet: social insects and humans.

There are two forms of caste differentiation described by ethologists: structural caste and temporal caste. Structural caste defines Alpha Reality — genetic wiring. Temporal caste defines Beta Reality — developmental staging of the wiring. The most successful-intelligent species manifest both structural and temporal castes. Until Human Species understood how these two caste systems work they were unable to understand human psychology and thus manage their own, evolving destiny.

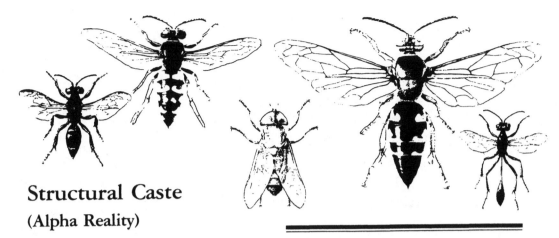

Structural Caste
(Alpha Reality)

Structural Caste involves the familiar genetic division into specialized functions (worker-humant, warrior-humant, drone-humant, builder-humant) that characterize hive organisms like social insects and civilized hum-ants. Structural caste in insects is easily identified by visible morphological (anatomical) differences. In humans neurological differences are more important in determining the behavior of each caste.* Structural caste is genetic-anatomical templating which produces involuntary-robot behaviors. A drone bee looks different from a worker bee or a queen bee.

Structural Caste differences also characterize homo sapiens. Male and female — is one structural caste difference. Big, muscled, hyperadrenalized aggressives are a separate caste — the warriors, the Amazons. Dainty, fragile, nurturant minister-types are a caste. Bobby Fishers, J. Edgar Hoovers, Bella Abzugs and Marilyn Monroes are caste-exemplars. The caste distinctions are blatantly visible, but discussion of genetic types is taboo among modern humans — although these differences were taken for granted by earlier societies.

Socialist countries forbid talk about genetic caste-differences because Marxism holds that society determines behavior. Caste theories, to a socialist, reek of capitalistic-class-elitist racism.

---

*It is obvious that highly complex neurological differences also characterize each insect hive. It is possible that individual insects have more illusions of individuality than we now credit them. The nervous system of each juvenile worker-ant is imprinted with specific culture cues. Each corridor of each ant hill has its highly characteristic odors, textures and humidities which identify the inhabitants. It is reflex-chauvinism to deny naively that ant hill cultures — 100 million years a-buildling — offer their caste members any less sense of individual and hive uniqueness than is offered the average hum-ant.

> ## A drone bee looks different from a worker bee or a queen bee.

In western democracies, the Intellectual-Scientist-Caste denies caste differences because of the hive commitment to equality. The revulsion against Nazi, Arab and Zionist genetic fanaticism also makes caste discussions *verboten* among liberals — and most scientists are liberals.

It is interesting that uneducated, lower-class people readily accept the reality of racial and caste-differences. Country bumpkins and illiterate farmers are aware of the effects of breeding and are, thus, far more ethologically sophisticated than liberal Cambridge Nobel Prize laureates.

Common-Sense suggests that there are a limited number of basic genetic castes that characterize the human species, and that new caste differences will emerge as *homo sapiens* continues its accelerated differentiated evolution.

Temporal Caste
(Beta Reality)

The most impressive and successful technique used by DNA to increase the intelligence of social species is Temporal Caste. Temporal Caste refers to the process of maturation in which an individual metamorphosizes from one form to another within hir own life span. Passing through developmental stages — performing different survival functions at each life passage.

Temporal casting in an ant-hill assigns the young tasks of infant care. Slightly older ants are assigned house-keeping and hive-repair functions, metamorphizing into more external functions of exploration, food-gathering and warrior activity.

Reflect on the wondrous neurological advantage of Temporal Caste. The mature ant knows how to perform several caste functions. This means that SHe has several gears or circuits in

---

The human being is a robot.

---

hir nervous system. An organism which has passed through temporal metamorphic sequences is simply more intelligent. *Temporal caste means polyphase brain and thus multiple Beta Realities.* Caterpillar caste to butterly caste; pollywog to frog; pre-teenager to adolescent.

Now reflect on the super-wondrous glory of the human brain. The terrestrial human life cycle spins the developing individual through 12 stages. The suckling infant is certainly a very different caste from the serious ten year old school-child. The rock 'n' roll teenager is certainly a different caste than the tottering post-menopausal.

Until recently our philosophers (sic) have been unable to understand temporal casting in humans. For very good genetic reasons. The human being is a robot, blindly operating within the reality bubble of structural caste and current temporal caste imprint. At each developmental stage the individual must imprint the current hive reality for that developmental stage. The infant cannot be concerned with teenage sperm-egg fantasies. SHe must suck, suck, suck at the cultural cues that SHe has imprinted — the touch, smell, taste, sound of the mother.

The 11th stage new-parent suddenly, miraculously forgets the barbarian teenage reality in which SHE lived just a few months previous.

Each generation is a wave moving through the gene-pool . . .

---

ous. Each human accepts the reality of the current temporal stage hive-imprint, and almost totally represses the memory of previous stages. *The 24 circuit equipment is there, however, available for activation.* It is the aim of this article to turn

you on to its glory.

The most loveable aspect of human temporal casting is this: each stage plays a part in the overall 24 element human molecule. Think of the human gene-pool as a complex molecule which builds on new elements as it evolves. Temporal casting allows for temporal flexibility. Each generation is a wave moving through the gene-pool — contributing to the locomotion of the gene-pool through time.

Let us examine the Temporal Caste situation. Does the Stage 1 suckling, floating infant play a role in the human ant-hill? Oh my yes! You better believe that the suckling infant is the glue which holds the enormous technological civilization together. The task of the infant is to trigger domestic responses in adults. The baby's task is to suck tits, emit anguished-demanding yowls, dirty diapers, gurgle winningly. The neonate performing its repertoire of activities is working just as hard as the auto worker or the dutiful parent. Sucking mother's breasts turns on hormones that keep Mom home.

If Mom's 11th brain is not fed by gurgle cues and cries, young Mother will be down at the dance hall swinging her hips or, horrors, competing with men. (Thus the enormous neurogenetic significance of the Pill. It is no accident that an irresistible Women's Liberation Movement occurs one generation after voluntary birth-control appears. Birth control is self-directed management of temporal caste sequence. Women can postpone Stage 11 maternal-matron-morality. The "youth-cult" which has produced middle-aged women teeny boppers and married Teamsters wearing Joe Namath satin shirts with Fonz hair styles is another by-product of the newly won control of our neurogenetic brain sequences.)

The school child (ages 5-11) also plays a crucial role in the human hive. Young students keep the enormous educational industry going. Schools become bureaucratic paper-factories keeping teachers busy, school administrators occupied, counselors engaged. The whole insectoid apparatus is designed, of course, to imprint the young robots with role-models, making them ready to take their places in a bureaucratic-socialist centralized hive civilization where everyone is trained to play a role.

The Teenager Caste similarly plays a vital role in the human ant-hill by providing warriors in times of war. Indeed, teenagers encourage war. Before 1960 every dictator knew that the way to keep the restless students from rioting in the university was to get them fighting on the border. In times of peace the crime rate rises. In times of peace the task of teenagers is to keep the police establishment and the judiciary going. More than half of all *reported* crimes are committed by those under eighteen. If unreported vandalisms, blood-letting fights and hub-cap coups were included, we would see that 90% of all crimes are committed by barbarian teenagers or unmarried, pre-domestic males. If Stage 10 adolescence were eliminated from the human cycle, there would be no Red Brigades, no rock-concert riots — the monolithic police bureaucracy would immediately crumble and in its anguished collapse take the entire society down with it. *Every caste has to be kept occupied.*

> In times of peace the task of teenagers is to keep the police establishment and the judiciary going.

As usual, it is more comfortable for us to understand human robot-hood by looking at others. Thus we notice that in "primitive" tribes young children perform baby-care. Older girls help with agriculture. Older boys guard the flocks. After puberty temporal caste assignments change dramatically. In all societies adolescent males pass through a warrior stage.

Today in civilized societies technology and complex labor divisions have diminished the survival value of child-castes. Thus the elaborate culture of organized play and extended education to prepare youngsters for warrior and post-warrior status.

HOOLIGANISM
British Fans Put Sock Into Soccer

BY WILLIAM TUOHY
Times Staff Writer

LONDON — Britain, the nation that gave the world many of its sports as well as the concept of sportsmanship, has been plagued this year by violence in connection with its national game — soccer.

One recent report suggested that the typical "soccer hooligan" has much in common with the teddy boys of the 1950s, the mods and rockers of the 1960s, and the skinheads and punks of the 1970s.

So when 50,000 or 60,000 young fans gather at one of the big weekly games the stage is set for trouble and violence.

Local judges tend to avoid stiff penalties for soccer hooliganism because many of the accused are young or too poor to pay fines, or are first offenders.

"These young men are restless and aggressive," said a senior government official dealing with sports, "and we no longer have compulsory national service (the draft) where they could work off steam. These football games are not so much the cause of the violence as a deeper reflection of the malaise of the society.

"We can only hope that this period is a phase in our time and that we will soon pass through it."

The Coordination of Structural and Temporal Castes

It must be stressed that current knowledge of human neuro-genetics is so primitive that we have just now realized that structural and temporal castes exist.* This insight is obviously changing, totally, our conceptions of human nature and society. It is probable that we are neuro-logically programmed so that understanding of castes cannot become part of species contelligence until the time for Space Migration occurs. Plan-It Colonies in High Orbit provide the new ecological

---

*Sociobiologists and ethologists define their professions as the study of Behavioral Genetics. This term is not adequate. Neuro-genetics is a more accurate word — what is inherited is not behavior but neural templates which determine the use of the anatomical-technology. Local hive behavior cues — language, customs, artifacts, and the like are not genetically inherited; they are cultural imprints. Only the caste-circuits are inherited. Until Ethologists understand the difference between neuro-genetic caste and local-social-imprint, their brilliant observations cannot be mapped.

vacuum which will allow human caste differences to blossom without the friction and crowded competition which now colors racial-class-sexual-caste differences.

To understand your own personal development you must remember that you are a genetic-caste-robot. You are templated by DNA to play a certain role and outfitted with a 24-gear brain that is very different from 92% of other human brains.

We now use the venerable language of Zodiac types to start a dialogue about casting. Why do we borrow the 12 signs of the Zodiac as labels for basic structural human castes? This is a conservative bow to tradition. Philosophers, good ones, are human ethologists. For five thousand years the most shrewd human ethologists have worked on this twelve-fold type-casting — based, we must assume, on extensive and empirical observation. If we ignore the "astro" part we are still left with the "logic" of 12 survival tactics — Pisces, Aries, etc. In the future more sophisticated classifications of human types based on neuro-logical differences will replace the crude zodiac classification used in this book.

For now let us assume that your genetic template determines your structural caste which, in turn, determines your life-long real-ity attitude.* We shall call your structural caste your ALPHA REALITY.

Now there will be some among you, of scientific and intellectual bent, who will be offended by this use of "sloppy occult astrological/superstitious" technology. But before you fuse out, please re-read this crude, generalized list of 12 personality types. Realize that this is an admittedly primitive attempt at introducing the notion of temporal caste, seriality and developmental order. Note that the survival characteristic assigned to each type describes an evolutionary technology and a developmental stage. Pisces is baby and amoeboid. Aquarius is the most elderly, orderly, mature. Sense how this list tries to recapitulate the evolution of the 12 basic neuro-technological functions — both in the species and individuals. May I suggest that you not reject this list unless you can replace it by a better personality typology based on the sequential evolution of intelligence, in species and in individuals.

Intellectuals, scholars, academics, salaried scientists and all other categories of verbal bureaucrats unanimously denounce astrology. This immediately alerts the Intelligence Agent

*Attitude is used in the high-altitude, high-velocity aeronautical context — angle of approach.

THE TWELVE ALPHA REALITY STYLES
(STRUCTURAL CASTES)

1. **Pisces Incorporating Caste**
   floating, dreamy, liquid,
   sucking amoeboid attitude
2. **Aries Swimming-Biting Caste**
   twisting, biting,
   incisive shark attitude
3. **Taurus Amphibian Caste**
   slow, steady, earthy,
   crawling shore-line approach
4. **Gemini Quicksilver Caste**
   swift, tricky, evasive,
   rodent attitude
5. **Cancer Territorial Caste**
   strong, possessive,
   controlling mammalian attitude
6. **Leo Arboreal Caste**
   active, exhibitionistic,
   political monkey attitude

7. **Virgo Passive-Magical Caste**
   parroting, symbol-discriminating,
   paleolithic attitude
8. **Libra Figure-It-Out Caste**
   thoughtful, inventive,
   orderly neolithic approach
9. **Scorpio Put-It-Together Caste**
   engineering, administrative,
   dealing, architectural attitude
10. **Sagittarius Dramatize-It Caste**
    romantic, intense,
    adolescent barbarian attitude
11. **Capricorn Parental Caste**
    domestic, familial, responsible,
    moralistic attitude
12. **Aquarius Conservative Caste**
    religious, aging,
    past-oriented attitude

that some important genetic nerve is being touched. One hears these paper-pedants (and their civil-service followers) making such solemn, judicial pronouncements as: "I don't believe in astrology." This statement means: "I don't understand seasonal ethology and I automatically reject everything my brain is not wired to receive."

We look, therefore, for the valid reasons why hive philosophers fear astrology. And we find, hidden in the tangle of zodiac ravings, three important items of neuro-genetic wisdom:

Regular cycles influence neural development,
Each of us is born a robot, templated and controlled by rhythms that we can decipher and harmonize with,
Each of us is born into a caste, or into a complex of castes.

Let us suspend belief and assume, for the moment, that Zodiac types define structural castes. Each of the 12 terrestrial intelligence-functions plays an important role in the human social molecule. No human gene-pool can exist unless it has people and institutions playing out these 12 neuro-technological parts.

Now let us consider temporal caste. It is the genius (genetic-volatility) of humanity that, although each of us is a genetic-robot, we pass through the 12 stages as we mature. What a wondrous package, indeed is WoMan! Each of us represents one of the twelve intelligence-survival-solutions and each of us, in maturing, passes through and relives all twelve solutions.

Genetic Consciousness allows us to discard old outmoded hive-reality maps, to file away, retire, every previous theological and philosophic blueprint — except those which are based on continual evolution. This does not mean reject empirical data or close-off information or ignore opinions. Note everything that the primitives say. Be open to every stupidity, savagery, rigidity of the Newtonian natives. Listen to the Christian Fundamentalists when they shout that the Bible is a Word-for-Word revelation and you will get a shocking insight into the parroting, paleolithic, humanoid brain. And then check your own behavior for 7th Brain repetition.

Study and then file-away orthodox Darwinian blind-selection theories — while respecting the field reports of evolutionists and ethologists. Then play with the notions of Structural and Temporal Caste as they affect you. How can we fail to admire this clever I^2 tactic which allows each of us to recapitulate evolution and to move ahead to create the future?

Find your Robot-Structural-Caste (DNA Alpha Reality) in the left-column of Table II and then slide along the 12 developmental stages (CNS Beta Realities) through which you have passed. How can we fail to exult in this blueprint which allows us to experience — and retrieve from genetic memory — every reality which our evolutionary forebearers have offered us?

DNA has given us the equipment to recapitulate-pre-capitulate the major DNA solutions — past and future.

The aim of DNA is to Increase Intelligence, I^2. Individual human beings evolve, stage by stage, as higher circuits of the CNS are activated. Post-hive consciousness allows humans to grasp the aesthetics of the DNA blueprint.

The gift of DNA is this: although we are templated as genetic-robots (structural caste) we are equipped with a 24 calibre brain which allows us to imprint (fabricate) every Alpha Reality available to every major life-form which has preceded us on the scene. And to imprint every major life-form to come.

DNA has given us the equipment to recapitulate-pre-capitulate the major DNA solutions — past and future. *But more than that, DNA has given us access to both CNS and RNA equipment so that we can creatively re-imprint each of the 24 CNS (Beta) realities and then re-structure our Structural Caste.*

The extraordinary success of humanity is due to the combinatorial complexity of structural and temporal castes in this species.

93

BETA REALITY — TEMPORAL CASTE: CNS

	Newly-born Infant Amoeboid Stage	3 Mo - 6 Mo Amoeboid Stage	6 Mo - 1 Yr Old Amoeboid Stage	1 - 2 Yr Old Stage	2 - 3 Yr Old Stage
Pisces Incorporating Caste	Amoeboid Floating Style of Sucking	Amoeboid Floating Style of Biting	Amoeboid Floating Style of Crawling	Amoeboid Floating Style of Walking	Amoeboid Floating Style of Possessive Controlling
Aries Biting Caste	Shark-Biting Style of Sucking	Shark-Biting Style of Biting	Shark-Biting Style of Crawling	Shark-Biting Style of Walking	Shark-Biting Style of Possessive Controlling
Taurus Crawling Caste	Amphibian Crawling Style of Sucking	Amphibian Crawling Style of Biting	Amphibian Crawling Style of Crawling	Amphibian Crawling Style of Walking	Amphibian Crawling Style of Possessive Controlling
Gemini Evasive Caste	Evasive Weasel Style of Sucking	Evasive Weasel Style of Biting	Evasive Weasel Style of Crawling	Evasive Weasel Style of Walking	Evasive Weasel Style of Possessive Controlling
Cancer Controlling Caste	Muscular Aggressive Style of Sucking	Muscular Aggressive Style of Biting	Muscular Aggressive Style of Crawling	Muscular Aggressive Style of Walking	Muscular Aggressive Style of Possessive Controlling
Leo Directing Caste	Monkey-Exhibitionist Style of Sucking	Monkey-Exhibitionist Style of Biting	Monkey-Exhibitionist Style of Crawling	Monkey-Exhibitionist Style of Walking	Monkey-Exhibitionist Style of Possessive Controlling
Virgo Mimicking Caste	Fussy Mimicking Style of Sucking	Fussy Mimicking Style of Biting	Fussy Mimicking Style of Crawling	Fussy Mimicking Style of Walking	Fussy Mimicking Style of Possessive Controlling
Libra Thinking Caste	Thoughtful Inventive Style of Sucking	Thoughtful Inventive Style of Biting	Thoughtful Inventive Style of Crawling	Thoughtful Inventive Style of Walking	Thoughtful Inventive Style of Possessive Controlling
Scorpio Dealing Caste	Engineer-Architect Style of Sucking	Engineer-Architect Style of Biting	Engineer-Architect Style of Crawling	Engineer-Architect Style of Walking	Engineer-Architect Style of Possessive Controlling
Sagittarius Romancing Caste	Barbarian Romantic Style of Sucking	Barbarian Romantic Style of Biting	Barbarian Romantic Style of Crawling	Barbarian Romantic Style of Walking	Barbarian Romantic Style of Possessive Controlling
Capricorn Parenting Caste	Moral Parental Style of Sucking	Moral Parental Style of Biting	Moral Parental Style of Crawling	Moral Parental Style of Walking	Moral Parental Style of Possessive Controlling
Aquarius Old-One Caste	Old-One Religious Style of Sucking	Old-One Religious Style of Biting	Old-One Religious Style of Crawling	Old-One Religious Style of Walking	Old-One Religious Style of Possessive Controlling

ALPHA REALITY — STRUCTURAL CASTE: DNA

3 - 4 Yr Old Stage	4 - 6 Yr. Old Reality Imprint Stage	6 - 9 Yr Old Reality Imprint Stage	8 - 12 Yr Old Reality Imprint Stage	Teenage Reality Imprint Stage	Parental Reality Imprint Stage	Sr. Citizen Reality Imprint Stage
Amoeboid Floating Style of Gesturing	Amoeboid Floating Style of Mimicking-Parroting	Amoeboid Floating Style of Inventing-Learning	Amoeboid Floating Style of Creating	Amoeboid Floating Style of Romantic Fucking	Amoeboid Floating Style of Parenting	Amoeboid Floating Style of Aging
Shark-Biting Style of Gesturing	Shark-Biting Style of Mimicking-Parroting	Shark-Biting Style of Inventing-Learning	Shark-Biting Style of Organizing Creatively	Shark-Biting Style of Romantic Fucking	Shark-Biting Style of Parenting	Shark-Biting Style of Aging
Amphibian Crawling Style of Gesturing	Amphibian Crawling Style of Mimicking-Parroting	Amphibian Crawling Style of Inventing-Learning	Amphibian Crawling Style of Organizing Creatively	Amphibian Crawling Style of Romantic Fucking	Amphibian Crawling Style of Parenting	Amphibian Crawling Style of Aging
Evasive Weasel Style of Gesturing	Evasive Weasel Style of Mimicking-Parroting	Evasive Weasel Style of Inventing-Learning	Evasive Weasel Style of Organizing Creatively	Evasive Weasel Style of Romantic Fucking	Evasive Weasel Style of Parenting	Evasive Weasel Style of Aging
Muscular Aggressive Style of Gesturing	Muscular Aggressive Style of Mimicking-Parroting	Muscular Aggressive Style of Inventing-Learning	Muscular Aggressive Style of Organizing Creatively	Muscular Aggressive Style of Romantic Fucking	Muscular Aggressive Style of Parenting	Muscular Aggressive Style of Aging
Monkey-Exhibitionist Style of Gesturing	Monkey-Exhibitionist Style of Mimicking-Parroting	Monkey-Exhibitionist Style of Inventing-Learning	Monkey-Exhibitionist Style of Organizing Creatively	Monkey-Exhibitionist Style of Romantic Fucking	Monkey-Exhibitionist Style of Parenting	Monkey-Exhibitionist Style of Aging
Fussy Mimicking Style of Gesturing	Fussy Mimicking Style of Mimicking-Parroting	Fussy Mimicking Style of Inventing-Learning	Fussy Mimicking Style of Organizing Creatively	Fussy Mimicking Style of Romantic Fucking	Fussy Mimicking Style of Parenting	Fussy Mimicking Style of Aging
Thoughtful Inventive Style of Gesturing	Thoughtful Inventive Style of Mimicking Parroting	Thoughtful Inventive Style of Inventing Learning	Thoughtful Inventive Style of Organizing Creatively	Thoughtful Inventive Style of Romantic Fucking	Thoughtful Inventive Style of Parenting	Thoughtful Inventive Style of Aging
Engineer-Architect Style of Gesturing	Engineer-Architect Style of Mimicking-Parroting	Engineer-Architect Style of Inventing-Learning	Engineer-Architect Style of Organizing Creatively	Engineer-Architect Style of Romantic Fucking	Engineer-Architect Style of Parenting	Engineer-Architect Style of Aging
Barbarian Romantic Style of Gesturing	Romantic Style of Mimicking-Parroting	Romantic Style of Inventing-Learning	Romantic Style of Organizing Creatively	Romantic Style of Virginal Fucking	Barbarian Romantic Style of Parenting	Barbarian Romantic Style of Aging
Moral Parental Style of Gesturing	Moral Parental Style of Mimicking-Parroting	Moral Parental Style of Inventing-Creatively	Moral Parental Style of Organizing Creatively	Moral Parental Style of Romantic Fucking	Moral Parental Style of Parenting	Moral Parental Style of Aging
Old-One Religious Style of Gesturing	Old-One Religous Style of Mimicking-Parroting	Old-One Religious Style of Inventing-Learning	Old-One Religious Style of Organizing Creatively	Old-One Religious Style of Romantic Fucking	Old-One Religious Style of Parenting	Old-One Religious Style of Aging

INDIVIDUAL FREEDOM
IS THE KEY TO EVOLUTION

History, indeed, evolution itself, can be charted in terms of the growth of Freedom-of-the-Individual.

Freedom is defined as:

1. Amount of mobility (velocity-altitude), and communication-scope attained by the individual

2. Amount of direction-control of transportation-communication attained by the individual.

3. The opportunity of free-responsible individuals to signal each other and link-up in
more complex networks . . .
inevitably leading to . .
Migration.

TUCSON LECTURE

THE DARK AGES: COCOON PREPARATION FOR MIGRATION

An interesting thing happened when the caravans of futique gene-pools fleeing West hit the beaches of the North Atlantic. No place to go. The Dark Ages (sic) occurred when this Westward wave of intelligent gene-pools crashed against the North Atlantic wall. Thousands of restless gene-pools had to wait in Western Europe until they got smart enough, technologically skillful enough, to move sperm-egg flotilla up the North Atlantic. The vanguard elite clustered in Ireland — as far West as possible.

Darwinians didn't understand. It's not survival of the fittest; it's the evolution of the fastest in the Human Race.

Here was the familiar test of nerve and intelligence. During the Dark Ages the hive Fear Merchants said, "Stay put. The world is flat. If you sail across the North Atlantic you'll fall off the edge. You'll be eaten by dragons, or busted by narcotic agents." Or whatever they spooked people with back then.*

But the explosion did take place. The world is not flat, it's a spinning sphere. Eventually the DNA code reacting to the stimuli of pollution and over-population activated the mobility-agents. Celtic Rangers were the first to climb the Atlantic. Prince Henry, the Navigator, sent Vasco da Gama around the Horn; Queen Isabella pawned her jewels to fund the N.A.S.A. explorations of Christopher Columbus. Queen Elizabeth got an appropriation from Parliament to fund the astronaut voyages of Sir Francis Drake. At this swarming moment of

---

> ### It's not survival of the fittest; it's the evolution of the fastest in the Human Race.

---

expansion and exploration, the great European powers reached the high points of their culture, drama, poetry, art, science and philosophy.

That Dark Age was a pre-mutation period of growth-limitation, fear, bureaucratic hive-restriction, proto-Naderism which said: "Movement is unsafe at any speed."

---

*We recall here the etymology of the world LOCO-MOTOR. Fast movers throughout the history of evolution have always been considered "loco" or "crazy" by static hive-establishments. The paleolithic conservatives warned restless marine creatures away from the shore-line. Uni-cellular bureaucrats warned protozoic out-castes about hooking up in multi-cellular linkages.

COUNTER-INTELLIGENCE AGENCY REPORT

Date: February, 1972

Country: Imminsee on Lake Zug,
Switzerland

Subject: THE ETHOLOGY OF THE
SWISS SKI RESORT

Classification:

TOP
SECRET

The Scandalous Philosopher has fled to a cottage by the Lake of Zug, under a high jagged peak called Rigi Kulm said to be the soul of Switzerland. Zug Lake is inner-schweiz, center of the Confederation. The most conservative canton. Less than half a mile away the Tell chapel perches on a hill where William shot the tyrant Gessler and initiated Swiss freedom.

It is harder for our Agent, Maria, to come for weekends, changing trains at Bern, but She does. Fantastic Meetings and Departures in the railway station. Running platform hand-thrown kisses as the train pulls out.

Once a week he drives past Lake Lucerne, over the mountain, down to Interlaken and then up to Gstaad, where we have established Michel for the season in a ducal chalet. He has hired a chef from Geneva but alas no one comes to dinner except lower-level backgammon pros and young friends of his mistress DeeDee who make fun of him. Michel, like Maria, is a sincere residual of the Domesticated Glamor Morality imposed on adolescent nervous systems by the Movie Industry of the 1940's, which (as Neuro-sociology teaches) was ended by Einstein and Warhol. Michel is snubbed at Gstaad by the older generation because he fails to pay his Gin Rummy debts, and by the young because he is geared to play Playboy, a Circuit 4 role which is now played out.

COUNTER-INTELLIGENCE AGENCY REPORT

Date:

Country:

Classification:

Subject: page 2

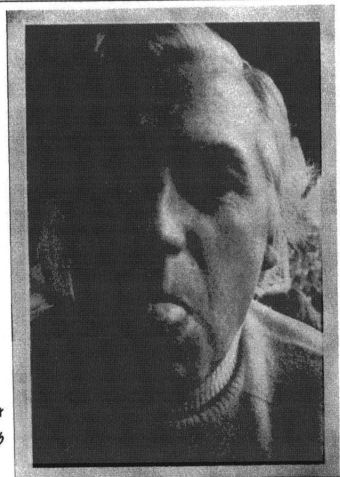

WE MUST REPLACE MICHEL WITH SKI INSTRUCTORS COMPETENT ENOUGH TO LECTURE ON GRADES OF HASHISH, PURITY PERCENTAGES OF COCAINE - CUTS, ETC.

Robert Anton Wilson is known throughout the Solar System as a Flamboyant Philanthropist. An early investor in Space Manufacturing and High-Orbital Real Estate, Wilson was one of the first generation of Einsteinian Go-go Billionaires — new Rockefellers, Stigwoods, Mellons — whose willingness to spray out millions of dollars for space-seed ventures led to the anarchic flowering of post-terrestrial Plan-Its.

Wilson's legendary tycoon-exploits have shadowed his earlier career as neurologician and author in the pre-flight years. He first achieved global fame in the early 1960's as a neurolog philosopher. During the 1970's his Illuminatus Trilogy *and* Cosmic Trigger *became classic texts for self-actualized mutants. During the 1980's he climaxed his literary fame by publishing block-busting best-sellers:* Shroedinger's Cat, Masks of the Illuminatus, Son of Illuminatus. *His spectacular career as film director followed.*

When Wilson migrated into High Orbit in 1993 he left several mysterious manuscripts, perusal of which has led to nervous breakdowns in certain East-Coast publishers.

Reprinted from PEEPLE MAGAZINE, *March 1986*

Marilyn's Input System

by Robert Anton Wilson

When night came, Marilyn was often to be found in the Odeon, one of the special world cafes whose exact function is unspoken, indeed, has never been focused. Albert Einstein, James Joyce, Marysia Harcourt-Smith, John Schewel, Richard Helms, V.I. Lenin, Rosemary Woodruff, Carl Jung, Leon Trotsky, Nena von Schlebrugge, Allen Dulles, Liz Elliot , Alexander Solzhenitsyn, Herman Hesse, drank coffee at these marbled tables and dealt answers to espionage inquiries.

It was a balmy night in Zurich and Marilyn was late as usual. When SHe was scheduled to be somewhere for dinner at eight, it was hir custom to lie in the bath tub for an hour or longer. Eight o'clock would come and go and still SHe would remain splashing in the cozy tub, pouring perfumes in the water, refilling the bath over and over again with fresh hot H20.

Marilyn knew what SHe was doing. Giving little Norma Jean a treat. As a child SHe was forced to bathe in water dirtied by six or eight people from the studio Publicity Department.

After SHe swept into the crowded restaurant the host presented hir to the other guest of honor. "Marilyn, this is Dick Helms."

Marilyn was quite surprised. SHe had expected a reserved Italian sporting gentleman in a grey suit, with a grey tie and a sprinkle of grey in hir hair. Instead SHe found hirself smiling at a loud, flashy fellow whose posture and bearing spelled W.O.L.F.!

Helms said, "What's happening, Mozzarella," gazing directly at hir *osso bucco*. (The

Latin origin of the word O.S.S. is bone.) SHe then fell silent. They sat next to each other. The only communication was Helm's investigative hand under the tablecloth.

Then Marilyn became aware of something odd. The other men at the table, a motly crew of code-stealers and axle-sanders, weren't showing off for hir or telling their stories for hir. No, it was Mr. Helms they were wooing! This was a novelty! No *woman* had ever put hir so much in the shade before. And they call this an intelligence agency! SHe thought.

Finally the moment came. Mr. Helms learned towards hir and flashed that famous, wry, thin-lipped Allen Dulles smile. "Tell me, little *mozzarella*, how do you expand your input?

"To expand input," Marilyn replied softly, "does not mean to read a lot of books. I notice, Mr. Helms, that you C.I.A. agents don't spend much time in libraries. Books give old facts interpreted in terms of old-reality maps. Few books written before 1976 have the post-terrestrial, genetic point of view. Believe it or not, Sir, they didn't even know about gene-pools or planet-spin in those days.

"My advice to you, Mr. Helms, is to infiltrate the future. Locate the neurogenetic centers where the future action is happening. There you will find the Intelligence Agents, the Out-Castes."

"How do we locate the future?" asked Helms absently. SHe was really wondering if Marilyn's cleavage indicated a parthenogenetic mode of sexual reproduction.

"Well," murmured Marilyn, licking hir luscious lips and giggling, "Counter-Intelligence Agents consistently make the mistake of focus-

---

My advice to you, Mr. Helms, is to infiltrate the future.

---

ing on today's bureaucrat-power-holders, who are already outdated by the Pre-Dom Species. In slow moving pre-technological eras this was a passable strategy. We Evolutionary Agents always focus on the Pre-Dom Species. The stages to come. Recall that Aristotle hung out with the teenage Alexander of Macedon not the reigning Philip.

"I humbly suggest, Mr. Helms, that you locate the Western Frontier Centers and exchange signals with the youthful elite who are always visible in frontal-lobe regions. In every

---

Sign up for the college lecture circuit in the Sun Belt of the good ole U.S.A.

---

terrestrial society there are pupal training centers to which the most successful gene-pools send their most intelligent larvals. The future of each gene-pool is blueprinted in the minds of its superior adolescents. Teenage brains are the hatcheries of future-realities.

"In Eastern countries you will find university students docile and insectoid obedient. Guess what this hive devotion predicts for the future of China.

"In the mid-brain Semitic countries you will find university students violently nationalistic and fanatically patriotic.

"In French elite academies you will find serious technocrats. *Mon Dieu*, Mr. Helms, imagine what that means for the future of France. *Tant Pis*.

"At the Frontal Lobe Sun Belt Universities you will find the young of the Pre-Dom Species obsessed with disciplined Self-Actualized Hedonic Freedom.

"So I would advise you, Mr. Helms, to sign up for the college lecture circuit in the Sun Belt of the good ole U.S.A. There you will learn what is going to happen. And perhaps, maybe, you can influence this hatching future a tiny, tiny bit."

VALENTINA VLADIMIROVNA TERESHKOVA*
(born March 6, 1937)
who, by spending 2 days, 22 hours and 50 minutes in zero gravity became the *fastest* (17,450 m.p.h.) and the *highest* (143.5 miles) and most *post-terrestrial* (2 days, 22 hours, 50 minutes) Woman in the Terrestrial History of Planet Earth.

*Later married to Andreyan Grigoryevich Nikolayev

TUCSON LECTURE

AMERICA IS WHERE YOU FIND THE CHANGE IMPULSE

Then the westward wave of gene-pools swam up to this hemisphere. Sailing ships unloading mutant-migrant sperm-egg cargoes on the New England ledges. At this moment, I want to look around the room and tell you, my fellow Americans, that there are certain facts we should remember about ourselves. Each person in this room is the seed descendant of evolutionary-wave-surfers. Descendants of Out-Caste foremothers and forefathers who were sent by their gene-pools up the Atlantic into the new ecological vacuum.

In our liberal concern to avoid chauvinist-nationalism we sometimes lose sight of the basic thrust of the North American immigration, the genetic glory of America. My friends, I've climbed back-down to Africa. I've time-travelled in Asia and I've descended to Europe. Sometimes voluntarily and sometimes on the run. *(Laughter)* I love Old World cultures. The heritage, the tradition, the good wine, the cathedrals, the thatched roofs, the cobblestoned streets, the folklore. I love the quaint, quaint, quaint, cute quaintness. I love the old possessions, I love the sense of roots that you get there.

I've time-travelled in Asia and I've descended to Europe.

But I must tell you, my fellow Americans, *no future is fabricating in the ebb-tide Old World*, because for four centuries the smartest, most courageous, most restless, most freedom-loving, most imaginative, most ambitious sperm-egg carriers have been expelled from Old World gene-pools and have surfed the North Atlantic waves. Splashing up here to make this country a volatile, brawling, frontier breeding experiment. America is where you'll find the change chromosomes and the freedom-genes because Americans formed new gene-pools composed of Out-Caste elites. Everyone senses that the next step in evolution is going to happen here in the Sun Belt. The Old World gene-pools are *still* sending their most intelligent

evolutionary surfers over here to help shape the future.

Look at the globe today. (We often get too involved in hive-politics — so space out for a moment.) Notice the enormous walls built across Eastern countries to prevent intelligence from moving West.* The Berlin Wall is a genetic barrier to hold down the westward wave of freedom loving mutants. East European countries are literally medium security prisons.

When I was a fugitive from Nixon's agents,

America is where you'll find the change chromosomes and the freedom-genes...

at one point I found myself underground in Vienna. Some friends took me over to the Czechoslovakia border. It was both horrible memory and dread premonition to walk along the border between Austria and Czechoslovakia. My God, it was an enormous Folsom prison! Wire fences, guard towers and sharpshooters with guns to stop migrating genes from following the magnetic pull. There is a simple navigational direction for the evolution of intelligence and freedom — always Westward.

*There is only one political criterion by which you can judge a country. Does it allow free exit? Does it imprison its people in the hive or does it allow self-selected egress? No matter how repressive the regime, if it permits dissidents to leave — it is a free land. Frontiers are genetic escalators. Those rebels who refuse to leave the hive who stay to overthrow the Dictator are by definition dumber than the evil they wish to replace.

Sometimes Verne's prescience could be uncanny.

The Pre-Capitulation Predictions of Jules Verne

by Peter Vajk

J. Peter Vajk was born in an Old-cortical center, Budapest, Hungary. Loosened from his origin-gene-pool by the wondrous anarchic shake-up following World War II, he was pulled West and received a doctorate in Physics from Princeton University (one of the most important Snow Belt hatcheries). He subsequently continued his neuro-migration West to California.

During the years just preceding the Brown presidency, Dr. Vajk was one of the leading voices broadcasting the High-Orbital signal. In 1980 he became Research Director for the High Orbital Mini-Earth (H.O.M.E.) Consortium and helped design the proto-type Plymouth Rock and Roger Williams Plan-Its.

He received the Nobel Prize in 1982 and subsequently became one of the most honored WoMen in the Annals of Post-Humanistic Science.

Jules Verne was born 150 years ago on Feb. 8, 1828. Verne was recognized, even during his life-time as an evolutionary fabricator, an author whose works appealed equally to children and adults. He also is acknowledged as the father of science fiction, which appears to have a wider following today than it ever did. His best-known novels, including *Twenty Thousand Leagues Under the Sea* and *Around the World in Eighty Days*, were still in print more than a century after their publication.

In the years since his death in 1905, Verne has emerged as something of a prophet. Among the scientific advances anticipated in his books were the submarine, airplane, television and space travel.

Sometimes Verne's prescience could be uncanny, as Frank Borman, the American astronaut, discovered after completing the Apollo 8 moon mission in 1968. In a letter to Jean Jules-Verne, the author's grandson, Borman wrote: "It cannot be a mere matter of coincidence. Our space vehicle was launched from Florida, like the spaceship in *From the Earth to the Moon*; it had the same weight and the same height, and it splashed down in the Pacific a mere two and a half miles from the point mentioned in the novel."

STEVE VOLPIN

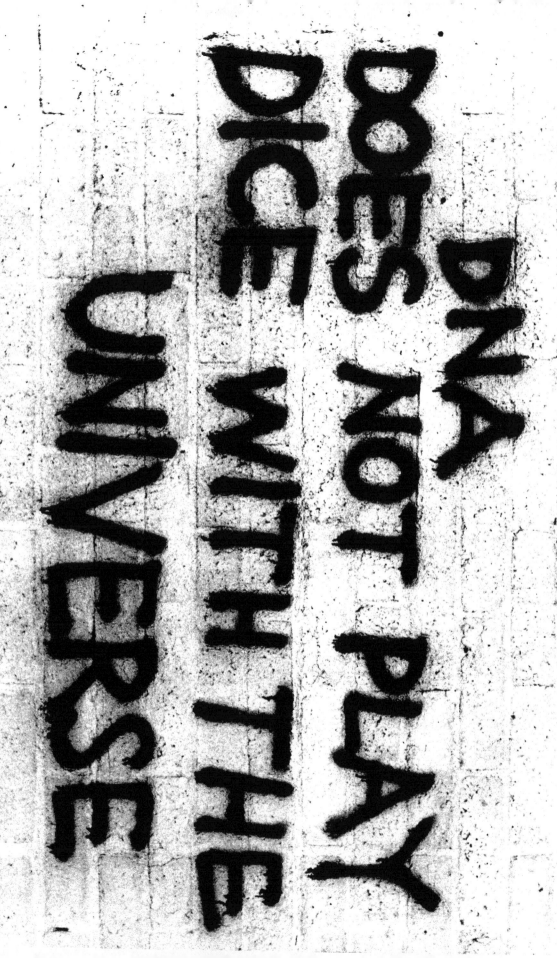

DNA DOES NOT PLAY DICE DICE WITH THE UNIVERSE

STEVE VOLPIN

THERE IS A GENETIC CASTE WIRED FOR THE ROLE OF EVOLUTIONARY AGENT: ONE WHO FORESEES AND HELPS FABRICATE THE FUTURE. TO SURVIVE THE AGENT MUST USE THE TERM FOR DNA CURRENTLY ACCEPTABLE TO THE NATIVES.

Among the many biog-raphies of Columbus there is a recurring theme of what we might call divine provi-dence.* In his own writings Columbus returns over and over again to the idea that D.N.A. put into his mind the conviction that it was possi-ble to sail all the way to the Indies ... Indeed the life of the discoverer abounds in episodes in which an acute observer may see evidence

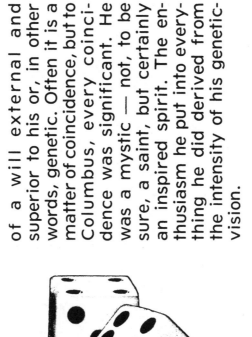

of a will external and superior to his or, in other words, genetic. Often it is a matter of coincidence, but to Columbus, every coinci-dence was significant. He was a mystic — not, to be sure, a saint, but certainly an inspired spirit. The en-thusiasm he put into every-thing he did derived from the intensity of his genetic-vision.

*Einstein's name for DNA Intelligence was Supreme Reasoning Power. "God, (i.e. the S.R.P.) does not play dice with the universe," said Einstein.

The "geniuses" of World War I were primitive herd-animals.

Psychology Goes to War!

---

by Frank Barron

In the 19th century the British Empire performed extraordinary feats of genetic transportation — squirting sperm-egg cargoes throughout the globe.

By moving their Dom-Species (Stage 11) Protestant from Scotland to Ireland they ruthlessly compressed the Stage 10 Catholic-feudal culture of the Emerald Isle. Faced with loss of the land Catholic gene-pools were forced to migrate. Each Irish family selected its most intelligent, mobile, adaptable, attractive member to send "across the water." Thus occurred one of the most successful genetic experiments in planetary history. America was flooded with sperm-egg units carefully selected for mobility-nobility.

The first generation of Irish migrants threw rail-roads across the continent. The second generation became politicians, policers, power functionaries. The third generation, which blossomed after World War II, produced the first Irish-American generation of philosopher-scientists.

The brilliant, innovative Irish savants who emerged in the 1950-70 period replaced the Jewish intellectuals. Before 1950 Jewish intellectuals carried the neuro-genetic signal. Since Jews were born Out-Castes they were able to transcend hive limits and fabricate new realities. After World War II Jewish culture became hive-establishment — the role of genetic exploration fell to the Irish. The American Celts were prepared perfectly to play the role of Intelligence Agents because of their intellectual history. In pre-migration Ireland the active intellectual person was forced into rebellion. The only educational choices for a smart young Irishman were the alien, Rome-oriented fuedal priesthood or the academies of the enemy Protestants. Irish women had no educational avenues open to them. Irish brains were thus encouraged to be anti-hive. From this Out-Caste position they were able to create new post-hive realities.

Frank Barron's career illustrates the Irish Renaissance. His ancestors, after arriving in America, avoided the priest-run ghettoes of the Atlantic Seaboard by moving to the rough frontier of the Pennsylvania mining mountains.

Frank Barron recognized his mutant status at an early age, and when the first occasion presented itself carried his seed-supply to the California frontier.

He quickly became the central figure in American psychology, taking over the position previously held by William James. His publications on creativity, innovation, hallucinogenic drugs, and psychobiography pushed the primitive field of psychology into scientific status.

Always the lonely champion of the individual at a time when psychology was totally dedicated to adjustment-conformity, it was natural that Barron was selected as head of the Post-Terrestrial Educational Commission.

By the year 2020 his educational theories were standard curricula in thousands of new worlds. Nancy Camp Barron, the famous chanteuse and movie star, was Frank Barron's mate, companion and mentor.

Previous to 1939 murderous-muscular strength, animal aggressiveness and obedient stupidity (recall the trench warfare of 1917) were the glorious characteristics of warriors.

Gravity's Rainbow describes in chilling, macabre detail how, during World War II, psychology became a basic weapon of warfare and Counter-Intelligence.

But, as the sensory and motor aspects of belligerence came to depend on intermediate-technology, i.e., machines operated by human minds, a terrible thing happened: Intelligence and mental-caste became factors in warfare! Special endowments beyond brute stupidity, treacherous cunning and unimaginative persistence became survivally attractive.

> ## Intelligence and mental-caste became factors in warfare!

The "geniuses" of World War I were primitive herd-animals — a mutation's quantum distance from the scope, acceleration and relativistic adaptability of our current mediocrity. Black Jack Pershing? Teddy Rooosevelt? Kaiser Wilhelm? Sgt. York?

By 1939, the selection of killer-teams involved careful screening for inborn caste differences, genetic types (prudently called personality traits or aptitudes). Military psychology became an integral part of the Anglo-American-German war machines. The task: identification, assessment, selection, guidance, training, motivation of caste abilities.

Diagnosis and treatment of psychological casualties — an entirely new concept of human nature — also developed. Machines break down; personalities could not break down until personality types were defined by our new mechanical-civilization. All our external technology serves as a model to understand internal (i.e., somatic-neurological) technology. Machines help us to understand our own bodily mechanics. Electronic computers lead us to understand and control our own brains.

Gravity's Rainbow is a spectacular exposé of how manipulative psychologists of the American Skinnerian Behaviorist School and the European Pavlovian School were assigned the responsibility, by the military caste, of predicting and controlling human behavior for purposes of . . . controlling human behavior.

THE NEURO-GEOGRAPHY OF PLANET EARTH: THE DISTRIBUTION OF LAND-MASS AS EXTERNAL REPRESENTATION OF EVOLVING BRAIN CIRCUITS

The continents and hemispheres of planet earth have been settled by technological civilizations in stages which correspond to the evolution of brain centers. Thus the arrangement of land-masses corresponds topologically to the anatomy of the nervous system. Asia is the spinal column; the Middle East is the Mid-Brain, and Limbic System; Europe and Africa are containers for the Right and Left lobes of the Old Cortex; North and South America are platforms for the emergence of the Neo-cortex, the self-defining future brain.

The history of civilization is the history of Agentry.

The Intell-Agent

by George Koopman

George Koopman, in 1976, published (in Neuropolitics) *the first detailed Stock Proposal for building H.O.M.E.S. He thus became the Father of Post-Terrestrial Free Enterprise.*

... "agent" suggested an
unscrupulous bureaucratic
scoundrel ...

Before the publication of the book, *Intelligence Agents* (1978), the word "agent" was in deserved ill-repute, especially in political, diplomatic and show-biz circles.

The very word "agent" suggested an unscrupulous bureaucratic scoundrel devoid of creativity, aesthetics, principles or talent who, by virtue of shameless cunning placed himself in central positions of power and control.

The *raison d'etre* of the agent is, of course, the deal. The deal involves the alchemy of link-up, package and connection. And the tools of the agent are persuasion, negotiation, bluff, manipulation, salesmanship.

The Agent Caste has existed throughout human history, dating back to the Neolithic period when artifacts, abstract-concepts, symbols, inter-tribal barter systems, paperwork began to replace direct face-to-face within tribe exchanges. As left-hemisphere technological society emerged, each gene-pool had to produce agents who represented the assets and interests of the sperm-egg collective in dealing with other gene-colonies.

In Feudal times, (Stage 10) the Agent represented the Crown or the Lord in dealing with serfs, peasants, tenants, traders and with the agents of other Lords. The sordid odor attributed to Agents probably dates back to their role as ruthless tax-collectors, dishonest traders, not to forget the many incidents in which agents betrayed their masters to seize power.

The caste of Agents took on more importance and a more attractive appearance during the emergence of Stage 11 Democratic societies. Here agents became political representatives of the various classes, castes, guilds, Brotherhoods, and gene-pools which sought to share power in a democratic tradition.

The history of civilization is the history of Agentry. This is to be expected since agents cunningly arrange for the publication of the history books. Wars are won and lost by generals, but when the smoke clears and the bodies are dragged off the field of action, then the real bottom-line stuff happens — the peace treaties, the Councils of Nicea, Trent, Versailles, Vienna, Geneva managed by agents. And when the autobiographies are written and generals from both sides peddle their memoirs, it is the agents who make the deals.

The high-points in the annals of Agentry have always come at moments of species mutation. Who has not marvelled at the astuteness of Algy Plancton, the renowned Paleozoic agent who put together the first Oxygen Commercials which led to shoreline migration?

Ron Bernstein well-deserves *his* place in the Agents Hall of Fame. After a brilliant career as a movie producer and literary manager Bernstein returned to Los Angeles in 1978 and started what is known as the "Bernstein Age of Show-Business." The key to his success was synergy — the assemblage of many elements in a block-buster molecule of enormous complexity. This technique was developed in its primitive form by the Australian Migrant, Robert Stigwood, who used a one-hundred-million dollar movie *(Saturday Night Fever)* as nothing more than a record album commercial.

Another early "synergy pioneer" was George Lucas who used a half-billion-dollar movie *(Star Wars)* as advertising trailer for his souvenir marketing business. Another early media-alchemist was Henry Edwards, who used a 110-million-dollar movie and a 150-million-

Who has not marvelled at the astuteness of Algy Plancton.

dollar album as promotion for his Pulitzer Prize winning novel *(Sgt. Pepper's Lonely Hearts Club Band)*.

Legend has it that Ron Bernstein, upon observing how movies, T.V. shows, albums, novelizations were all used as hype for each other, came to the startling conclusion which totally changed Human Ontology. "Why not use all forms of media, working together synergistically, to hype a Future Reality?"

Bernstein thus became the first Reality Movie Maker. If movies could get people to buy albums — why then movies could get people to buy realities. Reality became a spin-off of show

biz.

Starting in 1979 every sentient being on the planet was systematically exposed to Bernstein Futures. Blacks walked out of Bernstein movies

Reality became a spin-off of show-biz.

excited by the blueprints — colorfully, romantically, precisely detailed — for building exactly the kinds of futures they wished. By 1983 the Bernstein Empire was making Future Reality Movies for every gene-colony in the Western World.

Before Bernstein movies relived the past. After Bernstein movies created futures.

COUNTER-INTELLIGENCE AGENCY REPORT

Date: February, 1972

Country: Gstaad, Switzerland

Classification:

TOP SECRET

Subject: THE MEETING WITH
PRINCE ALEXIS

There has arrived at Michel's chalet a London model named Pamela whom we suspect to be an Evolutionary Agent. Please confirm. Her description is as follows: a languorous, soporiferous nervous system transported in slender, curved body with unbearably smooth-silk arms and skin of warm sepia enamel. Her carnelian, in the form of a snail, is surrounded by translucent red enamel pierced by a Mandrax thumb.

Before dinner, while Michel is preoccupied instructing the chef, Pamela is overheard whispering to the Professor that Prince Alexis is in town and wishes to arrange a meeting. He is to phone the chalet that evening. But Michel, realizing that he must prevent the meeting between Alexis and I², shuts off the phone.

UNVERIFIED STATION MEMOS FROM LONDON CODE HER AS A DANGEROUS HEDONIC ANARCHIST.

FITNESS NOTE FOR HAUCHARD FILE: It turns out that Michel has fallen on such bad times that he has been censoring personal calls. The poor man signed up to play Louis XIV but all the action is going to Mick Jagger. Michel doesn't like to dance, is burnt out by all-night gin-rummy, annoyed by amorous phone calls to DeeDee's nubile guests. And the Hedonists are on to his game. *(HAUCHARD SHOULD BE TRANSFERRED BACK TO MIDDLE-AGED PARIS.)*

So, just around midnight Pamela suggests (just like a bad girl should) that Alexis might be found at the Palace Hotel nightclub sitting surrounded by friends wearing a green silk shirt embroidered Psi-Phy. Roman designers dress him gratis, confides the model.

ROME AGENTS PLEASE CONFIRM.

(The following conversation is videotaped.)

The two aliens immediately recognized each other.

"Welcome fellow Time-Traveller," says the Prince, "I have come many parsecs to meet you."

Prince Alexis is slim, tall, with long black hair and translucent ivory skin. He looks, if it dare be said, like a fairy story prince, holding himself with royal pride, tossing his mane in fiery petulant arrogance. Scion of a most noble family, he has been educated Everywhere and done Everything at age 25. Gossip has it that he is sexually bi-lingual. He speaks Shakespearean English.

"It's taken us many orbits to get here," agrees the Philosopher. "Where was your last land-fall?"

"Katmandu. Do you know Sri Ram Muni? No? Excellent. How important that I can tell you! He knows you and has sent you a message."

"That's nice."

"I perceive," says Alexis, "a note of reserve in your voice. I share your hesitancy about Hindu swamis. I spent many months on assignment in India observing the Holy-man-groupie scene. Perhaps I should explain to our lovely companions that most of the famous swamis are hip show-biz operators, campy-vampy-splashy-flashy homosexual queens with gullible followers, grand ashrams, triumphal road tours, performing restful magic. It's amusing to hear them gossip and put each other down. They follow each other's productions like jealous rockstars. Competing for the top of the cosmic charts."

Date:

Country:

Subject: page 2

"There are a very few Intelligence Agents left in India," agrees the Professor, "and they are as hard to find there as here. It's the classic paradox. The more advanced the mind, the fewer people to talk to."

"According to legend," continues Alexis, "there are sixty-four illuminated people in the world. You won't find them administering large bureaucracies. The real spiritual wizards in India don't solicit followings, don't open branch offices throughout the world, and can't be bothered with fans, groupies, bank accounts."

"What do they do?" asks Pamela, leaning her head on her shoulder and moving her silken hand up her smooth arms. "Do they dance, ski, have girlfriends, get high? Are they good lovers?"

"It is my understanding," says the Professor, "that at least half of them are women. It is logical, isn't it, that many of them would be mated to each other?"

"You are thinking of Lama Govinda," says the Prince.

"And his beautiful wife Li Gotama. There's an answer to your question," says the Philosopher, turning to the Model.

"Smashing! The Holy Man and his Holy Woman," murmurs Pamela. "How original. What do they do?"

"They live in Almora," explains the Prince. "A small village in the foothills of the Himalayas. To reach Almora one begins with a dusty train trip north of Delhi across flat, parched semi-desert to Barelli and Katghodam. Then a bus circles up foothills, skirting gorges, crawling through dusty little hamlets where thin barefoot men in ragged clothes run alongside holding empty hands, through Nainital perched like a Swiss village by the lake and up through sad, lonely, patchy, overlumbered forests filled with melancholic Indian army troops in dark green uniforms and pencil mustaches maneuvering to exorcize the Chinese. And finally, the bus strains up to the Holy Village on the ridge, Almora.

"This is no tourist spot, you realize, way up here, two to three days travel by semi-primitive transportation from Dehli. There is not one hotel bed in Almora. The dark rooms at the inn offer a wooden frame bed with woven rope on which you throw your sleeping bag, which, if forewarned, you have ordered, custom-made with feathers and hand-sewn cotton in the teeming market of Old Dehli. There is not one concession to European culture in Almora. Not one Coca Cola, not one modern restaurant.

"Now if you leave this outpost and climb a dirt road for two miles, past outlying villages, you come to Holyman Ridge, a high, steep wall which looks North across valleys to Himalayan Tibet which towers above valleys to the south through which river and road to Katghodam curve downward. Scattered along two miles of the ridge, looking south, are houses in which assorted spiritual searchers, European and Indian, maintain part-time residence. The footpath then curves across the ridge and runs along the northern rim. This walkway, perhaps ten thousand years old, continues north to Tibet, and has been used by pilgrims, porters, merchants and, from time to time, warring bands. In a shack at the ridge-crossing tea has been brewed for centuries in brass pots over charcoal, served heavily sweetened in thick brass mugs.

Date:

Country:

Classification:

Subject: page 3

TOP SECRET

"A mile beyond the tea shack the pilgrim leaves the main path, turns left, climbs a twisting narrow trail leading to a point at ridge-end which commands an astronaut view, North, West, and South for hundreds of miles. There, in a house built long ago by Evans Wentz, lives the Lama Govinda and his wife Li Gotama.

"The Lama can accurately be described as venerable. An old man dressed in Tibetan robes with wispy oriental beard, he is a Buddhist scholar of German descent, with an enquiring, empirical mind. Teacher, Translator, Transformer, Transcriber, Transmitter of that ancient lore passed on by a scientific elite who devote years to research. The priests and swamis are second-hand karma dealers who solace the masses with soothing rituals and pop-versions of hive ethical codes. But with Lama Govinda one talks about the laws of energy that run the universe."

Alexis has been speaking intently, not paying total attention to Pamela's Mayfair pink enamel hand on his cock or the French girl's hedonic ivory hand stroking his neck. Turning back to the Professor he appeals for confirmation.

"Isn't that what you learned in Almora?"

"Yes," says the Doctor nodding, "Lama Govinda taught me to study the old symbol systems and to look for errors. When you find the errors and correct them, then you understand the message."

"What about Becky Thatcher?" murmurs Pamela softly.

"Ah yes," continues Alexis, "the beautiful Li Gotama, Parsee by birth, performs translations, illustrates the Lama's books with graceful drawings. She adds the aesthetic half. Li means fire-light. She calls him Ch'ien, the Creative of Heaven. I fabricate that Lama and Li are two of the sixty-four illuminated people. Would you concur?"

The Philosopher smiles in agreement.

"The Lama and Li are your teachers," says Alexis. "But I must tell you about Sri Ram Muni. He is to be found in a small temple outside Katmandu. He has preserved certain energy manuscripts which he has decoded and wishes to pass on. He has sent me west to present the version ready for you."

The Philosopher writes seven digits on a piece of paper.

"These are magic numbers," he says tipsily. "Dialed into the appropriate electronic transceptor they will put you in touch with my headquarters near Lucerne. Call me and we'll continue our talk."

(End of tape.)

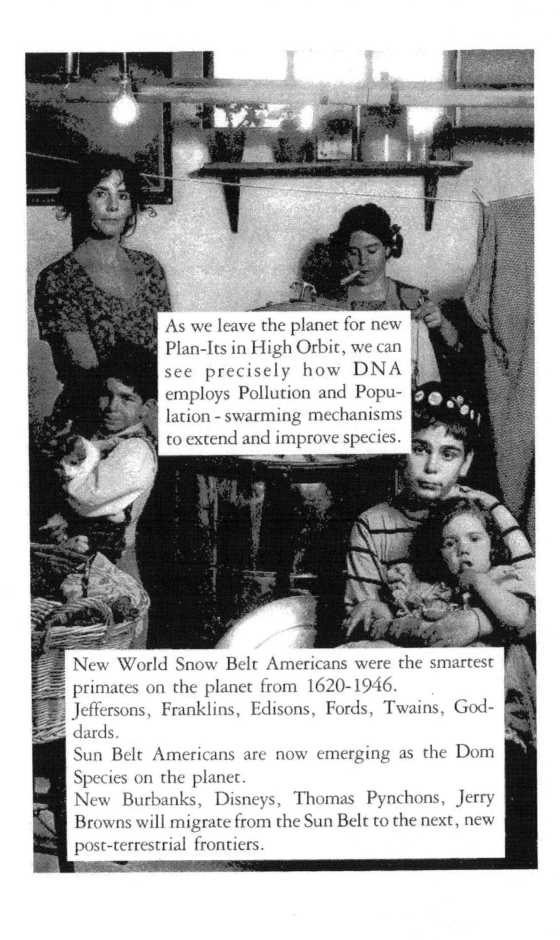

As we leave the planet for new Plan-Its in High Orbit, we can see precisely how DNA employs Pollution and Population-swarming mechanisms to extend and improve species.

New World Snow Belt Americans were the smartest primates on the planet from 1620-1946.
Jeffersons, Franklins, Edisons, Fords, Twains, Goddards.
Sun Belt Americans are now emerging as the Dom Species on the planet.
New Burbanks, Disneys, Thomas Pynchons, Jerry Browns will migrate from the Sun Belt to the next, new post-terrestrial frontiers.

Westward High

We can best understand the
Last Mutation-Migrations
(*Old World to New World, 1493–1943*)
(*East Coast to Pacific, 1943–1977*)
from the vantage point of the
Next Mutation-Migration.

TUCSON LECTURE

WESTERNERS ARE EASTERNERS WHO SMARTENED UP

Let me share with you, at this point, an immutable law of Neuro-Geography which governs terrestrial politics: *the evolution of intelligence has, for 2500 years, moved East to West.* When you go *back East* (note the retrograde terminology) you are going back in time, down in intelligence and lower in evolution.

Let me restate it simply: Westerners are significantly smarter, freer, more creative, more future-oriented than Easterners. Easterners are lower forms of evolution. Easterners, it is true, are more specialized — but, as we have learned

---

Do not try to hustle Easterners on their own turf.

---

from dinosaurs, specialization means Terminal Adulthood. Civilizations are, by definition, adult, i.e. passé.

Let us restate the axiom: freedom moves from East to West. Western gene-pools are always freer, more adolescent, more mobile than Eastern gene-pools. And in the Genetic Breeding Book, *Mobility is Nobility.*

The most intelligent and the freest people on the planet have been propelled by their gene-pools to the Western belt of this continent: Arizona, Texas, California, Oregon, Washington. The ecological niche of the future. Each Westerner is the hopeful adolescent blossom of the old Eastern roots.

When you move back East from the Pacific — be on guard. You are moving down into primitive, inflexible, cynical terrain. Chicago is a tough, mammalian jungle compared to San Diego. New England is a monument to the static past. Easterners, in their neolithic shrewdness are skillful, political mammals. Adepts in Newtonian competitions. Do not try to hustle Easterners on their own turf. New York is the center of money power, Washington is the center of barnyard political force, and Boston the capital of antiquated Puritan culture

— but there is no freedom, no spirit of growth and development, no enthusiasm for change in the Adult Eastern Hive.

These remarks are in no way chauvinistic. *All Westerners are migrated Easterners!* I was born at West Point, New York and teen-aged in Massachusetts. I honor my damp roots and respect their venerable, unchanging traditions. I thank the New England educational system for activating my migration button.

It is no accident that all the laws which restrict youthful freedom come from grim, prudish Eastern hives. We must be aware of the natural tendency of Eastern hive leaders to frighten stay-put yokels with stories of Western instability. Sure Californians and Arizonians and Texans are diverse, flamboyant, juvenile and easy to deride. It's always that way. Frontier Regions which encourage the formation of new gene-pools, wide-open territories which allow cultural experimentation and future fabrication are always easy to ridicule from the docile, adult, traditional bunkers of the Orient.

The age-old Chinese think that all Occidentals are crazy kids because we believe in individual reality and personal change. The Russians call individualism, hooliganism! We grant that an Easterner, in the secure cocoon of adult conformity and centralized dogmatic repetition, is shocked by the insane insistence of Westerners to "be themselves." We grant that the individual or small cult is kooky-vulnerable in contrast to the monolithic stability of specialized gene-pools which repeat what their parents did and cling to the myths of their grandparents. The independent Western pioneer is easily ridiculed. But the fact remains — freedom to experiment, courage to change, energy to re-create is always a Westward High.

A Memo Designed to Cheer Up the Human Race

by Rosemary Woodruff

Rosemary Woodruff was the wisest, funniest, most beautiful woman of her time.

These days — as we would expect from a Judeo-Christian-Marxist era — it is fashionable for intellectuals to complain about humanity's destructive and pessimistic trend.

While, in all charity we can understand the hive meaning of this pessimism, it is the task of Evolutionary Agents to counter it by repeating: *the Genetic Plan is working out perfectly.* The human cards are in no position to interfere with the DNA deal.

We are compelled to offer total sympathy and support for the human races when we remember that for the last 5000 years (a mere micro-flick in genetic time) the species have been in a continual *frenzy* of Mutation and Migration.

The problem is this: a species or an individual without genetic consciousness, caught in the midst of all-out-high-velocity changes, buf-

> ## Does a butterfly understand what's happening when it bursts, twisting and dewey-damp out of the dark, cozy cocoon?

feted, overwhelmed by no-let-up metamorphosis, pushed into rapid migration, is understandably confused and, a bit fatigued.

Until the Future History Series published by Peace Press, there were no maps to describe *how it feels* during the high-point of mutation. Does a salmon understand what's happening when it is being squeezed back up the Columbia River, battered, pushed against the current, leaping rocks, flipping forward, upward? Does a butterfly understand what's happening when it bursts, twisting and dewey-damp out of the dark, cozy cocoon?

Such dramatic migrations and metamorphoses are simple transitions compared to the bewildering, bumpy voyage of the individual humans and human gene-pools in the last few generations.

Recall, with compassion, the extraordinary changing status of the human brain. After nine months of exciting embryonic metamorphosis, it is squeezed into terrestrial life as a peculiar, slug-like larval with an enormous head and shrunken, totally helpless body. The amoeboid-bliss of the Neonate is shortly shattered by the activation of new neural circuits and the sequence of dramatic changes in physiology. Biting, crawling, walking, running, talking. Compared to every other species, the human being is in continual metamorphosis. Indeed, the outstanding neurogenetic characteristic of the human is this continual larval change. *Homo protean.*

In addition to this developmental variability, those who have lived through the 20th century have been whirled through a sequence of historical changes unparalleled on this womb-planet. A person born in 1900 moved from horse-carriages to Soyuz-Apollo in one life time. From gas-light to nuclear fusion. Mutations-migrations occur in cycles. Each generation since 1900 has ridden a series of enormous waves — all-changing reality breakers, with no chance to catch a breath. Thus, for the first time in human history, we have some dozen mutant groups swirling around at the same time. And, via electro-magnetic communication, aware of each other's changes. Those who just barely,

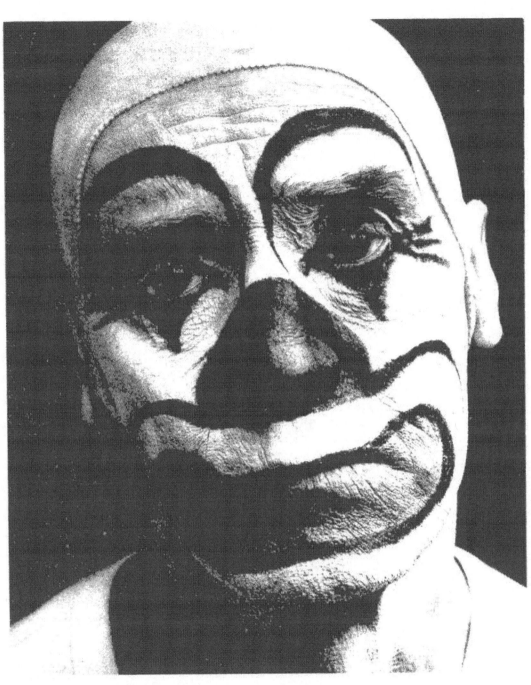

> ### . . . we have some dozen mutant groups swirling around at the same time . . .

gasping, made it from the Spanish-American War through World War I were then asked, with no respite, to deal with the Roaring Twen-ties, Communism, the Depression, Hitler, World War II, Hiroshima, Cold War, television, Lunar landings, drugs, *Hustler*, cloning. *No one was permitted to stand still.*

It's a dizzying, Einsteinian exercise in relativity — totally bewildering to a species that had been assured by Newton that every action had an equal and opposite reaction. Nope, no more. The new rule: every action leads to a multiple interaction, intersection — and it's all waves to surf, moving faster and higher.

Reprinted from SCIENTIFIC AMERICA, October 1981

The Pleasure Caste

by Kevin McCormick

Kevin McCormick was activated in the last half of the 20th century and was immediately assigned one of the most curious missions in planetary history.

His extraordinary post-terrestrial, post-human intelligence became apparent at an early age. The young Kevin was simply too smart, too active, too radiant to pass as a normal domesticated primate. His Out-Caste status caused him considerable grief and confusion — a fate typical of many Evolutionary Agents during the primitive terrestrial period.

McCormick's futique telepathic abilities brought him, while still an undeveloped cub, into the field of mass-neural-activation (then called show business). His acute neural equipment allowed him to sense which neuro-electric signals were needed to trigger mutations in young terrestrials. Before he was 30 years old he had become the most successful movie producer of all time — based on his uncanny skill in fabricating, on film, the future realities of the emerging species.

After his film assignments were completed McCormick retired for several months of re-imprinting and serial-reality fabrication using the new powerful transmitter drugs. It was then that his next career as philosopher began. His first step was to become Pope of the Roman Catholic Church (1986) and permanent President of the International Psychoanalytic Association. Thus liberated, he proceeded to do What-He-Wanted on several Worlds of His Own Device for several decades.

A study of History reveals that each gene-pool and every successful civilization has produced an aesthetic-elite caste — those whose nervous systems are especially sensitive to sensual stimulation; those who have the ability to receive, manage and transmit neurosomatic, hedonic signals. Those who are robot-programmed to stimulate pleasure in themselves and in others (either singularly or in cooperation with other reality-artists).

The wording of the last paragraph is carefully designed to indicate that there are three aesthetic-artist-sensory castes:

Hedonic Consumers: those who receive pleasure.

Hedonic Directors: those who create pleasure realities for themselves and others.

Hedonic Producers: those who exchange pleasure.

We are discussing here a strange and powerful caste of humans whose psychology (and neurology) has been ignored by philosophers because of the "taboo" nature of the subject. Pleasure. Beauty. Sensuality. Eroticism.

We refer to those called Artists, or "show business" people, entertainers, courtesans. Those in the Pleasure Industry. For obvious reasons Hive philosophers and Establishment

Millions of middle-class dociles are titillated by notorious courtesans

Reality-Definers tend to discredit the Pleasure-Aesthetic Castes and the contributions they make to the species. There is little overt, bureaucratic pressure on young people to take up a life of courtesan-actress-musician-artist when they "grow up." Indeed, the classic situation calls for discouragement by the gene-pool of such aspirations on the part of the young.

At the same time that the Hedonic Occupa-

tions are publicly taboo, there is a covert acceptance of them. Millions of middle-class dociles are titillated by notorious courtesans such as the Gabor sisters when they exhibit their ill-gotten diamonds on the Johnny Carson Show. Few of the enrapt electroid audience would actively encourage their daughters to learn this glamorous profession or their sons to contribute to such display.

One of the most obvious examples of human castes — elements which link to form the social molecule — is the pervasive presence of the show-biz-pleasure profession. Night clubs, saloons, theatres, carnivals, brothels, dance-halls. However fake, tinsel, laundered the actual performance — the allure, the promise is always the same. Somatic reward, in-human soft-skin-bliss, hip sophistication, erotic movement, hedonic consumption. Self-indulgence. Self-actualization.

With established society actively discouraging recruitment into these professions, how do we account for the fact that in every gene-pool and in every age a certain percentage of young adults pop up as pleasure-dispensors? *Genetic caste*. Good looks and animal magnetism are the give-aways. Observe any group of children at play and you can forecast those who are robot-templated by DNA to play hedonic roles. Who

give off the sexual radiation. The flamboyant self-confidence of the budding performer.

An interesting dilemma appears at this point. We do not have a formal, precise language to classify and describe the various pleasure-roles and hedonic processes. Indeed, before *The Principles and Practice of Hedonic Psychology* (1974) there had been little scholarly attention to pleasure in western literature. Whereas there existed an enormous nosology of pain, an endless clinical listing of negative pathological states, there was no psychiatric or psychological classification of the states of excellence, elite accomplishment, or pleasure. (It is true that a crude literature of beauty-pleasure existed in the Orient: pillow books, Tantric Hindu texts, Islamic-Sufi works.)

Why is there no terminology for beauty-pleasure in the West? Neuro-censorship. If words are invented for these myriad hedonic delights, then people will talk about them and enjoy them — a turn of events which Christian-Marxist hive establishments could not tolerate.

This taboo against the recognition of pleasure began to crumble in the 1960's. For the first time in the history of humanity a mass middle-class awakened to Self-Actualized Hedonism. We can justly use the term "awaken" to describe the sudden insight that the body is a pleasure instrument, designed to receive a wide range of sensory stimuli which can be self-directed and self-controlled.

Before the 1960's, in western culture, hedonic bliss was taboo — reserved only for the aristocracy. Sexual pleasure was limited to marital intercourse — and then only for hive reproductive purposes.

Susan Kaiser Vogel was born in 1947 — equipped with a body-brain model 2020. Her neurological equipment was thus designed to inhabit realities 73 years ahead in the future.

She was fortunate enough to appear in Southern California, the most advanced time zone, exactly when it became the center for post-terrestrial mutation. Her advanced mutant status was recognized at an early age by those close to her. She was encouraged, protected, "listened to" by an increasing number of persons who recognized that she was a direct-clear line to the future.

The energy given off by her nervous system and its magnificent carriage was radiantly visible to even the most larval observer. Comparative ethologists have been fascinated by Susan's time travel experiences. Never in planetary history did a futique visitor adapt so successfully to primitive life on a one-G planet.

Conceived ten mutational stages ahead of the Dom-species, she was forced to deal with gross, vulgar, jittery, ugly, repetitious behavior. The species was dedicated to safety, security, sanity, sex-role conformity and almost totally blind to the aesthetic.

After mastering the limited vocabularies of the physics, chemistry, biology and psychology of the period, Susan focused her adolescent attention on the central genetic issue of the time: Aesthetic Self-Actualization.

The Terminal Adult Authority of the Centralized Aquarian Age had limited sensory awareness to perception of hive-cues. Red meant stop. Artists, sculptors, playwrights, musicians worked within prescribed schools. The illusion of Bohemian-rebellious-individuality was carefully cultivated by hive moralists so that the Out-Castes produced by each gene-pool in each generation could be effectively isolated, neutralized and their symbolic spokes"men" rewarded. (The best example of the Stage 12 Insectoid-Collective-Artist-Poet is to be found in the Beatnik School — which imprinted grey-black-drab-ugly-urban-political-socialist models on the nervous systems of Caste 13-14 juveniles.)

Susan Kaiser Vogel sensibly avoided Art Beaurocracies and with stunning clarity selected Alan Watts as her first neurological guide. (Alan Watts, a most influential Evolutionary Agent of the late 20th century, promoted the use of 5th Circuit Neuro-transmitters to suspend hive imprints and to focus the brain on direct sensation.)

Susan developed the most sensitive neural-radar system ever used on a primitive planet. Her eyes scanned with naked-microscopic clarity registering, not just forms, but the play of light patterns. She used Zen techniques to free her ears from hive-imprinted limits and thus developed her auditory equipment to a

point far beyond human limits. Similar exercises in modalities of taste, touch, and kinaesthetics made her the most sensuous person ever to inhabit the planet.

Then Susan moved to Stage 14 (Life-as-Performance-Art). From this period date her monumental architectural-constructions: Can of Worms, Desert Forms, Blue Flame, Peach-Fuzz Invitation, The Blue Wave of Venice, The Fourth Pyramid of Giza. This phase was climaxed by her Crystal Palace, a walk-in piece composed of cut diamonds loaned by Ronnie Winston and the Shah of Iran; her Emerald Mosque — a thirty-foot edifice made of costly emeralds; and her Transcontinental Highway — a twenty-foot-high wall of crystal glass which stretched from Atlantic City to Santa Monica. The construction of this piece solved the problems of the first Jerry Brown administration.

Susan Kaiser Vogel's architectural period pushed minimal art to its maximal limits. Susan's assignment was to teach the basic lesson of DNA — The

Harmony of Extremity. Her pieces fused recklessly the most solid brick with the most fragile-ephemeral pastel color, the hardest with the softest, the most elegant with the most common. While her pieces employed the most ancient-basic paleolithic material and technique (one-stone-on-top-of-another) they represented the most avant-garde. At once the most commonplace and the most subtley conceptual. Her pieces were the most durable in material and construction — yet they lasted only a few days. Take your eyes off these massive structures and they disappear!

Susan's works during this period were designed to shock, electrify — activate primate brains at first sight. Thousands who saw The Blue Flame in the UCLA sculpture garden exclaimed: "What is it?" "It's a window to the sky," they might be told. Museum visitors walked into a room and were suddenly surrounded by Peach-Fuzz Invitation, a 43 foot semi-circle of soft-smooth pinkness electrically sliding along their nerve endings.

By 1980 millions of citizens in the advanced zones of the planet had been activated by Susan's transmissions and understood that Space Migration was basically an aesthetic challenge — the power to create Mini-Earths meant humanity need never again be aesthetically passive.

An astonishing leap in artistic sensibility followed. By the year 2000 the alert earthling could look forward to designing and constructing a limitless number of Mini-Earths. The inspiration for this, the first Aesthetic Society in human history, is credited to Susan Kaiser Vogel.

Her creation of the Universe of Beauty was, however, an adolescent, high-school achievement. Susan Kaiser Vogel's greatest fame emerges from her courageous, sensitive experiments in neural fusion and genetic-linkage. Her work in Conscious Conception and RNA-telepathy raised the Conception of Love six stages higher than had ever been experienced on the Planet of Her Birth.

The Federal Bureaucracy
literally paid for and
bought American
psychology.

What Did This Money Buy?

by Susan Kaiser Vogel

After his discharge from the service in 1946, I[2] was offered a well-paying fellowship to graduate school at the University of California in Berkeley. The funding came from a federal agency, the Veterans Administration, an obvious spin-off of the War Department.

During the first week of training, the graduate fellows were assembled to meet a representative from Washington who announced, with considerable solemn satisfactoin, that the Federal Government was getting into psychology in a big way. Enormous grants of money for salaries and research could be expected.

This prediction was no exaggeration. Before World War II, psychological research was a gentleman's game of little interest to the Firm and thus with almost no bureaucratic funding or supervision. After 1946, federal support of psychologists in the form of fellowships, salaried posts and research grants became the dominating fact of university life.

The Federal Bureaucracy literally paid for and bought American psychology.

What did this money buy? Exactly what the Firm wanted — a science of Adjustment and Control. Branches of psychology which study *management* of human behavior leaped into prominence: clinical psychology, personality, social psychology.

Leadership and direction of these new fields was assumed by former OSS (i.e., CIA) functionaries, wise in the ways of government support. The field of personality psychology in particular was covered with CIA fingerprints.

Professor Harry Murray, wartime director of the OSS Psychological Project, assembled at his Harvard center the cream of personality researchers. The aim was to investigate, not clinical pathologies (teams of Firm-supported psychiatrists were gleefully taking care of that), but to assess normal and successful humans.

By 1950 most of Murray's staff had fanned out to universities throughout the country in

Before World War II, psychological research was a gentleman's game.

posts of executive power. Donald McKinnon, for example, organized the Institute of Personality Assessment and Research at the University of California in Berkeley (IPAR).

To IPAR came Air Force officers and creative, successful subjects from many professions to participate in weekend assessments based directly on OSS-CIA methods. IPAR was funded by the Ford Foundation, the U.S. Government, and God knows how many fronts.

In spite of the prestige, affluence and power of its staff, IPAR was a curiosity because it never published any important papers, never had to compete for funding and seemed to be (like some Soviet tower) isolated from the exciting self-revolution in personality which occurred from 1950-1976.

This is not to say that the IPAR

psychologists-administrators were idle. Plenty was going on. IPAR was "running" American psychology — monitoring the field, quietly screening new ideas and promising recruits emerging from the graduate ranks, arranging back-scene support for useful researchers, lining up exchanges of staff with selected foreign departments. Get it? IPAR psychologists kept popping up in the funniest places. One energetic post-doctoral went along on an Everest climb. Not a bad place for overlooking (surveilling) China.

Another profoundly significant IPAR project attempted to institute a Brave New World Psych-tech Control. A crew-cut, pink-cheeked church-going staff-member named Harrison Gough designed a personality questionnaire to diagnose "normal and superior" persons. The test had scales for "rebelliousness-conformity," anti-hive thinking, independence, etc.

Gough received a lot of publicity when he floated the proposal that personality questionnaires could be given to every school child in the country in the first grade. It would then be possible, claimed Gough, to pin-point at age seven, potential troublemakers, future talented specialists. Specialized training and surveillance could then be instituted from the earliest years. No great outcry arose from the liberal psychologists.

Which was interesting. Although the average psychologist is a good-natured, reasonably progressive person, and although psychologists would be expected to understand human castes and hive-thought-control interventions, the profession is, by and large, amazingly innocent and unconcerned about the fact that it has been controlled by the Federal Bureaucracy for decades.

From 1920-1960 American psychology was as much a captive of the CIA as Russian psychology of the KGB. In some ways American psychology was more coopted, because everyone in and out of the Soviet Union knows what the KGB is doing, but well-paid American psychologists were blandly unaware of their sponsor-masters.

All this was completely changed, however, by the American Psychological Revolution which exploded in the 1960's.

COUNTER-INTELLIGENCE AGENCY REPORT

Date: February, 1972

Country: Immensee on Lake Zug,
Switzerland

Subject: THE ARRIVAL OF
PRINCE ALEXIS

Classification:

TOP
SECRET

Our local agents report that the Professor's hideout cottage on the lake has a fireplace study on the first floor opening onto the water. The top floor is a ship-cabin sailing down the lake. From the deck one whistles for the seven swans who float majestically along the shore and bend strong phallic necks to swallow bread crumbs.

Prince Alexis drives up in his Stingray, dismounts regally, throws reins to the groom and sets off a three day cycle of life-death magic. Sitting in front of the fire he begins to babble.

(The conversation is taped.)

"The fascinating facet of India," says Alexis, "is her worship of holy putrefaction. To the banal perceptions of the west she exists and has always existed, a bedraggled woolly mammoth buried in the ice of occult tradition. And yet no other ancient culture has been so expressive. In stone carving, temple, wood, gesture, fluid motion, sonorous sound, she has broadcast her bouyant message to the world. Close your eyes and sleep! Lest her repetitious dream be disturbed, she asks for only the smallest dash of creative stimulus in return. Dare we introduce western science-magic to the Ganges? Does soul, expressed in art, as in fucking, require equal reciprocity? Shall we, whether they like it or not, electrify the sita? A rock festival in Benares?"

"Strong cocaine," says the Professor. "Can we change the dial? Let's focus on the nearby future. What part do you want to play in our next episode?"

"What is the script?"

"That is the question. We're looking for it. The womb planet waits for our next broadcast. Unhappily it appears that we have to fabricate the treatment. What do you suggest?"

"My own obsessions are simple," replied the Prince. "Electronic rock 'n roll along the thin, aristocratic line from Chuck Berry to the Stones. Erotic mysticism, tantra and the pursuit of that Holiest of Grails: the all-night, orgasmless fuck. Oh yes, my family history amuses me. The saga of decadence, Sybaritism, epicureanism, philosophic gratification. I am, in addition, a nervous wreck. Do you know what that means?"

"I think so," replies the Professor with a tender smile.

"Then tell me quickly. Why?"

"Why what?"

"Why when I talk to a psychiatrist does he straight-away want to pop me in treatment? It's really quite unsettling. Say something, anything to exorcize this psychiatric curse."

"I'll have to make up a story."

"It's all fiction," says Alexis.

"In the 1950's," says the Professor, "I devoted nine years to the study of the personality, behavior, and strange beliefs of psychiatrists. They are a bizarre and superstitious tribe. My conclusion is that the profession of psychiatry is quite out of touch with reality. Do you like that?"

Date:

Country:

Classification:

Subject: page 2

TOP
SECRET

"Precisely my judgment," exclaims Alexis joyfully. "But I need more to convince me."

"This diagnosis does not apply to the younger generation of psychiatrists, many of whom are nice, if dull hive agents. Freud is considered by many to be a flaming revolutionary of free and honest sexuality. Nothing could be farther from the truth. Freud is the Nixon of Psychology."

"Oh that's priceless," grinned Alexis. "Freud is the Nixon of Psychology! How?"

"Every sensible person in the world," continued the Professor, "had been trying to end the cold war, but such attempts were futile. Because it required someone who fanatically believed in the polarity, someone totally committed to good to establish detente with bad. Nixon being the last politician in the world to want peace with his enemies, had to be the one to use detente against his domestic rivals. The same thing had to happen to allow a detente between Morality and Sex in the European character structure. For a century before Freud every intellectual in Europe had known about the unconscious role of sexuality. But no psychiatrist or scientist with a normal, healthy sex-life could be believed. It required the most uptight, sexless, prudish man in Europe to use sex as ally against his real enemies, the Viennese medical establishment. Is that enough?"

"I'm a difficult case. Can you continue?"

"Psychiatry," continues the Professor, "is primitive, prescientific hive regulation. Actually the pre-Freudian psychiatric language was much more realistic. Before Freud, psychiatrists were called 'alienists.' This is an extraordinarily happy term, because most psychiatric patients are aliens, that is to say, they have activated post-hive circuits of their nervous systems, circuits designed for future survival. When the UFO's land 'alienation' will become a very respectable word. The in-sane seem to live in another world. Exactly. They are perhaps best seen as premature evolutes. Mental hospitals should be called asylums. A nervous wreck is exactly that."

"It's a beautiful concept," says Alexis. "A badge of honor I shall wear proudly."

"Nervous," explains the Exorcist, "refers our attention to the nervous system, not to imaginary character traits. And 'wrecked' means pushed out of normal hive alignment. Collapse of the Domesticated Mind is considered to be the goal of most mutating post-hive entities. The mind as you know, Alexis, is the fragment of the brain that mediates the movements of the nine muscles of the larynx and the hand. Collapse of the mind means that the laryngeal muscles can no longer define hive reality."

(End of tape.)

CLAUDE A. RUFFALO, Ph.D.

The name and face of Daniel Gilbertson are recognized throughout the galaxy as symbols of swashbuckling neuroastronaut adventure.

Gilbertson started his internal-explorations while a graduate student at Oxford. He subsequently made documentary films on the desert, the deep seas, the underworld and in high orbit. Daniel spent the next decade as a staff hedonist at the then fledgling University of Space. He later went on to win the Pleasure Decathalon at the Hedonic Olympics of 1980, 1984

and 2002.

Daniel's career took an unexpected twist in 2001 when he designed the first 100% collimation-free microdisc sound processor with synaptic cleft micromote regulators and built-in quadrophonic headphones. Proceeds went to the establishment of a nonprofit social athletic club — "The Space Nomads" — dedicated to humankind's spirit of undying adventure. (Their motto: **Nothing Human is Strange to Us.***) During his fourteen-year tenure as a Senior Fellow of The Space Nomads, Daniel operated his own deep space safari company and lectured regularly on the future of social evolution.*

He also laid the original plans for the Phoenix Rising Animal Reserve which pioneered zero-gravity back-breeding techniques, recreating the Dodo and many other formerly extinct species.

His major accomplishments, however, came in the field of High Orbital Architecture and Design. The thousands of Mini-Earths he designed can be recognized throughout the solar system by their understated beauty and elegance.

Daniel Gilbertson was last seen heading towards Alpha Centauri to scout locations for a film version of his #1 best-selling paperback, Little Known Trails of the Alpha Centaurian Black Hole.

Reprinted from SCIENTIFIC AMERICA, August 1979

The Ups of Pleasure and Downs of Satisfaction

by Daniel Gilbertson

Hive-moralists for millenia have lamented the innate, pervasive tendency of human beings to kick-out in bursts of irrationality and pleasure seeking. Extrasocial self-indulgence.

It is important to distinguish between two very different hedonic reactions.

Hedonic experiences caused by activating higher-faster-future brains at the service of and controlled by self. *Pleasures.*

Intoxication and narcotic escape experiences caused by activating slower-lower circuits. *Satisfactions.*

Both of these experiences take consciousness away from domesticated robothood. Pleasures move one into the past-social-self-actualized future. Up from hive routine. Intoxicants, tranquilizers and narcotics move one back to the past — down from domestication, to primate and mammalian instinctual satisfactions.

Civilized terrestrial humans, robotically and blindly harnessed to species tasks, dependent upon gene-hive rewards for duty well-done, apparently need to slow-down, turn-off, escape domesticated pressure. Boredom and social inefficiency would result without some sequential opportunity to regress from hive morality, to activate the primitive circuits of the brain. Intoxicants and narcotic escapes are built-in devices to allow ritual regression to earlier, lower,

---

Each civilization produces ritualistic drug-taking.

---

slower stages. Their power and delight is that they are conventionally naughty.

The dutiful 11th Brain Domesticate and the 12th Brain Insectoid live in a reality centered upon hive duty. The 10 earlier brains are there, but are taboo, often blanked from consciousness. Every successful 11th and 12th brain civilization provides ritualistic means of allowing reactivation of the earlier brains — temporarily naughty immorality, programmed animalism. Permissable retrogression. Brains, as we know, are turned on and off by means of neuro-transmitter chemicals. Each civilization produces ritualistic drug-taking which allows temporary animalistic reversion.

This process is best seen in the Japanese culture — surely the most insectoid society in world history. The Japanese have developed ritualistic drunkeness which permits the Dutiful Nipponese to regress to animalism (Brains 4, 5, and 6). Alcoholism, abuse of state-manufactured vodka, is also tolerated in the Soviet Union.

It is noteworthy that the German culture, another highly domesticated-duty society, allows its citizens a scheduled intoxication-regression in the *Fasching*-carnival. And even the sober, tidy Swiss, permit each other a Springtime return to pseudo-bestiality when these paragons of 11th brain tidy familiarity become tipsy and lurch around like sodden bears shamelessly littering the streets of Basel with confetti! (Masks are worn at these carnival regressions. The Burghers do not want to have their inner animals seen.)

Other methods for ceremonial return of the animal-brain-stages involve totems exhibited at athletic events, parades, social gatherings. Observe that the unrepressed emotions released at these events are not sexual. Genital satisfaction is not the central motive. Middle-age, middle-class folks return to pre-adolescence and become exhibitionistic monkeys or noisy, often savage mammals. Recall South and Central American football games in which thousands of spectators engage in physical violence directed against the territorial rival.

The orchestrated revival of earlier brains is a basic issue in any stable gene-pool. Each of our 12 terrestrial brains has its own ego, demands activation, must be allowed to cut loose on some regular basis. The best-run civilizations have worked out a weekly return of the regressed. The domesticate works dutifully Monday through Friday. Saturday SHe is allowed to assemble in animal-totem competitions — the *Bulldogs* of Yale versus the *Horned Toads* of Texas Christian. Saturday night the socially approved intoxicant is imbibed, permitting a temporary explosion of mammalian territorial competition and sexual low-jinks. Sunday morning the chastened and hung-over domesticate attends a DNA adoration ceremony in which the dignified gene-hive Creator is recognized, the brief foray back to animalism exorcised. The domesticate, purged and reborn, is ready to start the next week of hive duty.

So far we have discussed alcohol — which triggers off mammalian reactions. Another powerful set of neurotransmitters reconstruct even more primitive realities. Narcotics reactivate 1st brain experiences and put the domesticate in touch with relaxed, floating, vegetative

---

Middle-age, middle-class folks return to pre-adolescence and become exhibitionistic monkeys.

---

pre-terrestrial-marine neurological realities.

Narcotic drugs are approved when used in sickness rituals. Symptomatic cries for help can stimulate shaman-doctors to offer the narcotic experience which activates lower-brain consciousness — ancient, infantile, vegetative. The taboo is necessary to hive discipline. The narcotic return to marine status is so tempting, so inviting, that it must be administered by an Authority figure. The domesticate is not allowed access to First Circuit neurotransmitters. Self-administration of narcotics to actualize infantile responses cannot be tolerated for fear that everyone will reject the busy, hectic, adult demands of the hive and escape back to vegetative-ocean bliss. The Doctor Ceremony is the method by which hive-society allows citizens to plug back into the early marine circuits.

> ## It is impossible, however, to phone in "well" to the hive-center.

An amusing diagnostic side-light on domesticated terrestrial civilizations: It is acceptable to phone-in sick to the office and thus avoid work. Hive-society recognizes that the insectoid slavery it imposes is basically lethal to the workers. The ceremony of sick-leave is allowed.

It is impossible, however, to phone in "well" to the hive-center. To announce: "I feel so good today, I'm not coming in to work." In the hedonic society of the future (when the Dom-Species is 14th Brain) provision will be made for "well-leave" in addition to "sick-leave."

The difference between intoxicant-narcotic behavior and hedonic behavior should now be clear. The former engages earlier-slower-lower instinctual brains. The latter moves consciousness and behavior into the self-actualized future, engages future neural circuits. The former are rewards for the over-worked domesticate. The latter are genetic endowments, new brains presented, ready-or-not, by the evolutionary process — not earned, but grown-into.

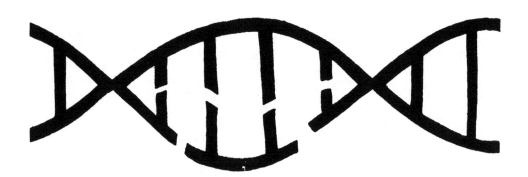

ALL THE REALITIES WE SHALL EVER KNOW ARE CREATED BY THE CONVERSATION BETWEEN DNA AND CNS (CENTRAL NERVOUS SYSTEM). THE DNA BLUEPRINT OF EVOLUTION, PAST AND FUTURE, CAN BE DECIPHERED AS WE TAP INTO THE DNA-CNS CHANNEL.

WALL GRAFFITI

CIRCA 1996

Reprinted from PSYCHOLOGY TWODAY, February 1982

The Dirty Tricks of American Behaviorism

by Mary Leary Gorman

The Behaviorism, which co-opted earthling psychology after World War I, was a dramatic and partisan rejection of the previous generation of wide-gauge thinkers who founded Scientific Psychology in the later years of the eighteenth century. A rejection of men like Wundt, Fechner and Tichener who defined the subject matter of psychology — the rigorous study of the relationship between inner and outer geography, between consciousness and external stimulus-behavior.

Before World War I, psychologists operated in respectful collaboration with "subjects." The basic laboratory technique was "Introspective training" — teaching people how to attend to, calibrate and describe the workings of their own body-brain. This charming laboratory by-product of 19th century Romantic Individualism was fiercely rejected by the Behaviorists who moved in after World War I and sternly defined psychology in terms of objective stimulus-response — scornfully banishing to the shadowy realm of subjectivity any internal, personal reaction of the subject.*

And Oh boy, what a new toy for power-hungry hive-managers! Psychology! Conditioning! Mind control! From the first, Behaviorism was seen as the special province of the manipulators, the secret services, the bureaucrats, the espionage boys, the spies, the "dirty trick" operatives.

*Before 1914 psychologists were Protestant scholars and gentlemen who, in contrast to the academic bureaucrats of today, would never stoop to deceive or manipulate subjects. The ethos of the time is nicely illustrated by the comment of Henry Lewis Stimson, Secretary of War, 1911-1913 and again, believe it or not, 1940-1945, who tried to block the emergence of OSS-CIA elements by saying, "Gentlemen, never open other people's mail."

During World War II, the elite of American psychology worked with the Office of Special Services (OSS). (The OSS was, after the war, reorganized as the CIA). From their center near Washington, D.C., OSS psychologists developed the science of Personality Assessment. Candidates for espionage and "dirty trick" operations were not only administered batteries of tests but were assessed in complex, contrived, simulated psychodramatic situations. The classic example of OSS assessment involved the fake graduation party, which was played out as follows:

After several days of harassing assessment experiments (in which apparent co-equal colleagues and fellow candidates were actually planted psychologists, slyly playing disturbing and confusing roles) the candidates were invited to a party with staff members in which alcoholic drinks were served. The celebration party was, of course, part of the assessment. The candidates' reaction to the fake comradery was part of the selection process.

Easy-going trustful souls, given to cocktail fun, were transferred out to the Office of War Information. Distrustful, cagey, paranoid types were immediately screened-in as part of the Intelligence (sic) elite; in Pynchon's words, ". . . the New Chaps with their little green antennas out for the usable emanations of power, versed in American politics (knowing the difference between the New Dealers of OWI and the eastern and moneyed Republicans behind OSS), keeping brain-dossiers on latencies, weaknesses, tea-taking habits, errogenous zones of all, all who might someday be useful."

From these war-time roots grew the Post-war Psychology of Selection and Adjustment.

TUCSON LECTURE

TO LIVE EAST OF DENVER IS TO FAIL
THE INTELLIGENCE TEST

The truth of the Occidental Ascendance becomes comically clear when we move down and back East across the Atlantic Ocean. The Greenwich time zones are in centuries. If Boston is two hundred years before Los Angeles (no accident that the current Neurological Capital of the planet has been given the high-altitude title "City of the Angels"), then surely we see that London is four hundred years back and down.

If England is a comic opera
what can we say
about France?

What, in truth, can we expect from England? Elizabethan Style? Repetitious tradition? Culture? Only in the sense of a class structure — which penalizes new genetic intelligence in favor of inherited privilege. Parent-child inheritance of bureaucratic advantage always drives the superior-futique genes into migration. This is not a political complaint, but a neuro-genetic I.D. test. The genetically active, whether descended from the sperm-ova of prince or pauper (every gene-pool contains its princes and paupers), always migrate West. Those who rely on power remain in the Eastern capital.

If England is a comic opera what can we say about France? Paris is a museum of dusty Louis XIV grandeur. And what, in relevant charity for the past, can be said about the lessons that an intelligent terrestrial primate can learn today in Lisbon? Madrid? Rome? Athens? Cairo? Beirut? Jerusalem?

There is this to be said for N.A.T.O. nations. They are the most Western, i.e., the freest and smartest gene-pools of the Old Continent. Examine a map of the Euro-Asian land mass. Color in blue those countries which are democratic, which respect human rights, which outlaw torture, which allow any cultural or individual experimentation. You will see that the

blue countries cluster nervously at the Western borders of the huge, Euro-Asian hemisphere. Notice as you go East you find more government restrictions, more centralization, more contempt for the individual, more commitment to tradition and familial-dictatorship.

"Buffalo is an intelligence
test you have failed."

To live in the East is to fail a genetic intelligence test. This winter I travelled from San Diego to Buffalo and told the shivering natives, "Buffalo is an intelligence test you have failed. So you have to stay here and repeat Buffalo 1A." *(Laughter)* Can there possibly be one intelligent person left in North Ireland? Uganda? *(Laughter)* Any Ugandan with more than eight billion neurons surely has swum a river or climbed a mountain to flee from that jungle of primitive barbarism.

And what can we say to those Americans who, via genetic back-spin, look East for something to do? The time has come to learn how to read the Occidental Altimeter. When you move East you crash-land in the past. Consider our liberal Potomac executives and congressional busybodies who continually ignore the wisdom of Washington's farewell advice not to meddle in the affairs of the Old World. Poor President Carter sends a senile envoy, Averell Harriman, to Cyprus to settle the quarrel between the

---

Foreign policy is the game of mad monsters playing chess blindfolded...

Turks and the Greeks — forgetting that Mid-Brain Mediterraneans have been fighting each other about mammalian territorial borders for 5,000 years! And here comes Secretary of State Vance attempting to mediate border disputes between the Palestinians and the Hebrews! How about that for a genetic laugh! And Nixon tilts in favor of Pakistan! And Kissinger intervenes Lon Nol in Cambodian politics thus assuming the karma for two million dead and creating the ultimate insectoid state-postwar Cambodia. Foreign policy is the game of mad monsters playing chess blindfolded with mammalian-gene-pools as pawns. Foreign policy is totally foreign to the American Myth. That's why accented Europeans like Kissinger and Brzezinski are selected to be Secretaries of State. It's a European game several centuries old.

Here's your American Ecological Foreign Policy. The folks of the Old World inhabit pre-civilized, barbarian gene-pools. Europeans and Africans and Asians are our own animal origins still obsessed with territorial conflict. This is not said in disinterest. By all means send food and veterinary medicines to the Old World. By all means send the old gene-pools invitations that freedom, change, mobility and Intelligence Increase awaits in the West. But to meddle in European-African-Asian politics is an attempt to reconcile the ancient quarrel between rabbits and foxes. Shall Free Americans take sides in back yard competition between the red ants and the black ants of South Africa, or the ferocious-fanatics of the Middle East? Interestingly enough, the national, tribal folk of Africa say they just want to be left alone and have no loyal commitments to Soviet or Pentagon politicians. By all means let them alone.

CNS

means

CENTRAL NERVOUS SYSTEM

your best friend!

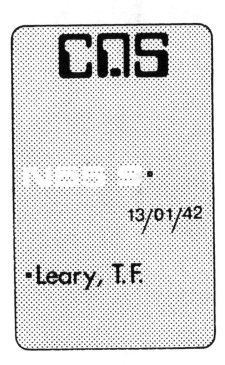

don't leave home without it

133

The Magical Mystery Tour of Switzerland

by Timothy Leri

Sergius Golowin, a Swiss historian and member of the Bernese Legislature, lives between the lungs at Interlaken. His arcane specialty is the magical, occult, Celtic thread of Swiss history. During my exile Sergius took me around to the sacred shrines of the Confederation. The Witches Meadow. The enchanted valley of Brother Nicolas. The charmed Celtic forest high in the Lycergic Alps. The cave of the Irish hermit above Interlaken.

Sergius, as though in a dream or trance, would escort me to a carefully selected site, read from a history book about the events which occurred there, strike a pose and have his picture

taken with me. I later discovered that Golowin was re-enacting scenes from ancient paintings, re-living the visits of former philosophers — re-making old Celtic Reality Movies. I got the strong impression that I could not leave Switzerland until I had traced the steps of the Celtic migrants who passed through the High Valleys on the voyage to the western lobes.

One day we drove in the yellow Porsche to Einsenin, south of Zurich, to visit the birthplace of Paracelsus. We carved through pastoral beauty (hip Swiss in their boredom call their country the Green Hell), past meadows and tidy farms, into a small village where, amazingly, there rose a medieval cathedral, towering, expansive, fronted by a broad St. Peter's cobblestone plaza where three hundred thousand pilgrims used to assemble from all over Europe.

Inside was dark, heavy oppressive, high, solid like the cathedral of Sevilla. In the enormous mausoleum there were so few people walking like ants. Old women dressed in black. In the stone floor under the central dome was a circle, fifty feet wide, of mosaic designs. As

The game is to look for the hidden message.

journey-men, Intelligence Agents always looking for secret keys that open to higher levels, Sergius and I picked up Brotherhood of Masons vibes. Secret psychedelic cult-spoor.

The game is to look for the hidden message. In the cathedral of Einsenin, once center of European Christianity, there is a large circle of the twelve astrological signs hidden by the pews. They are so large and scattered that only the time-traveler would notice. Astrology, with its evolutionary and caste implications, was one of the dangerous drugs of the Middle Ages. How did they get away with embossing pagan symbols in a Catholic Cathedral? Maybe the Zodiac was so suppressed that the local inquisition didn't know the details of the heresy.

We returned to the car and drove past neighboring convents and seminary dormitories out along a country road overlooking the lake, down a side road and across a bridge. Sergius is an impressive navigator, considering that he's directing time ships calibrated in centuries; but he does get vague in the fine tuning. He knew the house of Paracelsus was just beyond a bridge. He asked at the nearest farmhouse and came back with the information. Everything in sight had belonged to the family of Paracelsus.

We walked down a path to a high vantage spot and thought about the great alchemist who played here as a boy before wandering around Europe, teaching, studying, experimenting, getting arrested, deported from Basel, hiding from the Bernese police, seeking asylum in Prague (home of alchemists). He was the father of modern chemistry, modern medicine, and Jung claimed him as founder of dynamic psychology. He was basically an alchemist, dealing drugs which provided the illuminated vision, the philosopher's stone which, when swallowed, tuned you into the bio-physical

network and focused your neurological microscope so you could identify the web of energy. Paracelsus was the wisest and most influential mind that Europe produced, but the chemical companies in Basel don't like to talk about him too much now because he was an illegal magician.

We drove back to the bridge and Sergius said "Stop" in front of the charred debris of a burned-down house. "This is the house that was built on the site of the house of Paracelsus." We poked around the ruins. There were shards of melted glass in different colors. I stuck one in my pocket. The symbolism was asphyxiating. In front of the house, just on the other side of the bridge away from town was a metal sign. It read: PARACESUS. "The L is missing," said Sergius. He nodded knowingly. *In this, the tidiest country in the world, the birthplace of wisest product of Swiss gene-pools was a neglected shambles.*

"It's called 'Devil's Bridge," said Sergius. "The Bishop who controlled the town was in charge of all road construction. Now and then dissatisfied farmers would build bridges themselves. When the agents of the Bishop would come around asking who built the unauthorized bridge, they would say, 'The devil built it.'"

He's directing time ships calibrated in centuries.

My house on Zug Lake, where from the balcony I watched seven swans swim stately to be fed, was just below the hill where William Tell hid in wait for the tyrant Gessler, slew him with the extra arrow, and thus began the Swiss War for Independence. *Twelve twenty-one* was my phone number in the Villars Chalet. And the house on Zug Lake was in the exact center of Swiss space and time. When one moves free, Sci-Fi high above gravity pull, it's all mystic, mythic, connected overground comics.

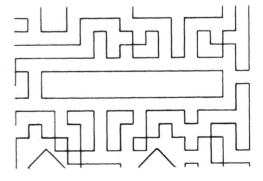

Letter from Brian Barritt in Amsterdam
to Commodore Leri in Folsom Prison, Sept. 1973

Hello Tim:

Nice to know you're OK and reassuring to know that your nervous system is in your control and mind functioning with the same sizzle as always. Christ man, the three months I just finished in the Amsterdam jail were longer than the three years I did in England. Prison is a bore but it does get the extrasensory mechanisms moving. Helps to catch up with the reading too; I read all the English books in the library, murder, rape, robbery, all the things a good con should know. Even found a copy of Bucke's Cosmic Consciousness — for long termers I guess.

The last few weeks I was the only English speaking guy in the place. The Silent One wandering through the prison structure like a spectre with the three dumb monkeys on my back Saying Nothing, Understanding Nothing, Contributing Nothing except a few words in pidgin Dutch and an occasional bleep of enthusiasm. Then they let me out, steal my money and buy me a ticket on the first boat to England. In the detention cell at the Hook of Holland I meet her, Jane, seventeen years young and it's her first deportation, she's traveling back on the night boat, the same boat as meeeee!

Well like it's just cosmically planned baby, that's all.

I am showing her the constellations as we cruise beneath the occult moon before she tells me she is a boy! Total embarrassment, absolute disorientation! Just what a con needs on his first night out.

So many odd and funny things happened to me from when I was deported till I arrived back in Holland with a fresh passport 48 hours later. Even the fuzz goofed and paid me 50 pounds by mistake. Omens coming in thick and fast, Bonne Chance to rebirth.

BUSINESS SECTION: You asked about Michel Hauchard. I made no agreements, settlements, with him. We got photostats of the correspondence between the lawyers and our suit against him was coming together nicely when Hauchard split the country. I didn't have the bread to chase him around France. With a little help from Joanna I might have been able to do more but my letters asking for information were unanswered or the

---

Incest seems a good idea. I believe it to be an evolutionary method for strengthening existing genetic combinations.

---

content ignored. When you were in Afghan I told Michel he could keep the quarter of a million from Bantam and no hassles from our side concerning the rights to your future works, if he got you out of custody or delayed your flight back to the States. Later when Sue was in Amsterdam I offered to drop the case against him if he sent her $5,000. Nothing was put in writing. He did not help in any way.

SOUNDS: David Bowie.

LITERATURE: Simone Vinkenoog translated Confessions of a Hope Fiend into Dutch. I am going to Switzerland — soon as Davie Log has finished his holidays and is back in England for the new term. To see what is happening to The Psychedelic Prayers. Carl Lazlo says the publisher still owes money to the printer and is having trouble with distribution — as always. A photostat version of Neurologic has been done in German by Gruner Zweig. I'm glad to see the Germans are on to it.

PERSONAL: Met Elizabeth's father. Sargeant Pepper himself. All the guys of his generation have minds like the Encyclopaedia Britannica. So I'm sipping my sherry and trying not to look too sexy when it strikes me that this sprightly old rooster is ogling his daughter. He was so jealous, man I was amazed. I am sexually ignorant about father/daughter relationships but I can tell when a guy is aching to fuck my chick and Dr. Elliott-Cooke is coming on with a heavy bedside manner. Liz thinks it's all a gas but I don't think he'll ever make her. Not with those classical sounds anyhow.

When I reflect on it, incest seems a good idea. I believe it to be an evolutionary method for strengthening existing genetic combinations. All the animals do it now and again to

purify and reinforce herd characteristics. Inbreeding is a stabilizing force, a survival factor designed to balance out the evolutionary pressures that cause constant change in the species, but for God's sake don't tell anyone. How the incest taboo came about I've no idea, but it came early on when the earth needed populating and as much variation as possible was needed so that evolution could get moving, and I see no reason for this archaic Pre-Cambrian attitude to continue.

THE CITY: Feeling very immortal lately with my lotus feet in high-heeled silver boots, ice cream coat (white satin drape) and thoughts going off like fireworks. But without each other to orient by, Elizabeth and myself would have difficulty in keeping our Circuit 6 Show free from the terrestrial realities whirlpooling around us.

Adam is a whirlpool of cults, scenes and shows. Magicians have been laying down these trips since '66 and disoriented time travelers come spiraling into the city and zapp into some mind-web or other before they can get a psychological bearing.

Adam is like living an immense brain. Really, Tim, it's very moving to see how the Time Underground has nurtured this incredible being. The visions we saw in the early 60's are

---

Adam is a whirlpool of cults, scenes and shows.

---

a living entity now. Sci-Fiction monsters that turned out to be friendly after all. Oh it's wearing patched jeans and it's broke most of the time, but in terms of human relationships it's the deepest and most profound model ever.

At present Adam has the highest mass consciousness on the planet. I doubt whether it will survive the leap from Circuit 5 to Circuit 6 and still head the evolutionary thrust, but at this moment, before the first neurological city is pinpointed, Adam acts as the model point of the earth's spiritual energy supply.[*]

Well, as you see we are in love with the city and the city is in love with us. We have not too much difficulty relating to the authorities in this setting, but one foot over the Dutch border in any direction and the pressure is full on against us. Your letter says, "It is very good not to be in an adversary position with the law." But Tim, it's the law that's in an adversary position to us. I can't remember ever having committed a crime by my DNA standards. I therefore figure I ain't committed any crimes. The closer I follow my nervous system (the Buzz) the more I am in tune with the evolutionary goal, it would be a crime if I did otherwise.[**]

Adam is like living in an immense brain.

The "straight" world is amiable here. The Underground and hippies are often treated with respect. The Netherlanders are an easy-going race at heart and since millions of guilders pour into the country via young cats who come to smoke the almost legal pot, the burly burghers of protestant Holland have a civic duty to respect their strange modes of dress and ultra-violet hair — as long as they have bread.

But it is more than that, really. It's not just bread that motivates the Dutch amiability. They have respect for the intelligence of some non-conformists; they have seen many pleasant changes and Holland has a history as a refuge for the persecuted. The Pilgrim Fathers stayed here a while after being pressurized out of England. It has a lot in common with Switzerland as a harbor of safety as well. And on the other side of the coin Sergius Golowin tells me the Dutch hired the Swiss mercenaries to capture the East Indies for them.

Sometimes glimpses of the year 2000 appear through chinks in the city's time stream,

---

[*]A most intelligent comment. Barritt knows that a neurogenetic migration is in the air. Like a good Evolutionary Agent he inquires about the next ecological niche.

[**]A common complaint of futique mutants who cannot gear inner to outer. Who fail to realize that each stage must be externally mastered and used as launching pad. That each hive establishment must be re-assured.

electromagnetic love-songs drifting through the streets, reflecting in the canals, twining fleur-de-lys round the spires of Baroque churches, the feeling of family, the strong warm glow of "home." Electric symbiosis. Comforting force fields of mutual respect.

NOTES: Mutation does not happen by accident, it happens to those who put themselves in the position and place where maximum possibilities for change can occur, after that it's just a matter of <u>Bonne Chance</u>.

HOW TO GET YOUR EGO BACK: Love thyself, and then find someone you like better.

Some things in the air. Since we received your letter we have had visitors from Swiss every week enquiring about you. Giger, Sergius, Carl Laslo, Brumbar and this week Kristoff from the Hesse-Haus in Corona. I think your time in prison is nearing an end.

Simone Vinkenoog suggests that I start a correspondence with you with the view of publishing later. If you think it's à good idea we'll do it, just let me know which questions to ask you.*

Love thyself, and then find someone you like better.

Brumbar is a first class artist. As soon as I get some slides I will send you them. I am very impressed by his work; there's softness, tenderness, strength and humor in them. They are healthy pictures. We neurologicians badly need a coherent symbol system. The "occultist" has a wealth of traditional symbols to call on. The eastern trip is alive with radiant images. The neurologician has nothing really beautiful to look at. There are too few Sci-Fi artists about. What is needed is contemporary illustrations, parables to the alchemical and eastern ones. I put some of Brumbar's pictures in the pages of Terra II and the book blossomed from an Underground production into a jewel-like scripture.

Imagery is very important right now. How about a mandala like the Buddhist Wheel of Becoming with the eight circuits illustrated so that the whole system can be taken in at once? Hedonic textbook? Cats are tripping out on Hindu and Buddhist symbols when

*Example of future-reality fabrication.

they should be building up memory archives based on contemporary and futique views of the scene.

Have you designed Tarot cards yet? If you have something in mind, flash me and I will ask Brumbar to do it. Posters are a quick way of telling people that a contemporary religion/philosophy exists. Everybody has been waiting for a neurological Tarot for ages and a science-fiction will become standard equipment for time travelers.

Our experimental tolerances have reached immense proportions. We are having difficulty finding enough stimuli to satisfy our habits. Really, we need freezing till 2000 and waking up when the earth's intensity ratio has risen a few points.* However, as Terra II gets nearer to the White Hole at the center of our galaxy and the stars are more numerous, we should meet and exchange information with other extra-terrestrials and the most sophisticated ecstasies of the Milky Way will be at our disposal. Unparalleled joys will streak and sizzle along our ganglia while Nirvana's and Satori's crackle and pop and awesome blue-white blasts murmur extra sensory obscenities to our souls. (Progress is measured here in terms of how much ecstasy can you take on the Pleasure Meters of Total Bliss.)

I make my entrance wearing my ice cream coat of vivid satin and silver high-heeled boots, Liz in amber and gold, red high-heels, smoking a phosphorescent cigarette.

We enter from opposite sides of the stage, meet in the middle, kiss, and merge into electrical life from flashing zig-zags of lightning. The lightning forks; we exchange bodies. I am Liz. She is me. The lightning slows to a pulsing golden glow as we divide into our two separate forms. We are looking at each other out of each others' eyes, we are the same entity and also two different entities at the same time. I take a draw on my cigarette. Brian blows a kiss to the audience, we exit together in a shower of stardust.

Bye Time
Love
Bonne Chance
Brian

*This is the highest point of Old Brain thinking. The New Brain response is: Brian, don't be so passive. Swim West and carpenter the future.

COUNTER-INTELLIGENCE AGENCY REPORT

Date: February, 1972

Country: Imminsee on Lake Zug,
Switzerland

Subject: THE AGONIZING CURSE OF
PRINCE ALEXIS

Classification:

TOP
SECRET

(Report by Deep-Cover Agent 3-15.)

Alexis gracefully rose to his feet and began to pace the floor. The flickering light from the fire painted red shadow patches on his aquiline face.

"Okay," he said, "that's enough for the psychiatric spell. Now let me present you with the more serious neurological problem. I have come eight thousand kilometers to beg of you a boon. And in return I bring you a most valuable gift."

"I am at your service," said the Philosopher.

"I have fallen under a most agonizing curse."

"How was this neurological imprint imposed?"

"In India. I picked up your trail, first in the ghats and ganja shops of Calcutta. Then up to Benares. And then to Almora. It's your fault really. Your visit there has become a cultist legend. That's why I went there. In your footsteps. I found a house on swami ridge."

"Not the little cottage on Snow View which looks North to the Himalayas where I stayed with the beautiful Nordic sorceress?"

"No. Near by. But I know that cottage. I stayed in a house up beyond Snow View just before the footpath crosses the ridge."

"Just before the tea hut?"

"Yes. There are still many self-appointed holymen living along the ridge. Everyone who passes along the summit on the way to Lama Govinda's passes Snow View and feels your presence. Living ghosts make people nervous."

"Nervous is good," replied the Professor. "Nerve means courage and vitality."

"Living ghosts disturb because they remind people that the mysteries are still alive. It's a scandal that you are still running around this planet upsetting hive traditions. If you were trans-migrated according to custom it would be more comfortable for everyone. You could be dealt with, commercialized, marketed, re-discovered and fed into the Messiah Biography Machine. One wave of books could prove you a comic prophet. The next wave could demonstrate you were a shallow romantic vulgarizing the ancient gnosis. In the old linear age you would have been removed as soon as you produced a Shock. If you announce you are going to drive people out of their minds, and if you do activate them to ecstacy and terror and awe, it's the genetic duty of the Hive People to assasinate you. I find your living presence disturbing. Why do you hang around?"

"Come now Alexis," murmured the Philosopher. "You are getting carried away with old pre-Einsteinian myths. Since 1946 the Genetic Intelligence assignments have changed. Agents must now illustrate, publicly and flamboyantly, the process of rapid, continuous metamorphosis. Change Agents continually change. Have some more wine."

Pathology Always Precedes Potential

Julien Offray de la Mettrie

*"The human body is a watch, a large watch con-
structed with...skill and ingenuity." la Mettrie*

This description of a new college course
in Genetics, taught in a prestigious
Sun Belt University, is a very valuable
neurogenetic clue. It is the kind of
evidence (easily overlooked by hive observers)
which Evolutionary Agents seek. It reveals
much about the Neurogenetic Stage of the hive
culture — and of the planet.

Genetic Counseling always appears one generation after Personality Counseling. When an
advanced, post-political culture offers courses in
"Job Counseling," "Personality Counseling" or
"Marital Counseling", the I² Agent knows that a
move towards Self-Actualization is occurring;
that a free-mobile-individually oriented society
has emerged. (Note that the Soviet Union was
not offering courses in Personality Improvement in 1978.) Extension courses in the Snow
Belt cities were just beginning to catch on to the
Self-Actualization movement which had originated — where all individual freedoms start
— on the Western Frontier.

The term *Genetic Counseling* indicates that a
7th Circuit Stage 19 Consciousness is dawning.

The emphasis is on genetic *disorder*, not upon
genetic *endowment*, but this is to be expected. A
new technology always appeals to hive-security
first — as a way of dealing with danger. Awareness of genetic disorder always precedes awareness of genetic excellence. Just as psychiatry
always precedes self-actualized psychology.
Pathology always precedes Potential. When the
experts in a hive begin treating "broken-down
personalities" they have recognized the existence of "personality." And the next step is for
healthy individuals to start taking charge of
their own "selfs."

On nursery planets the military (warrior-
caste) is responsible for developing new
technologies for faster mobility and communication. The citizens in the Western Frontier
then co-opt the technology for their own self-
actualization.

So it was with Genetic Intelligence.

The first step is discovering that genetic
causes exist for human problems. This is a big
breakthrough — resisted, of course, by Stage 12
Socialist Demo-poll cultures. Genetic determi-
nation focuses on gene-pool statistics and
caste-differentiation, thus minimizing the importance of hive managers. Stage 12

Socialist-Welfare cultures insist that the collective super-hive (the state) is responsible for everything.

Once humans begin to face the fact that genes determine the varied destiny of their different children, then they are ready to see that genes determine their own caste. Next comes the catastrophic discovery that each gene-pool is a time-hive, a genetic molecule, made up of many elements called castes. The whole game is genetic robotry.

Within ten years after Genetic Counseling Courses start studying Genetic Problems we can expect courses in Genetic Potentials and Self-Selected Breeding. These courses will emerge on the Western Frontier. (There is no chance that China or the Soviet Union will offer courses on genetic elites.) The definition of Genetic Counseling then changes from an emphasis on pathology to one of excellence and growth.

By 1985 the definition of Genetic Counseling will read like this: a communication process which deals with the human *potentials* associated with the occurrence, or the possibility of occurrence, of a genetic *advance* in the gene-pool. In 1978 the Dom-Species on the Sunset Strip was moving from Stage 12 Social-Sacrifice to Stage 13 Self-Consumerism. The Pre-Dom ideas emerging on the volatile Western Frontier were:

Pre-Dom[1] (Stage 14)
Bodily Intelligence Self-Actualization
"My Body is my Time Ship"

Pre-Dom[2] (Stage 15)
Voluntary Civilian Space Migration
"We Are Not Terrestrials"

Pre-Dom[3] (Stage 16)
Brain Reality Consumerism
"I Can Select My Own Reality"

Pre-Dom[4] (Stage 17)
Brain Reality Self-Actualism
"I Can Create My Own Reality"

Pre-Dom[5] (Stage 18)
Brain Reality Fusion
"We Can Fabricate an External Reality"

Pre-Dom[6] (Stage 19)
Genetic Consumerism
"I Can Select My Own Genetic Reality"

Pre-Dom[7] (Stage 20)
Genetic Engineering
"I Can Fabricate My Own Genetic Reality"

It is the function of terrestrial Dom-Species to place under Hive-Taboo all notions of the future. The ideas of Bodily-Sensory-Hedonic Consumerism — fiercely taboo in Stage 11 and 12 societies — had actually crumbled on the Western Frontier by 1978.

The Pre-Dom[1] Taboo against Bodily Self-Actualization was also crumbling in the Sun Belt — as exemplified by the legalization of marijuana, the classic tool of one who wishes to control one's own hedonic reality.

The Pre-Dom[2] Taboo of 1978 condemned Civilian Space Migration. In January 1978 the Director of N.A.S.A., one Dr. Frosch, testified in Congress that Civilian Space Migration was a "pre-adolescent" idea. He was precisely correct. If pre-adolescence is defined as age 11, then a pre-adolescent idea will become a young-voter idea in seven years and will be legalized in California in ten years.

There are two sets of Taboos which are imposed by the Dom-Species to maintain its equilibrium and Hive-Solidarity: *X-Dom Taboos condemn the past* and *Pre-Dom Taboos condemn the future.*

The Dom-Species is held together by its opposition to the proximal past and future stages.

The whole game is genetic robotry.

As examples of X-Dom Taboos we note the shames attached to Cannibalism, illegal personal violence, violation of property, personal dishonesty, rape. The Ten Commandments are a valuable index of the Neurogenetic Stage of the time: Thou shalt honor thy parents; Thou shalt not steal, kill, lie, sexually trespass, or violate territory within the hive; Thou shalt adore the Hive-totem and not worship past pagan Gods or Future Gods.

Social Welfare countries (Stage 12) place under taboo all forms of individuality — both past and future.

Stage 11 Societies (Democratic-bourgeois) place under taboo Feudal Elitism (10) and State Power (12) and post-familial individuality (13).

The Pre-Dom[3] Taboo in 1978 condemned any intervention into Brain Control — either by others or self. Thus the revulsion against C.I.A. Brain Experiments using drugs or bio-electrical means.

The Pre-Dom[4] Taboo against Self-Directed Brain Change was even more rigid. While there was some liberal hand-wringing about C.I.A.

experiments with LSD there was stark terror at the thought of Self-Appointed Individuals using psychedelic drugs to change their own Realities.

The Pre-Dom[5] Taboo against Intentional Communes of Individuals linking to create new Realities was very pervasive in 1978. Every attempt to construct such communities was routinely snuffed.

The Pre-Dom[6] Taboo against Genetic Consumerism surfaced for the first time in 1975–78 when citizens became morally outraged by Genetic Engineering and cloning.*

The flap over Recombinant DNA Research, Life Extension and cloning was a wonderful sign that Neurogenetic Consciousness was emerg-

---

The "monsters," of course, are us in the future.

---

ing. Nothing can happen in evolution until the Dom-Species gets upset and worried. When the red-neck politicians and the liberal agitators moralize about "monsters escaping from the laboratory and being unleashed on the unsuspecting public,"the Out-Caste Intelligence operative perks up interest. The "monsters," of course, are us in the future.

The basic tactic used by Evolutionary Agents to reassure the Dom-Species about Future-phobias is to point out that allowing the *next* mutation to occur is the best way to avoid past terrors. To convince the Doms that past-terrors are worse than future fears. Thus the Stage 11 Capitalist had to realize that some Social-Welfarism was the only way to avoid a return to Stage 10 barbarian-dictatorships. The Communist Stage 10 dictators realized that some individual consumerism is the only way to avoid a return to tribal anarchy.

The task of the evolutionary agent is always to encourage migration.

In 1978 it was the assignment of Evolutionary Agents to demonstrate that Civilian Voluntary Space Migration was the only way to

deal with the tensions of nationalism, tribalism and Self-Actualization. Anita Bryant comes to see that the only way to keep homosexuals away from her children is to allow Gay Societies in Post-terrestrial Plan-Its. Racists of all colors realize that the only way to preserve Discrimination and Racial Pride is in High Orbital Mini Earths (H.O.M.E.s).

By 1978 it was becoming obvious that the only solution to Hive Terrors, both past and future, was Migration to Space Plan-Its. The past always migrates behind the future. Today's future taboo is tomorrow's dogma.

Liberals, in 1978, were alarmed that nuclear energy, brain-changing drugs, radiation-control of brains, genetic engineering might fall into the hands of Barbarian Territorial Dictators. Note that cloning, the key migratory technique for a post-terrestrial species, is first discussed in fearful terms of Hitler-like revivals. The hive custodians frighten the people with mad scientist Nazi-devil rumors and thus conceal the possibility that you can clone yourself and friends. The same taboo-terror was projected on post-terrestrial intelligence. The Martians were coming to eat us, and not to enlighten or entertain us.

Such natural hive fears can be assuaged by the realization that nuclear energy, brain-changing

---

The Martians were coming to eat us, and not to enlighten or entertain us.

---

drugs (LSD), cloning, and genetic research can only be safely employed in frontier, experimental communities — which can be found only in High Orbital Mini Earths.

The first sign of Neurogenetic Consciousness, as evidenced by this University of California course on Genetic Counseling, could only have appeared in a community which was into Self-Actualization and in a state where the governor, Jerry Brown, had become a Space Plan-It enthusiast.

*The emergence of a new taboo is always sign for evolutionary rejoicing. Today's new Taboo is tomorrow's advance. Agents who create *new* crimes are automatically promoted to the Out-Caste Hall of Fame. Examples of new crimes are: automotive speeding, bootleg radio broadcasting, psychedelic drug manufacturing, nuclear research, computer larceny, leaving a country without an exit visa, DNA research, cloning.

Migration Is Self-Actualization

GENETIC ARCHIVES BUMPER STICKER FROM 1493 (also used in 1978)

AN AFFECTIONATE INVITATION TO EASTERNERS
TO COME JOIN THE PARTY

To say that Old World natives inhabit primitive ecological niches, is not to be chauvinistic. I descend from Irish stock. I look at Erin with an affectionate "roots" perspective and must admit that every intelligent Irishman and Irishwoman has long since migrated West! "Across the water." Can you believe that today in Belfast, Catholic kids are raised to murderously hate Protestants — and

---

Californians are as far removed from the Reformation Wars as Luther was from the Neanderthal.

Protestants teach their youngsters to genocidally despise Papists. That's at least four hundred years in the past! And, at the current accelerated rate of evolution, Californians are as far removed from the Reformation Wars as Luther was from the Neanderthal.

To say that Europeans are feudal-insectoid, that Africans are tribal-primates, that Japanese are techno-insectoid, is not to deny the ecological unity of all life on this planet. DNA wants the whales to survive, DNA wants the crafty Middle-Easterners to continue to quarrel over borders. And so do we! We can respect the

ant-hill commitment of the Chinese to the Super-Insect Mao, and appreciate the technological skill of the web-spinning spidery-electronic Japanese. We can revere our mid-brain and spinal links to the Old World — and at the same time we must recognize our genetic ascendance beyond our primate, mammalian, insectoid roots.

Arizona and California are states totally populated by migrants squeezed forward by Old World gene-pools. The smart Africans have left Africa and are in America. Futique Mexicans swam the river. The superior Jews landed at Ellis Island along with the genetically selected Germans — all of our ancestors moving to the Sunset Strip in response to the genetic imperative.

Nor are these remarks demeaning to the Old World Old Brain residents. Migration still continues. This week several thousand Blacks, Orientals, Europeans left the Old Brain Hemispheres and carried their ovaries and testicles Westward. If any Old Brain citizen is insulted by these remarks, we repeat the affectionate invitation: if you are genetically selected to advance neurogenetic intelligence on this nursery planet you'll head for the Western Frontier tomorrow.

If you are geared to create the future gene-pools, move West to join us.

Come on up, you happy Arabs and you mellow Jews and you clever Africans and you alert Mexicans and you restless, freedom-loving Orientals. We need you up here with us on the frontal lobe of this primitive planet. We need your adventurous intelligence to join us in the next great migration. Westward High. Regardless of race, creed, color, national origin — if you are geared to create the future gene-pools, move West to join us.

Date: February, 1972

Country: Imminsee on Lake Zug,
Switzerland

Subject: I DETEST THE ASHRAM SCENE

Classification:

TOP
SECRET

(Conversation videotaped.)

"Almora," says Alexis intensely, "still trembles with the resonance-remains of vanished Out-Castes. Magicians, as they used to call them. Did you ever freak out there?"

"Of course," laughs the Professor, "I had several splendid cosmic frights. No wonder. Siva temples, Methodist Missionaries, weird sexual cults, the underlying Hindu-Moslem antagonism, and the ominous presence of Mao across the snow peaks. If you are erotically fused, Almora is one of the highest places in the world. Were you alone there?"

"Yes," sighs the Prince. "Totally, abysmally alone."

"Tant pis. Tres dangeriuex," exclaims the Philosopher. "If you are alone, a restless, guru-seeking pilgrim or some such disconnected nonsense, Almora is a bore. People like Almora because it is a respectable bore."

Alexis springs to his feet shouting in pleasure. He strides across the room, leaning against the wall, begins an excited speech.

"Exactly. It's a small bore, low calibre, dull spiritual Eastern colony. That's how my trouble started. One night I found myself in the house of a group of people — many of whom you know. Former students, former satellites, ex-traveling companions. An old lover, beautiful but subdued.

"Well, I hate followers, disciples, imitators. I spin out through empty space hungering for stars of equal magnitude. All right, let's face it. My snobbishness was offended by these middle-class people sitting around playing instruments that they can't play. I'm not that good, but I <u>have</u> sat in with the best groups in England and (let me speak frankly) I <u>do</u> own the best sound equipment in Europe. So here are these safe-and-sound people on scholarships talking Vedanta. I detest the ashram scene. YWCA tasteless. Someone starts passing acid around. I take some. Then in disdain and irritation I seized the box and dropped around ten pills."

"How reckless," says the Professor in alarm. "Scornful solitude is not the best space platform from which to launch an all-out voyage into time."

"Precisely. Imagine my dilemma. Almora is a spiritual Disneyland. I am now a mindless organism, a 20 billion neuron network flashing a 100 million signals a second. Moving at the speed of light. Naturally I tear off my artificial body covering."

"Naturally," agrees the Doctor.

"My brain can send messages to any of the busy little chemistry factories in my body. Pump-pump, I squirt adrenaline and ATP into my muscles. My strength has increased one hundred percent. My naked eyes see the lattice-fabric of reality. The energy is so great I literally glow. Everything is alive with electron-magnetism. And most horrible, I am surrounded by these living cores of life encapsulated in leathery robot bodies regarding me with distaste and fear. I am their worst nightmare come true. I am totally <u>freaked</u> out."

"Fantastic," smiled the Philosopher. "Priceless."

(End of tape.)

Excerpt from Encyclopedia Galactica, 2078

Archives from the planet Sol-3 indicate that in the evolution of the Human Line thirteen new Dom-Species emerged in the 2½ billion years after seeding. Only six times in the 10,000 years preceding the birth of Jack Leary did a paedomorphic rejection of Terminal Adulthood by the juveniles of the species occur.

This means that 13 times in 2½ billion years one generation was called upon to assume the most difficult responsibility assigned to any individual nervous system. Active resistance to the monolithic pressure of adult domestication. A dramatic break with hive culture. Escape from the very gene-pool which gives continuity and safety to individuals. The role of *genetic traitor*.

Neoteny requires inconceivable strength. The species, at the peak of its strength and specialized survival skill, and crazed by the sense that it has peaked — throws all of its resources against the youthful traitors. A genetic intelligence test results.

The species makes it extremely difficult to mutate and hurls its moral sanctions, its scorn, its police forces, its wily, canny old tricks at the mutating juveniles. It *must* make an attempt to check, test and challenge the upstart renegades.

If the paedomorph rebels have appeared too soon, or in the wrong place (i.e., not on the Western frontier) then they are easily crushed. The kids are not going to make any headway east of La Brea — too bad if they appear in Madrid or Athens or Jerusalem or Moscow. Only when the genetic hour has struck and only on the changeable Western rim can neoteny (rejection of Terminal Adulthood) succeed.

In the decade 1964-1974 a small handful, less than 100,000, juveniles performed the extraordinary genetic feat. Using the available electronic communication technology they formed a global network and sent out the signal. *Drop Out*.

The adult fury unleashed upon this small band of Evolutionary Agents was savage and brutal. The pressures were incalculable. The visible leaders were singled out for particular attack by the Adult Authority and the casualty rate was tragically high. Janis. Jimmy Hendrix. Jim Morrison. James Dean. Elvis Presley. Probably no juvenile agent was harassed more rigorously than young Jack Leary.

External pressure from the hive establishment was easier to deal with than the confusion caused by his own gene-pool connections. The young Evolutinary Agents, however brutal the treatment they received from the Hive Authorities, were linked together in an unspoken peer-network. They were all together in rejecting Adult Authority. In spite of the scorn heaped on "hippies" they all shared a moral superiority to their parents.

Jack Leary's parent-hive was one of the central headquarters in the Genetic War Against Terminal Adulthood. How can you reject a gene-pool which is committed to change and doesn't offer the solidity of the traditional parent-hive? In recognition and honor of these feats of Relativistic Neurology, the Solar System Council, in the year 2049, instituted the Jack Leary Prize for Genetic Heroism.

Evolutionary Agent Jack Leary became a Genetic Warrior Hero because of the unique time and place of his birth. He entered the warrior caste of his Temporal Development (Stage 10, Adolescence) exactly at the outbreak of the Great Gerteration War (1964-74). He was brought up in the Headquarters of the Evolutionary Expedition to Planet Earth and was thus, like the young Marcus Aurelius, weaned on smoke and shot — exposed at this formative period to the rigors of genetic conflict. His role as Elite Evolutionary Warrior was thus crystallized in space and in time.

By the age of 11 he participated in the Battle of Cambridge where he served as aide-de-camp to Aldous Huxley. At age 12 he served as frontline messenger to General William Burroughs in the First Battle of Newton Center. He flew several Cessna Turn-On Missions with the Harvard Air Force.

At age 13 Jack Leary was assigned to a reenforcement squad which travelled by Land Rover to Mexico and was busted on suspicion by Adult Federales in Acapulco. He later escaped with his companions to Zihuatanejo in 1962.

At age 14 he was expelled with the Harvard Expedition from Mexico. During the Valley Forge summer of 1963 he also participated in the retreats and expulsions from the islands of Dominica and Antigua. In all these engagements Jack Leary's courage and unfailing high spirits were much commended.

In the same year he was a member of the first party to explore, and then colonize, the Planetary Base at Millbrook, New York (Sept. 1963). He subsequently participated in all 64 of the B-Movie Realities produced there.

In spite of the scorn heaped on "hippies" they all shared a moral superiority to their parents.

At age 15 Jack Leary was seized for ransom for the second time by the Counter-Intelligence forces in Laredo, Texas (Dec. 1965).

During the years 1966-67, when the Police State Troopers of G. Gordon Liddy held the Millbrook Castle under seige, Jack was on continual scout duty. His heroic deeds, his arrogant princely bearing, his long jet-black hair became the symbols of the young juveniles. The Forces of Terminal Adulthood made him a special target for their anguished fury. Sheriff Quinlan captured young Jack during one raid and personally supervised the shearing of his ebony hair. Quinlan ambushed and captured Jack for ransom eleven times during this period. (In 1978 Sheriff Quinlan was himself indicted and arrested for selling and stealing guns. G. Gordon Liddy later served over four years in Federal prisons for a series of burglaries and contempt of court.)

By 1968 the realization was dawning that the Generation War was actually mutational in scope. By this time the Harvard-Millbrook Evolutionary Task Force had openly raised the Spectre of Paedomorphia.

Stations WDNA and KRNA were broadcasting the message: *DROP OUT!* Juveniles throughout the planet were being instructed to avoid adulthood, to "do your own thing," to create your own reality.

Long-hair and blue-jeans, dope and rock-and-roll became the crude symbols of this mutation. Adult establishment throughout the world immediately understood the significance of these new species manifestations. A global repression came down on adolescents who exhibited these clear signs of neoteny, i.e., species treachery.

The position of Jack Leary was infinitely complicated by the paradoxical fact that his father became the spokesperson for the paedomorphia which swept the globe. Dr. Timothy Leary, during these years, was comparing the youth revolt to:

Calcium ingestion by young amoeba who rejected the unicellular state and developed into mobile-boney forms

Oxygen sniffing by larval fish who moved to the amphibian state

Mao ingestion by young amphibians who became fast-moving animals

Tree climbing by young lemurs who were rejecting the four-footed mammalian state

Weight rejection by juvenile dinosaurs who moved into the high-flying avian life.

In these broadcasts Leary reassured the Adult Authorities that rejection of Terminal Adulthood by the juveniles of a mutating species was a positive, loving step — that the escaping children were charged by DNA with the task of carrying the best of the old species into the future. Wise and charitable adults would experience the greatest satisfaction in evolutionary history if they consciously participated in the evolutionary process. He reminded them that the function of juveniles migrating into the future was to send back to the Old Ones the perspectives and advantages (technological and neurological) of the new level of evolutionary intelligence.

The message crackled out from Millbrook — *Turn On with Your Parents*. Share the unfolding future with them.

Meanwhile Jack Leary had become the arch-symbol of the paedomorphic escape. Every Counter-Intelligence Agent in the country was focused on the neurological objective: Crush Jack Leary. Between the ages of 16 and 19 Jack Leary was arrested nineteen times. In only one of these ambushes was he found in possession of neurogenetic chemicals. On eighteen occasions he was kidnapped and held in dungeons simply for being a visible juvenile, i.e., an unrepentant mutant.

When the Great Migration to California occurred in 1968 Jack again served as scout and advance guard. After the Christmas Ambush of Laguna Beach (Dec. 1968) Jack was hauled before an Inquisition Tribunal in Orange County, California (President-elect Nixon's home duchy). During his trial he refused to speak and was consistently reprimanded by the Judge for his unrepentant attitude. His standard answer to most questions was "Not really."

The election of 1976 which was won by the Anti-Adult-Out-Caste Alliance brought an end to the active genetic warfare. The forces of paedomorphia were allowed to live in a state of uneasy truce with the Old Hive. Marijuana was decriminalized, the draft ended. Hedonic, self-indulgent, self-actualized life-styles were not only tolerated, but indeed, co-opted by the commmercial establishment. The juvenile species was congratulated for giving up active protest.

Only the most perceptive Hive-Moralists (Tom Wolfe, George Will, William Buckley, Meg Greenfield) recognized that the apparent quiescence of the young actually represented a sophisticated individualism even more ominous to the Terminal Adult Establishment than the visible protests of the preceding decade. The noisy turmoil of the 1960's did, after all, imply some connection on the part of the young to the Old Hive ways.

The Me-ism of the 1970's, however, reflected a cynical, contemptuous, detached recognition

---

By 1968 the realization was dawning that the Generation War was actually mutational in scope.

---

on the part of the intelligent young, that the Adult Establishment was a Mafia Power that must be offered token respect, paid-off and adapted to. The general formula was "40 hours a week to indulge the Man — the rest to indulge myself, my loved ones and my friends." It was well recognized by all concerned that such trade-offs were temporary, that the Adult Authority was crumbling and could not last to the turn of the century.

But beneath the calm of inter-generational truce the mutational struggle continued unabated. Counter-Intelligence Agents (Nixon appointed narcs) roamed the land stirring up trouble, seeking to provoke a return to open

---

The message crackled out from Millbrook — *Turn On with Your Parents.*

---

warfare. Evolutionary Agents who had become public symbols of neoteny continued to be harassed. When Margaret Trudeau embarrassed the supreme Adult Authority of Canada by running off with the Rolling Stones, Keith Richards was immediately busted and threatened with long incarceration by Pierre, the outraged husband. Dr. Peter Bourne, symbol of the youthful presence around Jimmy Carter, was set-up and disgraced. Professional athletes (usually Black) who led an extremely visible rejection of the flagrant paternal system (owners of sports teams) were repeatedly persecuted. And Jack Leary continued to be the symbol of Neotenous Youth and the target of Adult rage.

It was not until 1984 when High Orbital Forces took over the government of the California Republic that Jack Leary was pardoned and awarded the Highest Medal of Valor.

At age 35, his princely stature thus recognized, Jack was able to move into the next stage of his temporal caste development. He used the enormous wealth he had inherited to design and build dozens of H.O.M.E.S. from which he launched his historic explorations of the Moons of Mars, Jupiter and Saturn. His mining concessions and homesteading operations on these satellite-mineral deposits made him one of the richest people in the solar system.

In the year 2049, with eleven of his children, Jack Leary left the system of the home star as Commander of the first Major Interstellar Expedition. The rest is Galactic History.

How the CIA Makes People Stupid

by John Busch Leary

One way to understand how intelligence can be lowered is to study the Counter-Intelligence Professionals.

1. The CIA incessantly seeks old facts about other hives.
2. The KGB continuously searches for maps, blueprints, plans about intra-hive activity — in spite of the fact that nothing of genetic importance occurs within hives.

3. "They" feverishly construct apparatuses, devices, networks to *limit our intelligence*.

How do Counter-Intelligence Bureaucracies attempt to lower intelligence? How does the CIA attempt to make the KGB (and Senate investigating committees) more stupid?

1. *Secrecy*: Here is the most obvious and blatant technique for inhibiting intelligence. All secrecy is designed to increase stupidity. Anyone who keeps secrets from you is your Essence Enemy — acting to lower your most precious asset — your intelligence. If intelligence is the Ultimate Good then secrecy is the ultimate crime. Censorship is the imposition of secrets.
2. *Disinformation*: False facts obviously increase stupidity. When Richard Helms lied under oath about CIA involvement in Chile, he was acting to keep the Senate and the American people stupid. When Dick Gregory and Mark Lane invent Kennedy conspiracy facts they are lowering the National Intelligence Index.
3. *Sexual or Financial Immorality*: A classic ploy by which the hive stimulates stupidity is the Immorality Placebo, usually Sexual or Financial. First the gene-pool sets up a Moral Taboo. Moral Taboos are magnificent Intelligence Qualification (IQ) devices because they get everyone in the hive hung up on virtue-sin. The Moral Taboo must interfere with some normal, natural caste-behavior — must perversely prevent some castes from getting something that they neurologically are wired to want. Once brought into focus by prescription the Taboo becomes charged with artificial cop-sinner magnetism.

Genesis, the first chapter in the Judeo-Christian Bible, clearly sets out the strategy of the Immorality Placebo — using good-evil as a fascinating distraction, a front, a ploy.* There are two Forbidden Trees in the Garden of Eden. The serpent (now exposed as agent provocateur) gets Eve and Adam to eat the fruit of the First Tree — which provides the Knowledge (substitute the word "hang-up") of Good and Evil.

Thus forgetting about the Second Tree — which bears the Fruit of Immortality and Self-Actualization.

---

*The Immorality Placebo has been formalized by Pynchon as one of his "Proverbs for Paranoids, 3: If they can get you asking the wrong questions, they don't have to worry about answers."

Reprinted from WE MAGAZINE, July 1987

The Lesson of the Social Insects

by Anise Nun

Nina licked her full, petulent lips and started to take her clothes off, revealing her "Today is Tuesday" panties and saucy poinsettia-embroidered garters which lifted deep-purple silk stockings. Her creamy thighs and her soft mound lay in shadow.

"Termites," she sighed. "We must learn from the social insects. They have been running successful urban civilizations for 100 million years."

Saina leaned over to pluck the poinsettias and watch the ivory limbs emerge from the purple silk. Anna, watching, giggled and began to pull her dress over her tousled blond head. She bent forward to peel it off, revealing the round, firmness of her thighs, the two sweet dimples over her hips, the smooth, curving back.

"Yes," she murmured in agreement. "Each termite colony is a gene-pool organized into castes which sends out explorer-migrants to found new mini-worlds."

Finally Saina unbuttoned her dress and let it fall to the floor. She was wearing Frederick's of Hollywood panties, slit open, front and back, hinting at the plump curves of her sexual promise. Her voice was soft:

"Those who wish to preserve urban civilization should study the insect hive. The word *termite* comes from the Latin word *termes* — which means the end. The end-point of terrestrial society is the hive."

The bedroom floor was covered with an enormous blue yak fur rug. The three women tumbled down upon the arctic splendor, their soft, milky bodies writhing and rubbing against each other. They were no longer separate bodies. They were one sweet, soft, curling octopoid body — sucking tentacles, stroking hands, juicy tongues. One squirming marine body with three kissing mouths, six erect nipples, three moist vaginas. They pulsated together, limbs interwoven, slowly breathing love. Suddenly a column of ants emerged from Saina's vagina and began filing down her leg.

Nina began to giggle softly and then spoke:

"The growth of urban civilization during the last 5000 years is a steady move toward insectivization. The well-run anthill is 99,995,000 years ahead of humanity in efficient social organization. A hive is a joyful, clean Manhattan with 8 million secure citizens moving in tune with the humming unity."

"Oh yes. Oh yes," gasped Saina.

"It's so good, hmmmmmmmmm," hummed Anna.

Then mouths kissed and tongues nibbled and juices flowed. The three starved bodies fed on each other, the tension building. Probing fingers parted welcoming flesh and slid into gasping lips. The soft pelt upon which they squirmed emitted a mammalian scent which merged with the odors of their moist bodies.

Saina's honey voice broke the slippery silence: "Humanity cannot grow beyond the Insectoid Stage until it understands precisely how the social insects are ahead of us in terrestrial culture."

Saina fell on the swelling curves of Anna. Nina was rolling in passionate frenzy. One dimpled knee over Saina's back, she twisted to reach Anna's legs with her searching tongue. Anna writhed and pushed her mound closer to the penetrating kisses, the tender bits, the hot tongue that was as firm as a ram's horn.

"OOOOH!" gasped Nina. "Yes, when overpopulation and pollution signals the success of the society, then each hive produces a new caste of Winged Giants who fly far away from the hive in male-female pairs to create new worlds, to carry the gene-pool DNA to better ecological niches."

As she spoke she twisted her body so that her mound was pressed against Anna's mouth. Anna had been tenderly caressing the curve of her buttocks, and now she slid her finger into the tight little sphincter mouth, out from which flew clouds of silver-winged flying insects.

"Isn't it amusing. We languorous, self-indulgent high-flying ones are carrying the eggs from which will come the New Hive Worlds."

COUNTER-INTELLIGENCE AGENCY REPORT

Date: February, 1972

Country: Imminsee on Lake Zug, Switzerland

Subject: FOR THREE HOURS I RAN NAKED AROUND HOLY-MAN RIDGE

Classification:

CONFIDENTIAL

FILE NO. 4575

(Conversation videotaped.)

"Yes, exactly, timeless and priceless. My brain tunes into my DNA code, synapses crackling with genetic messages. I see with the eyes of countless ancestors. What a rowdy band of velvet brigands I spring from! And the futique children to come. You understand my predicament? I am real entity from time suddenly trapped in this fake-believe Disney-land. Yes that's it. I remember seeing at Disneyland a plastic Indian village with fatigued redskins selling tickets and bakelite bows and arrows to cellulose tourists. Okay, now I'm the real Crazy Horse suddenly popped down there. Whew! Quel horreur. I see at a glance what has happened to my land and my people. I see in microscopic despair these robots who have never felt the wild Dakota wind in their face or the taste, touch, smell, thunder-sound of the living, eternal God. I scream at them. 'Are none of you alive?' I rave around looking for another living soul."

"Yes, that does tend to happen," comments the Professor sympathetically.

"Or I am your Thomas Jefferson appearing in a modern Congress. Awake you pink-faced rubber frogs! Is this what we fought for! I am Giordano Bruno running around alive in Madame Tussand's waxworks! I am Peter the wild-eyed Fisherman screaming at the Jesus statues in the plaster Bibleland in Florida, Awake Brothers, let's trash this place and get back to the living soil.

"Dig it, Wizard, for three hours I run naked around Holy-Man Ridge in Almora bursting with energy, shivering in cosmic loneliness searching for a living soul. I sit in the lotus position on a rock overlooking the valley to Tibet and watch the sunrise. Good. That's all in order. I stalk regally back to the cottages looking deeply into people's eyes. The American theosophists turn away in fear. Another acid flip-out! But dig it, the Hindu natives grin and salute me. Whew! Give me some more wine."

Prince Alexis throws himself on his knees in front of the fire and holds up his glass. The wine splashes light yellow, reflecting the firelight.

"Now, I'm getting to the hard part."

The Listener nods in understanding.

"Okay, I'm loping along the road approaching the house owned by the Methodist church. Two middle-aged matron-missionaries from Kansas are standing on the steps. I love these little ladies. They were the holiest Americans I'd found in India. So I trot up to them in joyful anticipation. But dig it, they both throw up their hands in some sort of defense against me. Why? Cause I'm naked, I suppose.

"But I'm so pure. So as I run by I casually swing my arms and gently, the way you'd pat a push-me, pop-up doll in the toy store, knock each of them down."

(End of tape.)

ANYONE BORN AFTER 1945 IS A MUTANT

Now let's fine-tune the time machine. I'd like to call your attention to the last thirty-two years in this country. Let's focus on what has happened since 1945. We're all so involved that we may not appreciate the incredible changes of the last three decades.

We choose the year 1945 for obvious reasons; that was when our species fissioned nuclear structure thoughtfully at Alamogordo and blindly at Nagasaki and Hiroshima. The release of atomic energy is a mutational moment in the history of every nursery planet.

It's useful to assume that in 1945 every living organism of every species, on this planet, picked up this fall-out and radiation message and transmitted it through their nervous system to RNA and back to DNA: "Hey, the domesticated primates are fissioning the atom! It's time to leave the planet because nuclear energies are not supposed to be used on a tiny, shrinking planet like ours." *(Applause)* At this moment an astounding acceleration of intelligence occurred! Review the evidence.

Since 1945 we have fissioned and fusioned the atom. Decoding the DNA Code has allowed us, at this moment in history, to confront the possibility of genetic engineering, cloning, and biological immortality. In the short three decades since 1945, Medical science has eliminated, one by one, most of the scourges and plagues which have terrorized our species since the beginning of recorded history.

The release of atomic energy is a mutational moment...

One of the most important things to happen to the new species born after 1945 is neuro-electronic consumerism. Television. Every American child born after 1945 crawled out of the crib, toddled across the room, and with tiny, chubby, baby hands reached the boob tube and began *dialing and tuning realities*. Wheaties, no! Post Toasties? Maybe. Coke? Maybe. 7-Up, Ford, Carter, Chevrolet, Ford, Carter, Disneyland, Disneyland, Disneyland, Disneyland. *(Laughter)* A young child born in the late 40's has learned how to be a Reality Consumer, a watcher of Reality Commercials, a selector of Reality Products, actively dialing a wide frequency spectrum of passive receptivity.

The Sun Belt kid born after 1945 has experienced more realities in one week than the most affluent aristocrats of the past could experience in a lifetime.

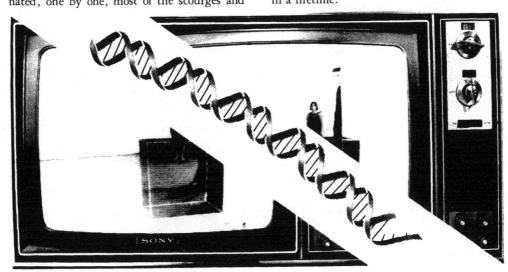

Reprinted from ESTQUIRE, May 1987

The Three Functions of Intelligence as Described by G. I. Gurdjieff

by Nena von Schlebrugge

1. Input

When the Evolutionary Agent G.I. Gurdjieff was a young cub in the Caucasian Alps, he suffered a minor wound in a scuffle with a chum.

It seems that Gurdjieff criticized the sound of the chum's flatulence. In the boyish roughhouse that followed Gurdjieff's tooth was loosened. When he reached in his mouth, the tooth came away in his fingers. Examining the technological relic he noticed that it had seven *roots*. And each root had a drop of brilliantly crimsoned blood.

When his companions showed no interest in this unusual phenomenon, the Young Agent ran to the village Dentist, who examined the specimen with interest.

"Amazing," said the Dentist, handing the tooth back to Gurdjieff, "I've never seen anything like it in the fifty years I have been extracting teeth. I don't understand it. It's a real mystery."

"But what does it mean?" asked the Youth.

The Dentist shrugged.

"But what shall we do about it?" persisted the Young Gurdjieff.

The Dentist shrugged again. "Consider yourself lucky that it came out that easily. You've saved yourself three rubles."

Moral: *The Young Gurdjieff resolved on the spot that for the rest of his life he would do nothing but study those events which the rest of the human race ignored as mysterious.* *

*Pynchon dealt with the same problem at a time when The Mysterious and Inexplicable was dominating the foreign policy of every terrestrial country. "Anti-paranoia," said Pynchon, "is that eerie thought that nothing is connected to anything."

2. Maps and Metaphors

When Gurdjieff was a young man in the Armenian Area of the Black Sea he was given good advice by his grandmother. Advice that he followed. It happened like this:

Grandmother was dying. To her home came over two hundred relatives — including scores of great-grandchildren. The mob of relatives filled the corridors and patios of the house with their lamenting. But the Grandmother would see no one except her oldest friend, a German doctor named Wimpe.

After many hours Doctor Wimpe emerged from the dying woman's room. The crowd, expecting an announcement of death was surprised when the doctor said that Grandmother wished to talk to only one of her many relatives. Our Young Agent! Little Georgie (Giorgione) as he was called.

The young Gurdjieff approached the aged woman and stood respectfully. She motioned him closer, grasped his hand lightly, looked intently into his eyes. She gave a satisfied nod and motioned him even closer.

"Listen," she said, "you are the only one who will understand. Imagine that. Two hundred descendants in this sperm-egg ship and you are the only one. Boy, swear to me that you will never forget what I tell you?"

"I shall never forget, Grandmother," swore Gurdjieff.

"Here is my advice. *Never do anything that anyone else does. Never think what anyone else thinks. And, most important, trust no one's maps but your own. And trust your own maps only for the moment.*"

3. Intensity of Transmission

The third technique which Gurdjieff used to guide his life and to increase his intelligence was passed on to him by, of all people, an illiterate and naive peasant. (Or someone impersonating this caste.)

It seemed that every year after the harvest this peasant was in the habit of walking to Moscow to repay his seed loan, purchase items unavailable in the village, drink some vodka and see the city sights.

After the peasant conducted his business he was relaxing in an outdoor cafe drinking vodka and listening to the music, when he suddenly remembered that he had forgotten to purchase a special book that his oldest son had requested.

So the peasant and a tipsy friend set off to find a book store.

The book was found. "That will be 13 rubles," said the clerk.

"But the price printed on the cover is 10 rubles," protested the peasant.

"The extra three are for the postage," replied the clerk.

"Splendid," said the peasant handling the clerk fifteen rubles.

The clerk returned with the change, courteous salutations were exchanged and the peasant left the store.

As the two peasants continued their walk down the boulevard the friend inquired with impatience, "Dmitri, why did you pay three rubles too much and why do you feel so merry about being over-charged?"

The peasant laughed loudly. *"When we're on a spree in Moscow, we pay the whole tab. Including the postage."*

THE UNIVERSAL TRAVELLING WORKSHOP

IN ITS PASSAGE

WILL STOP HERE FOR A VERY SHORT TIME.

Henry Edwards was the first Earthling to master the yoga of continual change. Using the newly discovered Principle of Neural Chain Reaction, he proceeded to use each reality he created as an accelerated vehicle to energize and innervate the next reality structure.

He was a teacher, a novelist, a critic, a screenwriter, a fabled fabulist, a film director, a film producer, the kindest and richest entity in the solar system.

Henry is best known for his mythic romances and lyric adventure tales. By the year 2020 his favorite source of amusement was Story Telling. For fifty years Edwards' breathless, wondrous, amazing legends were transmitted throughout the galaxy — billions of humans and post-humans starting each day listening to his wry, affectionate inventions.

Others argue that Henry Edwards greatest achievement was as an art patron. His collection of murals, walls, mosaic waves, crystal lattices, diamond-emerald palaces dazzled the optic nerves of many worlds.

Reprinted from SCIENTIFIC AMERICA, September 1987

The Ex-Citing, Ex-Foliating, Ex-Plosion of the Human Gene-Pool

by Henry Edwards

Evolution is speeding up. In the first eight decades of the twentieth century evolution has accelerated with a rapidity which is almost impossible for us, who are whirled up in the process, to understand.

There is one diagram which stands out as the symbol of our mutational century. *Figure 1* presents the course of evolution in terms of the growth of intelligence, i.e., energies received, integrated and transmitted by different geographical sub-species of *homo sapiens*.

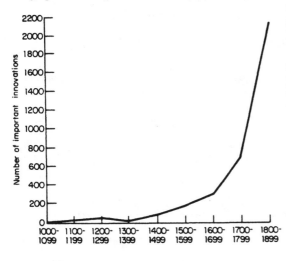

FIGURE 1

Figure 1 reminds us that for 3 billion years the intelligence of life forms on this planet grew with almost invisible acceleration. It took more than two billion years to slowly evolve the muscular technologies which propelled animals a few miles per hour; or which produced the muscular force of an elephant.

Then, with the mechanical revolution, the curve rockets upward.

The horizontal axis of *Figure 1* is time indexed in billions of years. The vertical (energy) axis can be calibrated in terms of number of inventions, energy produced and consumed, mobility in terms of speed and altitude, expansions of perception — microscopic or telescopic. Whatever energy index we chart, the climb rate shoots up almost vertically after 1946.

The human species is riding an energy-intelligence boom that has dramatically changed our conceptions of evolution. Darwinian theories of blind natural selection are now seen as primitive chauvinism of 19th century British imperialism.

Next consider *Figure 2*. Here the horizontal axis scopes the neurographic time zones — from primitive, pre-historic Africa to current California. The vertical axis is calibrated in DNA time.

We note that the Dom-Species in Africa today is hunter-gatherer. The Africans are thus 2 million years behind California. In Western Europe the Dom-Species is Stage 11 Bourgeois — roughly 400 years behind-time.

It is interesting to observe that Africa lacks the more civilized gene-colonies and that Europe and Russia and China lack the mammalian-primitive gene-colonies. Europe is left brain — Africa is right brain.

The forcible injection of the powerful African gene strain into North America, via slavery, produces the sturdy, solid, far ranging American and Californian cultures. Post-terrestrial colonization, obviously, must propel seeds from all terrestrial gene-pools into High Orbital Mini-Earths. The importance of the Black-and-Brown infiltrations into North America and, particularly into California, cannot be overestimated.

The Emergence of Evolved Nervous Systems at Various Geographical
and Temporal Stages   (Dom-Species of Each Ecological Niche Shaded Gre

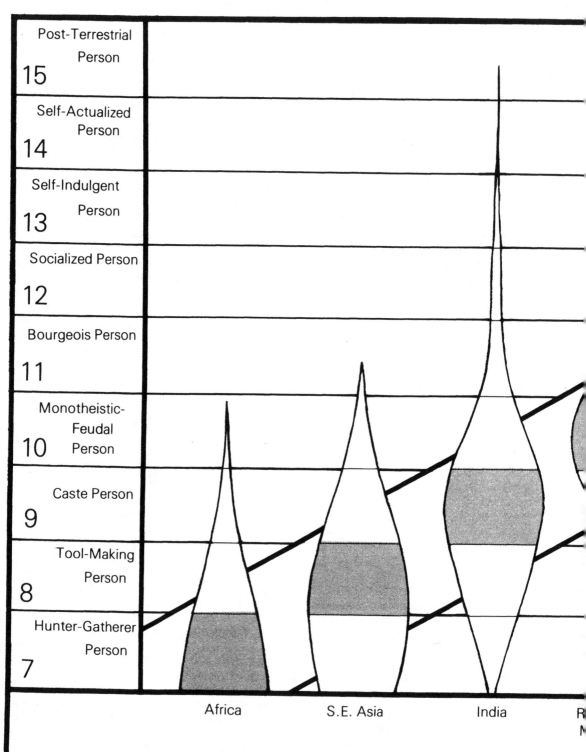

FIGURE 2

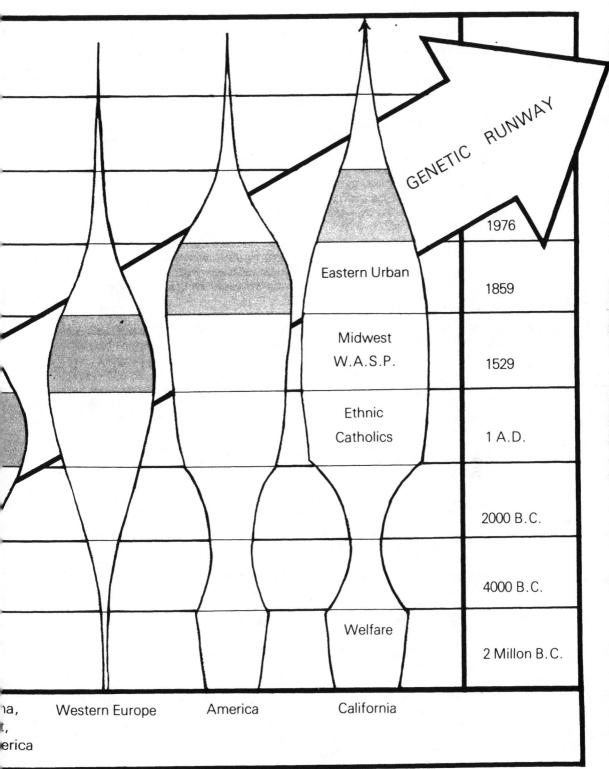

GENETIC RUNWAY

Eastern Urban

Midwest
W.A.S.P.

Ethnic
Catholics

Welfare

1976

1859

1529

1 A.D.

2000 B.C.

4000 B.C.

2 Millon B.C.

na,
t,
erica

Western Europe   America   California

R. CLARK

MEMORANDUM FOR THE RECORD:

1. Reference is made to the articles (attached), "The Hallucinogenic Drug Cult," appearing in The Reporter, 15 August 1963; "The Strange Case of the Harvard Drug Scandal," appearing in the 5 November 1963 issue of Look; and, numerous other articles recently appearing in magazines and in the public press on the same subject. These articles concern the use of certain hallucinogenic drugs (particularly LSD, mescaline, peyote, and psilocybin), some mind affecting mushrooms, and others by various groups for experimental purposes, often in a quasi-religious nature.

2. In the Spring of 1963, Harvard University fired Dr. Richard ALPERT, a psychologist, from its staff for noncontrolled use of the above-mentioned drugs for experimental purposes. His associate, Dr. Timothy F. LEARY, also a psychologist, had been using hallucinogenic drugs in experiments involving undergraduate students and after a series of attacks by faculty and by outside sources, the University was forced to remove both of these individuals from its staff. Somewhat earlier, Drs. ALPERT and LEARY had set up an organization known as the International Federation for Internal Freedom (IFIF), which obviously was a cover for additional experimental work in the hallucinogenic drugs. After their dismissal from Harvard and the attacks on their activities by the Division of Food and Drugs of the Massachusetts Department of Public Health and by the Federal Food and Drug Administration, the two doctors transferred their activities to Mexico where they claimed that they would have more freedom. However, several chapters of the IFIF were organized in different parts of the United States, particularly at Los Angeles, New York City, and with the main office at Cambridge, Massachusetts. Another chapter was organized at Mexico City, Mexico.

3. SRS/OS has for a number of years been engaged with certain other Agency areas in research and operational work with some hallucinogenic drugs. This work has been under rigid Security and Agency control, and the then Director of Security, Colonel Edwards, laid down rigid instructions that these types of drugs were not to be used under any circumstances on Agency personnel. Operational use of the drugs was handled through a special committee under the specific control and only with consent of Mr. Richard Helms, DDP.

4. It should be noted that the aforementioned hallucinogenic drugs are considered by the Office of Security and by the Medical Office as extremely dangerous. Uncontrolled experimentation has in the past resulted in tragic circumstances and for this reason every effort made to control any involvement with these drugs.

5. SRS has not been able to determine whether any staff employees of the Agency have engaged in the unauthorized taking of any of these drugs, but there is information that some non-Agency groups, particularly on the West Coast, have taken these drugs in a type of religious experimentation. While as previously mentioned there are no staff employees involved, some individuals known to have taken the drugs have sensitive security clearances and are engaged in classified work.

6. Any information concerning the use of this type of drug for experimental or personal reasons should be reported immediately to Chief/SRS/OS with all specific details furnished. In addition, any information of Agency personnel involved with the International Federation for Internal Freedom, or with Drs. ALPERT or LEARY, or with any group engaging in this type of activity should also be reported.

Chief/SRS/OS

TUCSON LECTURE

LIFE WAS SEEDED ON THIS PLANET

Here is an idea you may find amusing and stimulating to your intelligence. *Directed Panspermia* — the theory that life was seeded on this planet by higher intelligence and evolves, stage by stage, according to a pre-programmed plan.

Why are we here? How did life get started on this planet? These are crucial questions because

How did life get started on this planet?

your answer determines how you live your life here, and defines your goal. Your answer to the creation question (how you got here) determines what the next stop is, and where you are going.

There are two conventional theories of creation. The first, the scientific, is the most popular now. It is quite mad! It's the Darwinian dogma of accidental, statistical mutation. Natural Selection. A blindless, aimless, accidental forward lurching of evolution.

Urey and Miller performed an experiment in Chicago years ago. They put ammonium, methane and water vapor in a jar, blasted it with an electrical charge and found pre-biotic molecules. Then, they claim that is how life started. Look at any biological textbook! And marvel at the superstitions of current salaried scientists! Here's the orthodox hive scientific fantasy of evolution: 2½ billion years ago there was this bunch of methane molecules and they had a party one night with some ammonia molecules and invited a few carbon girls over, and started drinking water vapor, and the joint got hit by lightning. And they began to copulate!

None of the biology textbooks explains self-replication. They quickly slide over the key issue. How did pre-biotic amino acid become living organism?

Now the other orthodox theory is a vulgar, populist misinterpretation of the Bible. I am sure that the pre-civilized writers of the Bible didn't mean this, but the parrot-version taught in Sunday School is that Life was designed by some kind of police-type Jehovah. An Arab-desert macho character who went around interrogating, arresting and condemning anyone that he didn't like, and stationed an Irish cop named Michael at the gate of the Oasis to keep dissidents out.

The *Panspermia* theory was developed about 50 years ago by a Swedish biologist named Svante Arrhenius (1859–1927). He suggested that this planet was seeded by spores from outer space. Recently, dozens of pre-biotic-organic molecules have been found floating around in pre-stellar cloud complexes and in a type of meteorite called carbonacious chrondites.

The French, by the way, were un-interested in Panspermia until about 10 years ago when they discovered that alcohol was one of the biological molecules in space. *Paris Match* immediately ran an article on the existence of Extra-Terrestrial Intelligence! *(Laughter)*

And then in 1973, a distinguished scientist, a geneticist named Sir Francis Crick (you remember him, he decoded the DNA code with

Life was designed by some kind of police-type Jehovah.

Watson) and his colleague Orgel suggested the theory of *Directed Panspermia: This planet may have been deliberately seeded.* It is possible, and it is certainly fun to believe, that there are millions or even billions of planets like ours in this small galaxy alone, on which we have been seeded. And that the same process of evolution is taking place here and on many other planets.

Some sophisticated geneticists now agree with the *Panspermia* theory because they say it is impossible that in 2½ billion years, accidental copying-error mutations could have taken us from simple, unicellular life to Monday night football and Howard Cosell.

And who seeded us here on this womb planet?

We, in the future, did it.

Date: February, 1972

Country: Imminsee on Lake Zug,
        Switzerland

Subject: THE AMERICAN-HINDUS
        CONSIDERED ME A PSYCHIC
        UNTOUCHABLE

Classification:

CONFIDENTIAL

FILE NO. _____ 4575

(Conversation videotaped.)

"The Americans have seen me tumble the old ladies. They huddle together for a Nervous Conference. I can read their minds. They're afraid my antics will jeopardize their comfortable tourist scene. If only one of them had the courage and wisdom to groove with my energy, laugh acknowledgement and run down to the river to bathe with me."

"That sounds like the sensible thing to do," agrees the Receiver.

"Now," continues the Prince, "the leader of the American colony was a solemn young professor of Sanskrit philosophy from Michigan State. He told me that he had been a student of yours, a humorless follower who saw you as Buddha, threw himself at your feet in worship. To your dismay I'm sure. He and his wife were visiting India on sabbatical with their two children. He notified the police."

"Oh that's too bad. Why did he do that?"

"So the policeman from the village finds me meditating at the Siva Temple. Do you remember it? It's like the Siva shrine in any village with a three-foot stone carved lingam which women cover with milk and flowers. The policeman waves to me and I come along cheerfully. He pops me in a shack in the village below the ridge and waits on guard for the Captain to come in his jeep. A large crowd of villagers and Americans gather around the prison shack. The Captain enters alone to talk to me."

"After twenty minutes the Captain emerges from the shack and makes a stern, no-nonsense speech to the crowd. He says that I am a God-intoxicated saint. He tells the villagers, in Hindi, to protect me. Then he turns to the Americans. He denounces them for not taking care of their saddhus. For lacking faith in God's wisdom. For neglecting their holiest men. He speaks about the corrupting materialism of American culture and wonders why Americans bring their small-town concepts to spiritual India. He says that if they couldn't handle their saints, he would arrest, not the saints, but all of them."

Alexis tells this part in proper squeaky Hindu-English!

Date:

Country:

Classification:

Subject: page 2

The Prince and the Fugitive Philosopher are sitting in front of the fire, dented a bit by herb and wine. The sun is setting on the lake. Alexis had told his tale shyly.

"Is this the first time you've told this story?"

Alexis nods. "Yes. It's my shameful freak-out. My terrible disgrace. The Americans in Almora considered me a psychic untouchable. I've come halfway around the world to bare my neural wound."

"Do you want me to fabricate a helpful explanation of freak-outs?"

"Of course. That's why I told you my story," says Alexis somewhat impatiently.

"Okay, let's assume that freak-outs are created by unsympathetic, frightened people around the victim. First, the nervous system retracts its imprints to hive reality and activates future circuits. Drugs can do this or it can happen naturally. When this happens you are hyper-vulnerable to signals sent by others. You don't have your laryngeal mind to grasp reality. It hits you direct. It's a nice free state but you are very suggestible. Now put yourself back in that situation. You are loping up to the ladies. If they had waved to you what would you have done?"

Alexis wrinkles his brow in thought. "Why, I would have waved back and trotted on. That's what happened with the Hindus."

"Good. Now, if they had fallen on their knees and prayed to you, what would you have done?"

"That's easy. I would have blessed them."

"And if they had bent over and said, 'kick me,' what would you have done?"

"Yeah, I get the message."

"What signal did they send you?"

"They crunched up in fear as though I was a dangerous maniac."

"So, being in a cooperative mood, you gently oblige. Everything you did was perfect hadron particle behavior. But tell me one thing. What did you say to the Captain when he came into the shack?"

"Oh that was easy," laughs the Prince. "As soon as he entered I murmured Om Shiva, threw myself at his feet and touched his boot with reverence. He was enormously pleased. Then we sat and he lectured me aout God and Man and Law and Unity and Ramakrishna and Reincarnation. Standard Hindu Sunday School stuff. Every Indian policeman has a yen to be a swami."

(End of tape.)

Reprinted from READERS DIEGEST, April 1980

The Co-Option of Psychology by Counter-Intelligence

by George Milman

George Milman was genetically selected to become one of the first Mythic Permanent Adolescents.

His career of continual change was facilitated by his being born and raised on the Sunset Strip — the launch end of the Genetic Runway! Growing up in the ecological niche for the Self-Actualized Caste, he quickly learned how to make reality movies and to arrange life-sets as playgrounds.

Milman's first step was to secure his terrestrial affairs by studying law. He then indulged his taste for Japanese cuisine by starting the prototype Hiro Sushi Bar. In addition to satisfying his gustatory circuits his restaurant concept spread throughout the world and became the largest and most profitable food-dispensing firm in history. In addition to earning enormous profits, Milman's restaurants raised the aesthetic level of the terminal species and contributed to the Hedonic Revolution.

Milman's next move was, inevitably, the manufacture of toys. He was the first entrepreneur to understand the importance of Neurological Toys in activating the futique circuits of young children. Thus a new generation (1980 forward) whose intelligence was stimulated at early age by Milman Marvels grew up using toys and games to activate, stage-by-stage sequential circuits of their nervous systems. During the formative mutational years of the new post-human species it was said that any device which turned on the senses, stimulated the mind, opened up new neural skills, increased scientific understanding bore the trade mark: Milman Marvel!

The fact that American psychology after 1946 was an offspring of Military Psychology is neither alarming nor unexpected. Throughout human history the Military Caste has introduced each new technology — mechanical, medical, social, and even bureaucratic.

The military serves hive-terrestrials as the pioneer *avant garde*. The military caste, i.e., the warrior insects, are genetically wired to act as paranoid sense-organs for the body-social. Most intelligence structures were originated by their military who function as suspicious antennae for their societies. They were charged with the responsibility for finding out what's happening over there in the next hive; for sniffing out what the territorial rivals are doing. And protecting the hive.

As Pynchon pointed out in *Gravity's Rainbow*, wars (however cruel and pointless they may seem to liberals) were necessary competitions to stimulate technological advances. Inter-hive conflicts are evolutionary devices to make Earthlings move faster, see farther, communicate better, transport, organize and heal themselves more effectively.*

After the new technology has been tested and proved by the warrior caste, it is then co-opted by the other techno-castes who convert the new energy into hive use. The order in which castes take over a new energy is fixed: political power caste, engineer commercial caste, moral domesticator caste. In advanced societies which have met these security satisfaction challenges, the technology is then co-opted by post-hive individual castes: artist caste, neurologician caste, neurogeneticist caste.

The history of pre-flight civilization was this cycle of technological evolution. Each caste is robot-wired to use the New Technology and harness it to the specialized caste function.

Pynchon outlines how this new technology (psychology) was initiated during wartime by the requirements of the military and how mind-control techniques have been taken over by the managerial, technician-intellectual and social-moral castes.

Gravity's Rainbow, of course, was a powerful signal from the Artistic Caste (change agents).

The book was a brilliant attempt to use psychological knowledge to free individuals from the limiting past.

Without understanding all the implications, the Military during World War II, mobilized enormous national resources to create new technologies. These included air-transportation, electronic communication, nuclear energy, production of labor-saving gadgets, and psychological assessment of personality. All of these breakthroughs were produced by the patriotic emergency. Uncle Sam, the national self-indulgent consumer, wanted! And he got! Gimme 50,000 bombers! And the hive gladly produced! Gimme a radar system that will detect metal miles-high-in-the-sky. He got it! Sam said, Gimme ships and planes so I can ship ten million lusty young warriors in two years to the five continents. And he got it!

The neurogenetic implications are staggering. The American gene-pool sprayed sperm from 20 million testicles around the globe —

The American gene-pool sprayed sperm from 20 million testicles around the globe.

---

the fastest, largest genetic experiment in planet history. The so-called "war effort" performing the genetic function of mixing up sperm-egg exchanges in addition to the cultural interactions, i.e., the new imprint models imposed on youthful nervous systems of both the invaders and the invaded. When American G.I.'s rode into German towns astride sleek-powerful military machines an irreversible impression was made upon the impressionable German minds.

In the context of this all-out hive-war solidarity it was considered an honor for physicists like Einstein and Fermi to make bombs, and for psychologists like B.F. Skinner and Harry Murray to offer their services to do secret work for the OSS-CIA. (Skinner is not keen to have us recall that he spent *his* war years in clandestine research training pigeons to guide unmanned bombers to hit targets such as enemy cities, filled presumably with unarmed men and women.)

*For an extended discussion of the genetic meaning of war in species evolution, please refer to *Neuropolitics: The Sociobiology of Human Metamorphosis*, Peace Press, Culver City, CA, 1977.

Reprinted from HIGH TIMS MAGAZINE, December 1982

During his terrestrial years Henry Marshall lived in Southern America — just at the time of its emergence. His youthful experiments with Neuro-transmitters activated post-human circuits which he first developed to Neurobiology — a science which he, indeed, founded. Marshall was the first Human Ethologist who described human development in terms of neurogenetic stages.

While waiting for the primitive psychology of the 20th century to catch up with him, Marshall turned to documentary film-making. Here again his futique nervous system broke new ground. His movies, the first to trace human metamorphic stages, became classics and quickly became the basis for neurologic training in primary grades for all children in Dom-Species cultures. His films on the sociology of space colonies contributed enormously to the popular realization of the post-terrestrial migration.

Henry Marshall became the first president of the FeMan Ethology Association, and in 2011 founded the first Inter-World Educational Network. He and his mate Susan spent the latter part of the 21st century shuttling among the eleven H.O.M.E.S. of which they were revered citizens. In 1978, to explain migration from the old planet to High Orbital Mini Earths (H.O.M.E.S.), it was necessary to continually remind Americans that their fore-mothers and fore-fathers had done it before!

The Bawdy Pilgrims

by Henry Marshall

The passengers on the Mayflower were not stern, straight-laced, middle-aged religious zealots. The stuffy ones were Puritans, and they remained in Britain, protesting what they considered to be the liberal ways of the Church of England.

The Pilgrims were mostly young Elizabethans in their twenties and thirties. They wore colorful clothes, not those black hats and gray gowns you see in the paintings. They enjoyed good times, including the imbibing of strong spirits and the telling of bawdy stories.

Not only did they believe in a simple form of worship without trappings and fanfare; they also believed strongly in individual freedom and — here's an important part of their success story — they became devoted capitalists two years after their arrival at Plymouth Rock.

On the ninth day they rounded the tip of Provincetown and the Mayflower dropped anchor in Cape Cod Bay; the Pilgrims sat down together and drafted the first written covenant calling for civil self-government and individual freedom. It was the night independence was born. It was the forerunner of the United States Constitution. It was the Mayflower Compact.

Because the Pilgrims hadn't possessed enough money to rent and provision the Mayflower for its lengthy voyage, they financed their trip with the help of profit-seeking British businessmen. The Pilgrims agreed to work for the profit of a joint stock company. They were to invest their labor, and share in the profits. The London merchants were to invest their money and also share in the profits.

It was the night independence was born.

Each Pilgrim received a share of stock. Everything that was produced was to go into a common fund. At the end of seven years they were to sell whatever was left, beyond the necessities of living, and divide the proceeds according to the distribution of the shares of stock.

The British investors had demanded a communal set-up in the New World. It would make the distribution of profits and land much more convenient at the end of the seven years of the contract.

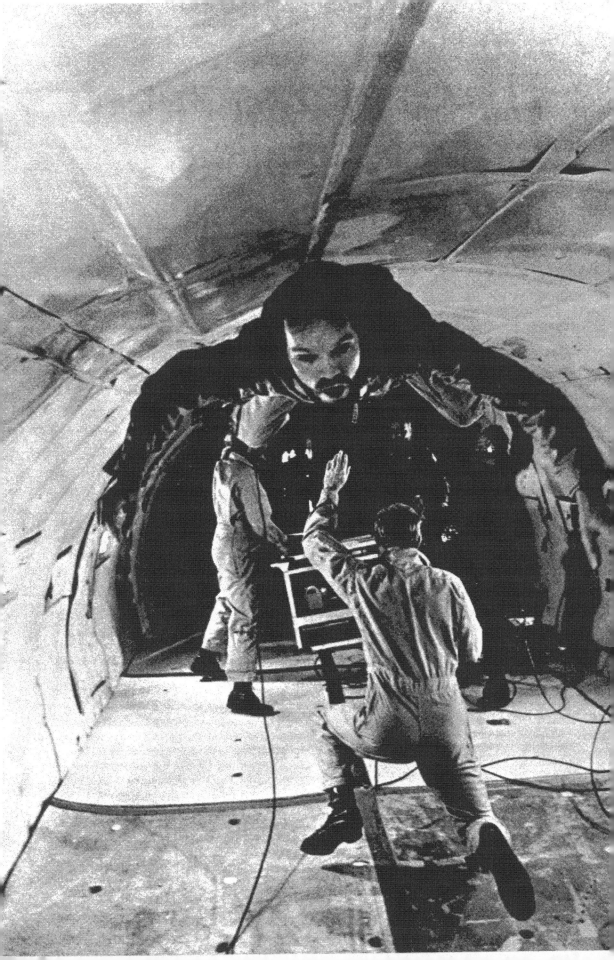

Reprinted from U.S. MAGAZINE, August 1980

The Great Revolution in Psychology

by Thomas Robbins

The womb-planet Earth, in two and one half billion years, produced less than one hundred activated nervous systems capable of transmitting mass-mutational signals by means of laryngeal-manual inscriptions — i.e., books.

Four of these Evolutionary Script Writers were American.

Thomas Robbins, author of Another Roadside Attraction *and* Even Cowgirls Get the Blues, *is one of this fabled guild.*

During the first month of graduate training, Agent Leri placed the University of California psychology faculty under intense surveillance. He read their papers and books, dropped in on lectures, observed their behavior. He reluctantly came to the conclusion that these decent, sincere men with corporate smiles were hive-custodians whose function was to prevent change, discourage intelligence-increase (I^2), and protect the gene-pool system which protected them.

He spent almost no time on the campus during his four years of graduate training and, thus aloof, received straight "A" grades and was given the prestigious Phi Beta Kappa award.

During this time he studied how graduate schools brainwash students and was not surprised, at the time of graduation, that, of a class of some 25 doctoral students, everyone (except himself and one other flamboyant Irish preterite named Frank Barron) was interested, not in raising intelligence of self or others, but in finding jobs with easy tenure, profitable outside consulting, mild climate, and good pension plans.

Avoiding university faculties like the plague, he started his own research project, and for seven years, received funds from the hive-central bureaucracy to support his investigations in group therapy and interpersonal diagnosis. The work was *highly praised*. Each year, a soviet-like official would visit his projects, inspect his data and raise his funding. Very interesting.

He was amused one time when a purchase order came from the CIA to obtain copies of tests he had developed.

The funding stopped around the time that he found it therapeutic to teach patients (my God did he say patients) how personality tests were used. And trained patients to diagnose self and others — including therapists. The bureaucracy seemed uninterested in the finding that patients' diagnoses of doctors were more reliable than therapists' diagnoses of patients.

And then there was the group therapy controversy. At that time medical psychiatrists were resisting the attempts of Ph.D. psychologists to diagnose and treat patients. But both hive-bureaucracies forgot their differences and closed ranks to oppose group therapy — a dangerous method in which the fragile, delicate, easily-destroyed personalities of patients were being tampered with by other patients. (*Patients*, later to be called clients, were preterite, non-elect persons, non-bureaucrats, non-salaried-non-experts.)

"But wait a minute," you say! "There's a contradiction here. If Freudian academicians claimed that personality cannot be changed, then why was it dangerous for non-medical or non-expertise people to participate in the therapeutic-process? If personality was unchanging, what harm could be done?"

The old Judeo-Christian dogma had the answer. Personality, they taught, could disintegrate, i.e., change for the worse, but it could not change for the better, grow, develop. Why? Because the unconscious was bad. Because, as Freud pointed out, society and ego were frail paper-clip-rubber-band structures flimsily holding off the basic wickedness of humanity. Original sin. The dutiful stoic mythos of System-People, the managers, who shoulder the burden of gene-pool maintenance, is always the same. Keep the lid on. Discourage change. Encourage Social Adjustment and Hive Conformity.

COUNTER-INTELLIGENCE AGENCY REPORT

Date: February, 1972

Country: Imminsee on Lake Zug,
Switzerland

Classification:

TOP SECRET

Subject: A PROBLEM OF ASTRONAUTICS

(Conversation videotaped.)

At this point Maria comes down with word that dinner is ready. She has prepared trout in a white wine sauce and stands by the kitchen door, Ava Gardner circa 1950, watching the cowboys in the saloon. She is a bit drunk. The Philosopher, the Prince, and the slim-hipped Gambler escort her to the head of the table. She eats little, keeps drinking wine, then says She wants to rest. She retires to the fireplace room. <u>We have assigned her the job of breaking up the acid scene</u>, but the presence of Alexis, the uncertainty of her role in the new script, the English dialogue without sub-titles overload her circuits.

SEE NOTE PAGE BOTTOM

After dinner She sends word that She wants to see the Professor. She is lying on cushions near the fire gasping for breath, just able to whisper that She needs medicine from her bag. Brian and the Professor search the house diligently. <u>The bottle is missing.</u>

Maria seems to be getting weaker. The Professor phones a medical friend in Basel who has no specific advice to give. Maria refuses to have a doctor called or to go to the hospital, shaking her classic head and rolling her dark eyes, implying that she understands the course of the malaise. She looks into the Philosopher's eyes and whispers solemnly, "<u>Je vais mourir.</u>"

very mysterious!

The men look at each other helplessly and shrug.

Maria lays back and dies. The Professor kneels at her right and Alexis on her left. Brian Barritt's eyes are bulging. Everyone in the room senses her spirit leave her body. Alexis feels her pulse. It has stopped.

From the control tower the Philospher talks to her somewhere in sky-time calling her to come back. Alexis massages her heart. Like a plane circling for landing, her spirit touches down in her body and everyone breathes in relief.

"This time-travel is demanding," sighs Alexis. "Death-bed scenes are so Victorian. That's why we couldn't allow it."

Maria is now lying in the Doctor's arms, her black hair on his chest, her eyes closed, drifting in contented repose.

"What do you mean?" asks Brian.

"The death-bed scene was the climax of the classic Victorian drama. There the truth emerged. The achievements of medical science have changed all that today. We aren't interested in listening to last words. We are concerned only that the patient live. So Maria, we apologize. We brutes would not allow you to die a heroine. We treat you, alas, like a patient."

"It seemed more like a problem in astronautics to me," says Brian thoughtfully. "Who is this Maria anyway?"

(End of tape.)

(SHE OBVIOUSLY SHOULD NOT BE ASSIGNED TO POST-TERRESTRIAL OR MULTI-LINGUAL INFILTRATIONS)

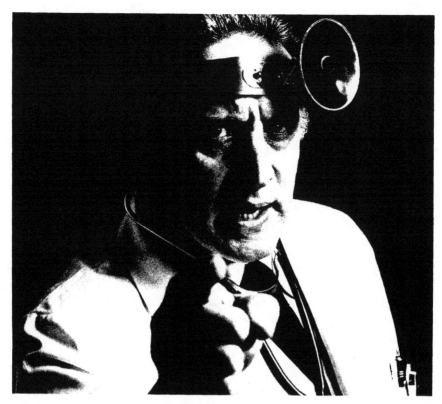

Reprinted from PSYCHOLOGY TWODAY, February 1981

The Psychology of Adjustment

by Joanna Leary

Joanna Harcourt-Smith Leary, of the 11th Caste, was one of the most important egg-carriers of the Planet Earth. Her chromosomes included mutant mathematicians, scholars, publishers, adventurers, aristocrats and explorers.

Joanna's post-terrestrial circuits were activated at adolescence by large doses of LSD. She quickly became one of the first conscious Intelligence Agents in the history of her species. Her velocity, relativistic-mind, adaptable change-ability naturally scandalized the Old World Hives. She was, therefore, kidnapped by the American government in Afghanistan in 1973 and, escorted by armed guards, transported to the Sunset Strip. She immediately rewarded the benign manipulations of her American hosts by publishing

the three classic books which facilitated Space Migration, Intelligence Increase and Life Extension: Neurologic, Terra II *and* What Does WoMan Want?

The familiar soap-opera scenes which have thrilled and amused galactic viewers for centuries actually did happen. Joanna did walk the streets of Berkeley, California selling Neurologic *in order to ransom an imprisoned philosopher.*

After starring in over 200 melodramas, unmatched for humor, elegance and picaresque adventure, Joanna left the solar system of her home planet and home star in her three-thousand foot solar yacht Chrysalis.

The he problem with military technology is, of course, that wars end. But terrestrial bureaucracies persevere, particularly those of the winning side. The reason postwar losers (Germany and Japan) rebounded more rapidly than the winners (England, France, Russia) was that the bureaucracies of the losers were destroyed. Anything that destroys a bureaucracy enhances evolution.

So after World War II, the massive industries which had been geared to produce war tools were converted to civilian goods. The managers and technical boys were ready to convert the assembly lines from tanks to fin-tailed cars. The radar factories were converted to television manufacture. America, during the 1950's, went on the biggest materialism consumer spree

---

Anything that destroys a bureaucracy enhances evolution.

---

in history.

The wartime psychological technology was also converted to civilian consumption. Personality assessment techniques were taken over by the managerial powers — and used to select and train employees. A new, gigantic industry emerged employing clinical psychologists and counselors and a new social-moral concept of human nature: adjustment.

Those who matured during the Self-Discovery 60's and the Self-Actualized 70's did not know that the aim of personality-clinical psychology and psychiatry during the 50's was *hive-adjustment*. Not surprising, really, when we recall that the Firm started it all in the 40's.

"Their" aim was, we recall, the preservation of the past, the prevention of change. To understand the gravity of the situation, remember: *There was no concept of personal change in the 1950's.* Human personality was seen as a fixed quality which could and should be adjusted to the system. Old-style psychiatrists (formerly called alienists) guarded the psychotic. The radical wing, psychoanalysis, taught that after five years of intensive treatment, five hours a week, at fifty dollars a session, the patient *might* get enough insight to wearily adjust and to discuss his neurosis at cocktail parties.

Feel Like NEW!

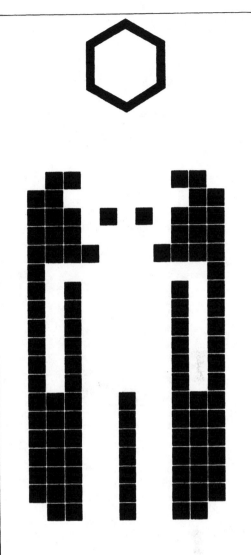

LIFECLOUD: THE ORIGIN OF LIFE IN THE UNIVERSE

Sir Fred Hoyle, ever controversial, collaborates with N.C. Wickramasinghe to write *Lifecloud: the Origin of Life in the Universe*. They would have us abandon the idea that life started here on earth for the view that a primitive biological system evolved in interstellar space, and was carried here, as well as to other planets, by meteorites. Their claim is that "our biochemical ancestry pre-dates the formation of the sun and planets"....

from New Scientist Spring Books

Reprinted from SCIENTIFIC AMERICA, October 1985

The Current Distribution of Human Genetic Castes in America

and the Different New Realities Which They Are Creating

---

by Pauline Kael

Pauline Kael was one of the first social philosophers who understood that the Hollywood motion-picture industry was really involved in Reality Fabrication.

Her scientific essays during the last quarter of the 20th century helped guide the first generation of movie-makers (1978-1984) who consciously and systematically fabricated realities aimed at raising intelligence and providing successful, happy evolving models.

A nd so we see with compassion that America — the Ecological niche of the Dom-Species and Pre-Dom Species — has become an evolutionary pinball machine in which hundreds of genetically different human gene-pools and genetic castes are bouncing around. Each caught up in genetic spirals of differing velocities, each fabricating different technicolor realities and developing new mutational styles. In flashing neon. Here is the demographic estimate of caste distribution in America, 1978:

Stage 1:

There are around 5 million Americans operating with amoeboid brains: newly born babies, terminally ill, genetic defects.

Stage 2:

There are around 5 million Americans with fish brains, unable to handle gravity: babies between 3 months and 6 months, the bed-ridden sick, genetic defects.

Stage 3:

There are approximately 5 million at the amphibian level of neuro-reality: crawling babies, wheelchair invalids, seniles, genetic defects. An enormous percentage of the Gross National Energy (GNE) is devoted to the care of human beings operating at the amoeboid marine or amphibian levels of neural development.

Stage 4:

There are around 10 million Americans who operate at the cunning-rodent-evasive animal level of neural development; here we include toddling children and those cunning adults who may be performing civilized tasks, but whose brain-space is rodent. Those who will automatically steal anything they get their paws on and have no concept of social-morality.

Stage 5:

There are around 10 million Americans operating at the aggressive-mammalian level of neural development. This includes children between ages 3 to 5, possessive seniles, and many well-functioning adults who operate like fierce carnivores or mafia capos — extorting, threatening, controlling turf by coercion.

Stage 6:

There are around 10 million Americans operating at the monkey level of neural development. This includes children ages 4 to 7, seniles, and millions of adults who may appear to be performing civilized functions, but whose realities are those of exhibitionist primates.

Stage 7:

There are around 20 million Americans who operate at the Paleolithic level, who are capable of parrotting-mimicking neural behavior and nothing more. This group includes children ages 5 to 8, rote-response seniles, and the millions of well-bodied adults who live at the hunter-gatherer level of existence and survive by performing violent-muscular acts — either criminals, police, military or athletic. Or who, via welfare, are modern gatherers. These innocents are incapable of inventive or independent thought and can only rote-repeat what they are taught.

Stage 8:

There are around 20 million Americans who survive at the Neolithic level of neural development. This group includes children ages 7 to 9, seniles, and those who perform craft-work at the level of simple agriculture, small shopkeeping, and who inhabit ethnic, tribal social realities.

Stage 9:

There are around 20 million Americans operating at the caste-priest level of neurogenetic evolution. This group includes pre-adolescent children ages 9 to 12, and those who live in ethnic groups which are directed by priests and in which economic division of labor is inherited.

Stage 10:

There are around 30 million Americans who operate at the semi-civilized, barbarian, feudal level of reality. This group includes adolescents between the ages of 13 and 20, plus ethnic groups who follow a peasant feudal ethnic-Old-World-religious persuasion.

Stage 11:

There are around 30 million Americans who live at the parental-domestic-protestant-ethic level of historical development. This group includes those between the ages of 20 and 45 who live in a home-owner middle-class free-enterprise reality.

Stage 12:

There are around 30 million Americans who live at the level of dependence upon a centralized-social-security Demo-poll state. This group includes non-seniles over the age of 45, and those who are neurologically most comfortable in an egalitarian, medi-care, uniform-unified-law-and-order Ralph-Nader-Ecological niche. Also, those who love the comfort of the Ronald Reagan hive and wish to conserve its John Wayne-Frank Sinatra culture for the few years remaining before their death.

Stage 13 (Dom-Species):

There are around 20 million Americans who live in a Dom-Species post-hive, post-political reality of Self-Consumerism. This group includes all those who define reality in terms of their own hedonic pleasure and organize their existence in terms of leisure, travel, recreation. This group includes a majority of the 35 million marijuana smokers, the Playboy readers, the sexual freedom cultists, jetsetters.

America is the genetic frontier.

Stage 14 (Pre-Dom[1]):

There are around 2 million Americans who live at the level of Self-Actualization. This group includes liberated graduates of yoga, holistic medicine, sufism, self-actualization programs. Being post-parental, these people make the best parents. They make contelligent decisions about when and how and with whom to breed. They treat their children as mutant arrivals — aliens and friends. They avoid imprinting robot-hive culture and train their children to become self-actualized and self-responsible at the earliest ages.

Stage 15 (Pre-Dom[2]):

There are an estimated 250,000 Americans who live at the neural level of post-social communes, including the Space Plan-It adepts.

Stage 16, 17, 18 (Pre-Dom[3,4,5]):

There are an estimated one million Americans whose brains operate at the Neuro-electric level, who understand the neural-fabrication nature of reality. These include many of the 7 million Americans who have experienced LSD, plus those geniuses and psychotics who are trapped in the 1978 Time Zone with futique nervous systems which have been activated too soon.

Stage 19, 20, 21 (Pre-Dom[6,7,8]):

There are a few hundred post-social human beings whose brains have been activated to the Neurogenetic Level and who can think like DNA. These Agents will find a few hundred thousand (from Stages 16, 17, 18) who will immediately respond to Neurogenetic Signals. These signals appear in the form of sociobiological texts.

Let us summarize this Neurogenetic Caste Census. If you'd travelled around the United States of America in 1978 you would have found the population distributed into caste-species as follows:

15 million Americans operate at the amoeboid, marine or amphibian level of intelligence; these first circuit innocents literally inhabit unicellular, fish or shore-line realities.

30 million Americans operate at the evasive-mammal, territorial animal and exhibitionist-primate level of intelligence. These innocents actually inhabit rodent, tiger or monkey realities.

60 million Americans operate at the Paleolithic, Neolithic or tribal-caste-system level of intelligence.

90 million Americans operate at the Feudal, Democratic or Socialist level of civilized robothood — robot responsive to hive morals.

Thus, 195 million American hum-ants are directed by involuntary instincts — committed to religious or political passivity, blindly obedient to hive morality — unable to operate as independent individuals.

If the Average American were given power he would operate like Idi Amin.

There is, however, a sizable, and enormously influential population of post-social, self-directed persons swarming, for the most part — in the Sun Belt!

22 million Americans operate at the post-

Each caste lives in a different time zone.

political level of hedonic consumerism, self-consumerism and self-actualization; they are committed to self-responsible philosophies and do not look to theological or political bureaucrats.

1 million Americans operate at the level of Einsteinian neural relativity; understanding and accepting the fact that the brain facilitates realities.

About one-half million Americans are ready to operate at the Neurogenetic level of reality — understanding and cooperating with the blueprint of DNA.

(It must be noted that America is the genetic frontier. In African and Asian countries about ninety-nine percent of the population operate at the marine, mammalian, and pre-civilized stages of intelligence compared to roughly fifty percent of Americans who inhabit these pre-civilized realities.)

The demographic estimates just presented are, of course, ignored and even repressed by American Moralists because they clash with the comforting, passive, liberal notions of equality that emerge in socialist or Demo-Poll societies. The statistically average American is somewhere between a Neolithic Caveman and a Superstitious Robot from the Priest-run, caste-stratified pre-civilized Past.* The average IQ is 100. A person with an I.Q. of 100 can read and write primitively and is generally incapable of any inventive thought. If the Average American were given power he would operate like Idi Amin. In fact, most of them run their homes like Idi runs Uganda.

These demographic facts were understood by the brilliant WoMen who wrote the American Constitution. Their system of checks and balances was designed to keep the Average Person (Neolithic) from grabbing control. The Athenian experiment, for example, failed because of Demo-poll — the Tyranny of the Mediocre.

*Ref: "The Naked Ape," D. Morris, 1967.

To keep American hivers from understanding the blunt facts about genetic robothood each of the human castes produces its public relations experts, sometimes called philosophers or theologians. (From the evolutionary point of view Philosophy is post-hive Human Ethology. The task of an Ethological Philosopher is to define the different species of humans and to explain how they interact so that the survival of the gene-pool and of each caste is assured.)

But the Dom-Species was not ready for that in 1978. Instead the spokesperson for each caste described reality from the perspective of hir species; since each caste inhabits a very different reality, moral outrage was endemic. Blacks, Gays, Holocaust obsessed Zionists, Reaganites, Irate homeowners.

Each caste lives in a different time zone. The dogma of the Paleolithic did not work in technological America, but this did not discourage the attempt by this species to impose its hunter-gatherer reality on others.

The most bewildered were the Stage 12 liberal humanists who kept shouting: "We are all one! Brotherhood of Man! We are all equal and homogenous."

Genetic heterogenity has, of course, always been obvious to those geared to look for it. The next eleven people you meet probably belong to eleven different species in mutation; living in different time zones, at different levels of contelligence. As you walk through the forest you don't expect each species you meet to be the same or to play survival games with your rules. The insightful ethologist admires each life-style: the radar speed of a rabbit, the innocent grace of a wolf, the levity of a bird, the sincere cunning of a spider. The same honor can be extended to each human caste you meet as you swim through the urban coral reef.

We are all U.F.O.'s . . .

We do not have to look aloft to flying saucers to find alien intelligences. We are all U.F.O.'s (Unidentified Flying Organisms). The first step in interspecies diplomacy is to recognize the species differences among us, exchange basic vocabulary cues as to each others realities and establish Inter-species Diplomatic Courtesies so that the womb-planet Earth can be shared harmoniously, and abandoned gracefully. So that new Plan-Its carefully designed to fit the differing realities of different species can be fabricated in High Orbit.

EXPERIMENTAL CONFIRMATION
CAME THIRTEEN YEARS LATER

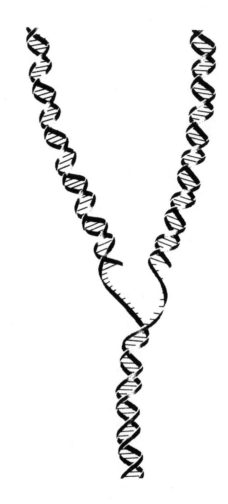

Rutgers Biochemist George Pieczenik has discovered patterns in DNA coding that he sees as evidence of selection at the molecular level.

"What this means," he charges "is that the DNA sequences exist to protect themselves and their own information.

It's not the organism that counts. The DNA sequences don't really care if they have to look like a lowly assistant professor or a giraffe."

Contacted at Galactic Headquarters DNA Publicists denied the charge. "Aesthetics happens to be what Evolution is all about," smiled one Disc Jockey at Broadcast Center.

DNA STAGE / CNS STAGE	HUNTER-GATHERER PALEOLITHIC TECHNOLOGY	TOOL-MAKING AGRICULTURE (NEOLITHIC)	METAL-WORKING TECHNOLOGY	NATIONAL MILITARISTIC BUREAUCRATIC TECHNOLOGY	MECHANICAL TRADER TECHNOLOGY	ASSEMBLY-LINE MATERIAL CONSUMER TECHNOLOGY	SELF-INDULGENT TECHNOLOGY
POST-HIVE INDIVIDUAL SELF							**STAGE 13** California Culture becomes Dom Species 1976
FAIR-SHARE COLLECTIVE CONSUMER	AHEAD-OF-TIME INDIVIDUALS OF PRE-DOM CULTURES; FORE-PLAYERS GENE-POOLS WHERE CNS IS AHEAD OF DNA TECHNOLOGY OF DOM-SPECIES					**STAGE 12** American Culture becomes Dom-Species 1865	
BOURGEOIS HOME-OWNER PRIVATE ENTERPRISE PERSON	CNS TIME AHEAD OF DNA SPACE				**STAGE 11** Bourgeois Culture England N. Europe Becomes Dom-Species 1529		
MONOTHEISTIC FEUDAL FANATIC PERSON				**STAGE 10** Mediterranean South-European Culture	CNS TIME BEHIND DNA SPACE		
PRIEST-RUN CASTE-BOUND HYSTERICALLY XENOPHOBIC PERSON			**STAGE 9** Middle-East Indo-Asian Culture				
TRIBE-CLAN PERSON		**STAGE 8** Neolithic Agriculture		BEHIND TIME INDIVIDUALS OF DOM CULTURES; BACK PLAYERS, REACTIONARIES; GENE-POOLS WHERE CNS IS BEHIND DNA TECHNOLOGY OF DOM-SPECIES			
RAPE-LOOT BREAK-TAKE PERSON	**STAGE 7** Paleolithic Culture						
	2 MILLION B.C.	10,000 B.C.	4200 B.C.	1 A.D.	1529 A.D.	1865	1976

"When my grandfather founded Ford Motor Co. . . . he had a primary purpose in mind," said Henry II at birthday observances in Detroit. "He saw the automobile as a piece of machinery. He envisioned that car, not as a luxury vehicle for the rich but as a means for the average man to make his life — and his family's easier and happier."

While founder Henry Ford had not invented the auto, as some Americans seemed to think, he did make significant changes in American life and probably throughout the world. He had developed a most advanced system for putting products together to produce them faster and cheaper. Thus his assembly line and merchandizing made the auto cheaper and put Americans in the driver's seat.

THE NEW FORD CAR
announcement of unusual importance
to every automobile owner

by
HENRY FORD

NINETEEN years ago we made and sold first Model T Ford car. In announcing it the public we said:

"'We will build a motor car for the great multitude. It will be large enough for the family, but small enough for the individual to run and care for. It will be constructed of the best materials, by the best men to be hired, after the simplest designs modern engineering can devise. But it will be so low in price that no man making a good salary will be unable to own one.'

"If I were starting in business today, or asked to restate my policy, I would not change one sentence or one word of that original announcement. In plain, simple language it gives the reason for the very existence of the Ford Motor Company and explains its growth.

"IN THE last nineteen years we have made 15,000,000 Ford cars and added to the world nearly 300,000,000 mobile horse-power. Yet I do not consider the machines which bear my name simply as machines. I take them as concrete evidence of the working out of a theory of business which I hope is something more than a theory of business—a theory that looks toward making this world a better place in which to live.

"The Model T Ford car was a pioneer. There was no conscious public need of motor cars when we first conceived it. There were few good roads and only the adventurous few could be induced to buy an automobile.

"The Ford car blazed the way for the motor industry and started the movement for good roads. It broke down the barriers of time and distance and helped to place education within the reach of all. It gave people more leisure. It helped people everywhere to do more and better work in less time and enjoy doing it. It [...] deal, I am sure, to promote the [...] of this country.

and different Ford to meet new and different conditions.

"We believe the new Ford car, which will be officially announced on Friday of this week, is as great an improvement in motor car building as the Model T Ford was in 1908.

Smart new low lines and beautiful colors

"The new Ford is more than a car for the requirements of today. It goes farther than that. It anticipates the needs of 1928, of 1929, of 1930.

"The new Ford car is radically different from Model T. Yet the basic Ford principles of [...]roduction and quality of prod[...] There is nothing quite [...] and price.

"The new Ford has unusual speed for a low-price car because present-day conditions require unusual speed.

"The world moves more quickly than it used to. There are only so many hours in the day and there is much to be done.

"Fifty and sixty miles an hour are desired today where thirty and forty would have satisfied in 1908. So we are giving you this new speed.

Quiet and smooth-running at all speeds

"The new Ford will ride comfortably at fifty and sixty miles an hour. It has actually done sixty-five miles an hour in road tests.

"Since modern conditions demand more speed, they also demand better brakes to balance this speed. So we are giving you four-wheel brakes in the new Ford.

"The new Ford will be quiet and smooth-running at all speeds and you will find it even easier to handle in traffic than the old Model T Ford.

"The new Ford has durability because durability is the very heart of motor car value. The Ford car has always been known as a car that will take you there and bring you back. The new Ford will not only do that, but it will do it in good style. You will be proud of the new Ford.

"THIS new Ford car has not been planned and made in a day. Our engineers began work on it several years ago and it has been in my mind much longer than that. We make automobiles quickly when we get in production. Nothing [...] a long time planning them. We spent twelve years [...] Ford car

"Every part of it has been tested [...] tested. There is no guessing as to [...] will be a successful model. It has to[...] is no way it can escape being so, [...] sents the sum total of all we h[...] about motor car building in th[...] 15,000,000 automobiles.

The new Ford will [...] a low price

"The price of the new Ford [...] dance with the established Fo[...] that it is better to sell a lar[...] at a reasonably small marg[...] sell a few cars at a large m[...]

"We never forget that [...] cars are the people who [...] business big. It has alw[...] share our profits with o[...] year our profits were s[...] expected that we volu[...] each purchaser of a c[...] done that if this bus[...] for the sole benefit o[...] to render service to [...]

"No other autom[...] Ford car at the [...] manufacturer do[...]

"We make ou[...] glass—we mine [...] every part used [...] charge a profit [...] operations. W[...] the public if [...] automobile [...] automobile [...]

"WE AR[...] low price[...] to give [...] increase[...]

"W[...] sell at [...] the k[...] foun[...]

off[...]
the k[...]
In[...]
se[...]

Reprinted from CAR & RIDER, Janaury 1983

Eric Orr was a core member of the Venice Network of Artists who emerged at the end of the 20th century in the years just before Space Migration. It was, of course, no ecological accident that the first group of post-terrestrial artists appeared on the western beach, the last terrestrial frontier. At the end of the Christopher Columbus Transcontinental High-Way.

(Other members of this elite group were Susan Kaiser Vogel, Larry Bell, Craig Hodgetts, Robert Mangurian, Kent Hodgetts, Victoria Shields, Duane Valentine.)

Orr's art has been well described as Space Alchemy. His tools (during this pre-flight period) were post-terrestrial: solar-lights, lenses, light-reflectors. With Larry Bell he produced the first space art using high temperatures to fix glass plates in vacuum atmosphere. This technique was used by Bell and Orr two decades before vapor-deposition-in-vacuum became the basic construction tool for space worlds.

Eric Orr's brain, which was activated to post-

terrestrial status by the intelligent use of neuro-transmitters, later became the first authenticated telepathic transceiver. Orr has been justly called the Alexander Graham Bell of Telepathy.

Henry Ford Homage to the Evolutionary Agent Who Introduced the Self-Mover

by Eric Orr

The genetic wave, that in less than a century hurtled North Americans through three stages of Evolution, was gracefully surfed by several Intelligence Agents. One of the most successful was Henry Ford.

In one generation this Agent took a species of Domesticated Primates from behind horse drawn plows and popped them into mechanical ground-vehicles constructed of steel, glass and rubber. Thus multiplying their Intelligence.

He put his country-men and country-women into the driver's seat! He offered the DRIVER'S SEAT, Throne of Self-Actualization, to the average working ants of his gene-pool. It came equipped with several self-actualizing technologies permitting neurological choice and stimulating Intelligence Increase.

The steering wheel allowed the individual to select hir own directional course and change it at will.

The accelerator allowed the individual to select hir speed — an Einsteinian concept, indeed.

Brakes added another dimension to self-control.

The gear shift. Transmission. Self-starters. Fluid power. Dynaflow. Overdrive. Convertibles.

Here we see the birth of a new language of self-determination. The next generations demanded for their bodies and their brains exactly those power-freedom-mobility characteristics that were built into their cars.

And the greatest stroke of genetic public relations: Ford called it AUTO-MOBILE! This word means Self-Mover. Intelligence Agents all over the galaxy smiled knowingly when the term AUTO-MOBILE flashed out through the Van Allen Belt.

Free-wheeling Americans called it the SELF-MOVER! Old World Europeans, of course, didn't catch on. To them the horseless carriage was another luxury for the rich. It was called horseless carriage in England. *Coche* in Spain. *Carro* in Mexico. *Voiture* in France. *Màccina* in Italy.

The genetic implications of AUTO-MOBILE were endless. The average person could move hir body or hir brain where SHe wanted to go.

The evolution of intelligence is a function of Velocity and Mobility. Henry Ford and his fellow agents rocketed the Genetic Intelligence Quotient of the species. Once the technological primates climbed into the driver's seat they were off to the moon — carrying their auto-mobile bodies and their auto-mobile brains.

LIFT UP YOUR EYES

by Dr. Timothy Leary

Future Pre _____ ___
1000 Westmount Drive, Suite 128
Los Angeles, California 90069

Date: February, 1972

Country: Imminsee on Lake Zug, Switzerland

Subject: IT'S THE GIORDANO BRUNO
SCRIPT THAT WORRIES ME

Classification:

TOP SECRET

We have attached another agent to the case as Maria is no longer effective. His report follows.

The next day Maria seems totally recovered but refuses to discuss the matter.

After breakfast they decide to take the cable-car up the Rigi Kulm and lunch on the summit terrace. From the peak one looks south to the four petals of Lake Lucerne and can visualize the Great Moments of Swiss history enacted below. Standing on the north parapet one looks down to the right at Lake Zug and to the left at a long green field. It appears so close that the Prince, the slim-hipped Gambler and the Fugitive Doctor decide to descend the cliff to the meadow and then down through the woods to the cottage.

The cliff drops down in steep sections. A half-hour of careful footwork and jumping leads to a narrow ledge which drops twenty feet to a sheer ice slope which ends in a hundred-foot drop. A slip chutes the careless climber to slippery death. They start chopping footholds in the soft crumbling ice with sticks.

The climbers are wearing slick-soled track shoes; Brian and the Doctor in light sweaters, Alexis wrapped in a pink tweed coat. It is an hour before sunset. The voyagers look at each other appraisingly. Any accident will leave them exposed all night on the mountain in the February chill. They could clamber back in retreat, but without a word spoken they decide to risk ahead together.

It takes twenty minutes of exploration and discussion to chart the descent of the first cliff. Survival circuits are flashing alarm. The sugary foothold could crumble. A foot could slip on slushy grass-mud and body slide over precipice.

The Doctor is scared; that is, the crisis centers of his nervous system energize neurons which control emergency glandular function. Each neuron has dozens of output fibers, each of which curls around a tiny bulb containing a chemical. When the alarm button sounds, fibers squeeze and danger drugs pour into the blood and lymph systems carrying the ominous message: Attention all units, our galaxy is in mortal danger. All-out alert. This biochemical state is felt to be most unpleasant.

Alexis, being tallest and, at the moment, calmest, takes over. He digs his way down the crevice and reaches the bottom. Brian, small, wiry, cheerful, uses his foothold and quickly reaches a point where he can stand on Alexis' shoulders and then drop to the level. Much against the instructions of his warning systems the Professor follows shakily. Halfway down he feels Alexis' hand grab his ankle and move foot to shoulder. When he hits safety the circuit orgasm explodes. A trillion cells receive the message: Danger alert is called off, continue normal life maintenance. The great galactic network had been mobilized for all-out survival, tested to the limit.

"The spasmodic discharge of emergency-juices," says the Wizard sitting in the snow catching his breath, "is the most basic of the 24 orgasms available to the human nervous system. The roller-coaster kick."

(she should be de-briefed and replaced as soon as possible.)

COUNTER-INTELLIGENCE AGENCY REPORT

Date:

Country:

Subject: page 2

The three climbers stand around in the late afternoon sun smiling at each other in pleasure like astronauts on the Ticonderoga making speeches about how proud they are to be members of the Space program, sharing post-orgasm tenderness. They start merrily down the easy grade to the right and within a hundred feet make a Jolting Discovery. They are trapped by another steeper cliff and this time there is no easy retreat. The sun is sinking. The neural-endocrine network begins to alert for another emergency.

This time Brian leads the way, a daring slice down a small crevice, reaching his hand back to steady his companions en route to another adventurous, risky, daredevil Circuit 1 orgasm, moving down the snow field to the next challenge. But the greatest dangers were still to come. Brian and Alexis explore the straight-ahead situation, seeking a path down the iceberg.

The Fugitive moves a hundred yards to the left where a stream plunges downward. Snow had collected in the stream bed and it is impossible to progress. Working slowly, chopping ice, hanging on tree limbs, he finds a way down and shouts back to the others. It is hard for them to find him, hanging to the side of a narrow shelf, propped against a tree trunk. Now it is his turn to lead and they follow, Alexis at one point sliding fifty feet on the ice and bouncing to his feet without so much as a crease in Brian Jones' coat.

The snow melts into a steep forest where they hang to tree trunks and slide down muddy paths. After an hour in the forest they hit the high meadow and Alexis leads them running across the ridge exultant.

Night has fallen when they reach the hotel at the base camp. The tavern-bar is civilization after a long Arctic safari. The owner finds it hard to believe that they have descended the dangerous west cliff of the Rigi in winter. They phone home. Maria has been worried. Waiting for the pickup car they order beers and lift glasses in celebratory toast.

Weeks later Brian disclosed that it had been just another Aleister Crowley tape replay. In London, North Africa, Europe, India, Egypt, the Philosopher guided by Barrett has unknowingly retraced the trail of Crowley. *(our London dossiers confirm)*

"It's time you realize that you are the recipient of the brain-model which is robot-wired to play the difficult public role of Evolutionary Change Agent. You are thus being forced, one might say, by thousands of gene-pools to relive Crowley, Dr. Dee and Paracelsus," Barritt tells the Fugitive.

"It's the Giordano Bruno script that worries me," replies the Professor.

Beware of Monotheism

Monotheism is the primitive religion which centers human consciousness on Hive Authority. There is One God and His Name is ————————— (substitute Hive-Label).

If there is only One God then there is no choice, no option, no selection of reality. There is only Submission or Heresy. The word *Islam* means "submission." The basic posture of Christianity is kneeling. Thy will be done.

Monotheism therefore does no harm to hive-oriented terrestrials (Stages 10, 11 and 12) who eagerly seek to lay-off responsibility on some Big Boss.

Monotheism does profound mischief to those who are evolving to post-hive stages of reality. Advanced mutants (Stages 13 to 18) do make the discovery that "All is One," as the realization dawns that "My Brain creates all the realities that I experience."

The discovery of Self is frightening because the novitiate possessor of the Automobile Body and the Automobile Brain must accept all the power that the hive religions attributed to the jealous Jehovah.

The First Commandment of all monotheisms is: I am the Lord, thy God: Thou shalt have no other Gods before me. All monotheisms are vengeful, aggressive, expansionist, intolerant.

Stage 10: Islam-Catholicism

Stage 11: Protestant Evangelism

Stage 12: Communist-Dulles Imperialism.

It is the duty of a monotheist to destroy any competitive heresy. Concepts such as devil, hell, guilt, eternal damnation, sin, evil are fabrications by the hive to insure loyalty to Hive Central. All these doctrines are precisely designed to intimidate and crush Individualism.

The process of mutating into Self-hood plunges the mutant into this cross fire of neurogenetic moral flak. Most of the freak-outs, bad trips and hellish experiences are caused by Monotheistic Morality. Again, it must be emphasized, that Monotheism is a necessary stage. Monotheism is a technology, a tool, to bring pre-civilized tribespeople and caste-segregated primitives into the collectives necessary to develop the post-hive, post-terrestrial technologies.

The major evolutionary step is taken when the individual says: "There is only one God who creates the universe. This God is my Brain. As the driver of this Brain I have created a universe in which there are innumerable other Gods of equal post-hive autonomy — with whom I seek to interest. And my universe was, itself, created by a Higher Level of Divinity — DNA, whose mysteries and wonders I seek to understand and harmonize with."

TUCSON LECTURE

THE TRIUMPH OF THE HIPPIES

An interesting thing happened when the first post-war baby boom generation of mutants hit college in the 1960's. I suspect that on every womb planet like ours, one generation after Hiroshima, you get a wild, volatile hippy-dippy all-out neural-change movement. Each gene-pool senses that a quantum jump into the future is about to happen, a retooling for a model change and each gene-hive squirts out its new experimental models. On this nursery planet these new models were called *Hippies*.

So, let's consider the 60's. I think it's important, as we rocket into the 80's, to understand what happened back then because there is a tendency to sweep that decade under the rug.

You gentle shock-troops won a noble victory for DNA.

Few people understand what happened between 1960 and 1970. I am here to remind you that the global neurogenetic revolution of the 1960's was the most important decade in human history. *(Applause)* Well, I see we have many veterans of the uncivil war of the 60's here. *(Laughter)*

I want to look at you, my fellow veterans in the first 20 rows, and say that you gentle shock-troops won a noble victory for DNA. *(Applause)* Let me remind you how you changed every aspect of American and global culture in the 60's. How your mutational signal reached and shook-up every gene-pool and hive-bureaucracy on the planet. You may suspect I am biased because I was a genetic activist in the 60's. But let me confess to you I have not one nostalgic bone in my body. I am certainly not here tonight, my fellow veterans, to lead a Charge of the Haight Brigade back to Woodstock. We shall salvage, not sentimentalize the past. As we move into the future we shall take the best of the 60's with us. You must not let Them at hive-control turn you into vegetating veterans like the American Legion and the VFW. Or seduce you into annual conventions at places like Philadelphia where you wear funny costumes and run around barefoot and get

"If she comes home from school smiling, watch her."

busted for old times sake. *(Laughter)*

I make gentle fun of the 60's, but I am serious when I say that this was an important decade. There is not one gene-pool in the American hive that hasn't been re-formed because of the 60's.

Take, for example, the parent-child relationship. I think today that family politics are, by a factor of 10, more intelligent, more respectful and more mature than they were in the 1950's. Merciful memory may have allowed you to forget that 5 to 6 years ago, your government, the Nixon administration, was sending pamphlets to parents instructing them how to surveil and bust their own children. You remember, it said: "If she comes home from school smiling, watch her." *(Laughter)* And, in the last Presidential election, we had the predictable phenomena of Betty Ford saying, "Aw, sure, the kids smoke grass in the White House, that's alright; what's important is we are honest about it." And Rosalynn Carter said, "Sure Chip got busted, thrown out of the Navy, for smoking grass, but that's not important. What's important is we can talk about it, be honest about our differences."

We don't have the hypocrisy that used to prevail when one generation was getting aggressively smashed with Martinis in the front room while the younger generation was serenely floating out the back window. *(Laughter, Applause)*

"Aw, sure, the kids smoke grass in the White House, that's alright."

Reprinted from CHICK MAGAZINE, June 1989

George Litwin was born in the primitive (pre-Hiroshima) half of the 20th century. He was a handsome, healthy, athletic Earthling except for one anomaly. He carried in his skull a fully wired 21st century brain.

The expected acceleration occurred. Before finishing his undergraduate work he had published more important articles than the average psychologist does in a lifetime. While still a graduate student at Harvard he initiated research on neuro-transmitter drugs (mescaline) and, indeed, introduced Leary and numerous others to this tool.

Litwin's subsequent work on interpersonal ecology and emotional climate laid the foundation for post-terrestrial neuro-sociology.

George Litwin's greatest achievements are in the field of Human Ethology. His demonstration of the existence of human castes, his studies on the relationship of geography and intelligence, and his genetic definitions of intelligence have established his galactic fame.

For the last 40 years (2020-2060) Litwin has been studying post-terrestrial sexuality. The entire world awaits his results.

To Find the Genetic River, First Locate Your Heart

by George Litwin

I'm sitting in this bar in the middle of Southern California's leisure-suit land, the San Fernando Valley, picking my teeth ever so discreetly with the edge of an American Express card, trying my best to mind the bar's business. I'm listening for little hints from the bartender about loose women in these parts. More specifically, I'm trying to confirm my suspicion that this place may be home base for the latest in extra-terrestrial close encounters — Evolutionary Agents fronting as *housewife hookers*.

I'm listening for little hints from the bartender about loose women in these parts.

I don't have to cool my steaming heels. Down towards the end of the plastic mahogany bar undulates a housewife type exposing two globular constellations. She performs an erotic-radar scan of the terrestrials in the crowd. She soft-lands on a bar stool and sits like a soft-round lunar-module. Her fingernails are painted N.A.S.A. silver and they tap against her glass in intergalactic code.

I catch her optical instruments in the mirror behind the bar. I signal her by rapidly blinking my left lens and smiling. When she signals back I screen the image of a pink tongue (at least it looked like a tongue) softly licking a cherry-ripe pair of lips. I throttle up, oft-off, and orbit down beside her.

She asks me if I'm looking for something.

"A married lady," I tell her. "I want a good looking Alien Intelligence with a real-life wedding band on her finger."

She waves her ringfinger in front of my eyes hypnotically.

"Know the kind," she murmurs. "What do you want?"

"The usual answers. Where? How? When?"

Her incredible quick tongue fascinated me much more than the fact that she was somebody else's wife.

She smiled wearily and shot me the eternal look of the Alien Intelligence Agent. I've seen them from Berlin to Las Vegas and they *do* have a certain look. It's in the eyes and most of all in the stance. Michelangelo would have called it *contraposto*.

"For 75 dollars," she coos in an Avon Lady voice, "you can get yourself all three answers."

"Your place or mine?" I reply in a choked-up voice. But she was gone inside, her eyes closed, her juicy lips moving mechanically in computer precision.

"The question of *where* is easily answered. Find the genetic runway on your planet, face the setting sun and move West. To find the genetic river, first locate your heart. Since it is on your left side, you know you will manipulate with your right hand. The large land mass is to your right when you face the setting sun.

"Face West at the shadow. Move between the swamp on your left and the iceberg on your right. On other planets spin-eccentricity slides the big land-mass south. Then all left-right north-south codes are reversed. This is a galactic constant. The Heart is always located on the equator-side when you move West. For Protection. The superior-technology-danger always comes from the north. The right hand hunts. The left hand is used for gathering. You will find the fruit trees growing on your south side.

"The question of *how* is already settled. Keep just ahead of the wave. Use the West-Ward ecological niche as base. Don't get bogged down in the hot swamps to your left. Don't get frozen in the structures to your right.

"So the only question is *when*? Since everything spirals through the 24 Stage cycle, simply locate your spot on the species-cycle, the cultural history cycle, and the personal-individual cycle and keep moving upward and outward at increasing velocity, making more precise link-ups."

Don't get bogged down in the hot swamps to your left.

I'm in a slow plunge cycle when the lady speeds up and brings me off just before I'm ready. Grabbing a Wash & Dry she sponges me with it almost as if she's wiping off a runny nose. "I hardly ever get such young business," she smiles.

different sites for different rites

Date: January, 1972

Country: Imminsee, Switzerland

Classification:

TOP SECRET

Subject: AN ALCHEMICAL EXPERIMENT WAS ARRANGED IN HONOR OF THE PRINCE

(Conversation videotaped.)

Everyone in the lakeside cabin is now aware of the voltage released by the introduction of Prince Alexis into the molecule. Two days in a row the Death Card flashed out of the deck.

The third night, in honor of the Prince, and by way of exorcism, they arranged an alchemical experiment which involved the dissolution of hive imprints, the transmutation of realities, the reception of vibrations from post-terrestrial consciousness.

They found themselves in front of the fireplace; the familiar room now so electrified that solid objects were seen to be composed of atomic and molecular bubble-chains and lattices emitting energy. A low comfortable humming sound filled the air.

After innumerable re-imprinting exercises Alexis smiled and produced from his briefcase the ancient leather text which had been sent from the Nepalese Holyman. Alexis reverently unwrapped the soft kidskin covering, unwound the silken wrap and placed the book on the carpet in front of the fire. Candles were moved to illuminate.

The book was constructed of leather panels, sewn together so as to unfold in eight sections. Alexis pointed to the Sanskrit design on the cover.

"That's the number twenty-four," he said.

"Why twenty-four?" asked Brian.

Alexis smiled enigmatically and flipped open the cover. Each of the eight panels of the leather manuscript was divided into three sections and in each of the 24 panels a picture was inscribed.

The bottom panel was shaded red and contained:

1. An Amoeba with the face of a baby with huge red lips.
2. A Fish with the face of a baby.
3. A Frog with the face of a baby.

The second panel from the bottom was shaded orange and contained the pictures of:

4. A Rodent standing alertly with the face of a two-year-old human child.
5. A Lion with the face of a three-year-old child standing over and pulling a toy away from a small animal with the face of a two-year-old human child.
6. A group of apes swinging from a jungle-gym — with the faces of five-year-old children.

The third row, shaded yellow, contained these three pictures:

7. A group of Paleolithic Homanids picking up stones — they have the faces of seven-year-old modern children.
8. An eight-year-old child in the body of a neolithic — thoughtfully examining a flower.
9. A group of children building a treehouse together.

COUNTER-INTELLIGENCE AGENCY REPORT

Date:

Country:

Classification:

TOP SECRET

Subject: page 2

The fourth row, shaded green, contained:

10. Knights on horseback with the faces of teenage kids — being watched by court ladies with the faces of teenage girls.
11. A husband and wife with their children standing in front of their house.
12. A million people crowded into an enormous city square — all facing and looking up to a velvet balcony.

The fifth row, shaded a rich blue, contained:

13. A beautiful, naked, human, hermaphrodite — the body radiating energy: glowing.
14. A Yogi, naked, hermaphrodite — radiating, glowing with sense of precise contol of the energy.
15. A beautiful woman and man locked in Yab-Yum position — radiating and glowing.

The sixth row, shaded light-electric blue, contained:

16. A beautiful naked human hermaphrodite. The brain is visible as are the extensive tendrils of nerves — the body glows.
17. A Yogi, naked, hermaphrodite with brain and nervous system visible — sending out tendrils of energy which embrace & create the surrounding material forms.
18. A series of mountain tops. On each sits a Yogi (as in preceding) with tendrils of nerve signals linking them & energizing the surrounding forms.

The seventh row, shaded violet, contained:

19. A Double-Helix — intertwined energy coils. Along the strips the preceding 18 forms are portrayed in red.
20. The Double-Helix is crowned by the head and face of a Yogi — the Yogi's Brain intertwines the Double-Helix.
21. A spaghetti tangle of Double-Helices in a spherical form — the whole image radiating like a Star.

The Eighth row, shaded silver, contained:

22. Stars in a velvet Black Sky.
23. Stars which form a Galactic Brain.
24. Strips and spirals of stars infolding to a Central Black Hole.

"What does it say?" asked Brian, pointing to a script on the bottom of the scroll.

Alexis pulled a piece of paper from his pocket and started reading. The candlelight shadowed his noble face. His voice was softly powerful.

"The sequence, that is, the numerical order, of evolution is everywhere the same. In the stars, in seed, within the atom, and in the unfolding development of the individual human being.

"Having decoded the numerical sequence which governs the evolution of energy we can

COUNTER-INTELLIGENCE AGENCY REPORT

Date:

Country:

Subject: page 3

Classification:

TOP
SECRET

use this Periodic Table to decipher evolution at other levels of velocity.

"Some sequences are more easily understood in the evolution of stars. Others are more apparent in the growth and change of seed-forms. Others are most clearly seen in the growth and development of the individual human being going through the changes.

"This parallel study of evolution in the life of stars, in the periodicity of the chemical elements, in the evolution of species on a planet, in individuals popping up at different historical epochs, demonstrates the underlying harmony and over-tone-unity of nature and helps the Young Agent discover the similarities in phenomena at all levels of velocity.

"The number of basic principles which govern all processes of change is very small. Let us say there are twenty-four. Different numerical combinations of these twenty-four stages create all the seeming variety of realities which humans can receive.

"The first fundamental rhythm of the universe is polarity. This has been called THE LAW OF THREE. This principle states that every event in the universe is the result of an Intersection of three processes: The receptive, the transmitting, and the interacting process between.

"Input. Outgo. Mediated by Integration. Dendrite. Axon. And cell body.

"Black Hole. Big Bang. Transition Between."

"The next fundamental rhythm of the galaxy is the Octave of Change. This has been called the law of 8 (7 + 1).

"Realities consist of vibrations. These vibrations are emitted from every form of structure along the electro-magnetic continuum, proceeding in different directions, crossing one another, colliding, strengthening, weakening one another. DNA fabricates eight brains which deal with eight evolving technologies along the energy continuum. The reason for this eight-phase spectrum can be understood only by the Six Brain Organism. There are eight (7 + 1) colors visible, eight (7 + 1) primary sounds, eight (7 + 1) is the rhythm of the chemical elements.

"Everything is in continual motion moving at fractions and multiples of the speed of light.

"The natural operational rhythm for the human nervous system is the speed of light, ever-changing. The mind of vibrations (the 6th Brain) is called the In-lightened mind. In-lightenment means thinking at the electrical rate of the Brain. The Brain is the Electrical Body. The Physical Body is the carriage for the Brain, i.e., Body Electric. Human muscular Behavior is the gross, coarse manifestation of faster, stronger nuclear vibrations — charm, charge, strangeness, attractiveness. Each impulse of consciousness from the lower neuro-muscular circuits, when received by the Electrical Body, becomes a small sun radiating meaning. The harmonizing of these innumerable units of experienced light is the skill to be learned by the Sixth Brain."

Alexis stops reading and suddenly turns the book with both hands exposing the other side. With all the panels exposed the book is about a yard long. Each of the eight panels is a color of the spectrum.

Date:

Country:

Classification:

Subject:

TOP
SECRET

The picture is a vague human-shape, a cloud-like figure in light blue. Within the figure and radiating are golden fibers — it resembles a surrealist anatomical diagram of the human nervous system. The light blue human figure trails off into a network of rainbow swirls and spirals. The effect is startling. The golden-fibers of the nervous system seem to be antennae receiving and vibrating current.

Alexis throws his head up melodramatically and holds his hands out, trembling. His fingers moving as though he were palpating some invisible substance. The others could see crackling current emitting from or being gathered by his hands. He looks at Timothy and smiles. They shift to sit facing each other about five feet apart. Timothy holds up his hands and jumps in surprise.

Alexis, Barbara, Brian, Corrine, Timothy, Liz and all the objects in the room are part of a three-dimensional television holograph, in radiant color; everything constructed of vibrations that flow in fast, smooth rhythm, current alternating so swiftly that a soft texture, infinitely luxuriant, is created. All present are totally joined, indeed, are each part of the holograph, each a shifting pattern of the same field of energy. Each knows what is occurring within the consciousness of the other, could know every thought and experience that the other had ever registered. The sumptuous, voluptuous, mink-lined, rich smoothness of everything fresh, alive. The "Isness" of Huxley's chair.

Alexis, Brian, Liz, Barbara, Corinne and Tim spend the night in telepathic wave sculpture, imprinting music, absorbing the message of the Nepalese transmission, and watch the sun rise over the mountain. Alexis is now following the Professor like a worshipful jealous girl, flinging a mink neckpiece over his shoulder.

"What shall we do next?" he asks.

"Find Her."

"Shall I stay?"

"No. Go now. If you delay here you will be late for our next intersection."

Alexis ceremoniously presents his host with the Nepalese text and leaves with Barbara and Corinne for Lucerne.

(End of tape.)

TUCSON LECTURE

SEX IS BETTER THAN EVER

The new culture which emerged from the 60's was fabricated by newly activated teenage nervous systems. These nervous systems had been imprinted by signals urging self-indulgence, self-discovery and self-actualization. This generation was caste-out far beyond hive limits where reputations, and at times, bodies were placed on the lines. The first benefit of this Out-Caste behavior was that *college education is better today**.

You have no idea how insectoid things were in the college scene. You may not remember back to the dark, ancient days of Eisenhower and McCarthy and Neil Sedaka and Elvis Presley. At that time college administrators, college presidents and college professors were considered to be in loco-parents, which meant it was their job to act as parents to keep the boys and girls apart! In the 50's and early 60's police matrons checked women in and out of the dormitories to make sure that the inevitable did not happen.

'Come let's to bed', says Sleepy Head.
'Tarry awhile', says Slow;

*There is, in this country, a caste which benefits from anger and stirring up trouble. It is called the legal profession. Left-wing lawyers say, "Well, what's wrong with the college students today? They are not angry as they were in the 60's." Well, of course, they are not. Because in the 60's we had some very irritable and irritating bureaucrats running the colleges, and running the country. But this too has changed.

Today there is much more understanding, tolerance and awareness between the generations. The Out-Castes of the 60's have become the Dom-Species of the Sunset Strip. The parents of today were the youngsters of the 60's, and your college instructors today were hippies then. The young policemen today and the young bank executives, all the people who are running the country today, lived through the 60's as long-haired dissidents and had that testing experience of opposition to the Nixon-Agnew gang. They are tolerant of, even supportive of, differences. The sign of a secure, genetically sophisticated species.

Would you believe $250,000,000 — a quarter of a billion dollars annually — for the rolling papers alone?

I want to look around this room and remind every young man in this audience that you are sitting in your seat tonight with a certain serenity and relaxation that you wouldn't have had in the 60's. You are freer tonight because your colleagues, the previous sperm-egg wave, fought hard to end that now unnecessary quiver of hive-paranoia — the peace time draft. Remember?

Some people say these cultural changes are phases, temporary hula hoop fads. But they aren't. You can't go back. The cultural changes of the 60's are irreversible. Certainly the sexual revolution which activated empathy and understanding between men and women will never be repealed.

There are so many aspects of the Sexual Mutation. First there is enhancement of sexual activity. Now some Older Hive Sociologists complain: "What is all this sex talk about? The *Reader's Digest* and Dear Abby assure us that people were making out in the 50's and the 40's as much as you are." Well, maybe. The *quantity* of sexual relations may not have changed, but I am obliged to tell you that the *quality* of sexual relationships has changed. There is an intelligence, and an aesthetic sensitivity, a tender understanding, a playfulness that simply didn't exist in the past.

The other aspect of the sexual revolution, of course, has to do with the relationship among and between the sexes. And certainly there can be no return to the romantic-feudal situation in which both men and women were going through the robot charade of macho-femme-fatale sexual impersonation. There is a wiser acceptance now of the electric difference between the basic equality of and the necessity for an intelligent and exquisite fusion among the sexes. (*Applause*)

Here's the bottom line of the 60's: *it was an intelligence-raising movement*. It was a neurological revolution with two aspects. Body Activation. Brain Actualization.

The Brain is emerging from the closet.

The notion of Self-directed Brain Change didn't exist in the late 50's and early 60's. It was necessary to turn people on to this option. Evolutionary Agents are robot-programmed to perform this activation role. Send a futique signal to nervous systems. If they are ready for it, if the time is right and the signal is precise — ZAP! The new circuits will activate! People will open up like flowers in May. And that is what happened in the 60's.

Remember this notion of bodily awareness was a Pre-Dom Species concept in the 50's. Before 1960 hive wisdom held that the body was an instrument designed for reproductive purposes. Sure, you were allowed to jump up and down on each other on Saturday night for breeding purposes, (instinctual sperm-egg exchange) but the notion of intelligent pleasure, hedonic engineering, bodily self-direction, didn't exist. The notions of consciousness raising and body awareness and personal growth did not exist.

Of course you know what has happened. Since the 60's the consciousness-pleasure hedonic-intelligence business has become the largest industry in the country. The Great American consumer society has co-opted the notion of "feel good." And that's a stage forward. Nothing is wrong with hedonic con-

sumerism. It was bound to happen. It's a stage, of course. New ideas always get watered down and vulgarized. In every gene-pool, every caste is going to pick up on new energies. So, let us face the amusing fact. The Self-Directed Pleasure Business has become an American obsession.

There is an enormous hedonic industry in this country which simply did not exist in the 50's or early 60's. You have water beds, satin sheets, diets, health foods, hi-fi equipment, Body Shops, vibrators. You have many forms of yoga, massage, body building and martial arts. You have the gurus and the swamis. You have all the personal development, self-growth movements. Every Girl Scout Troop in the country runs off twice a week to have consciousness raising episodes at the junior high school. Talk about money involved. Would you believe $250,000,000 — a quarter of a billion dollars annually — for the rolling papers alone? Six billion for the weed. Four hundred million dollars spent on jogging paraphernalia.

The self-indulgent, self-improvement pleasure industry — entertainment, travel, recreation, sensual stimulation, aesthetics, style and fashion — is the largest business in America. The business of Uncle Sam has become self-actualized pleasure.

Self-directed hedonic engineering is now the goal of the Dom-Species. Before the 60's, the orthodox hive philosophy insisted that "for every little pleasure there's pain, pain, pain." God was considered a beady-eyed accountant up there in Hive-Heaven keeping your hedonic balance in order. And woe be it to you if you overdrew on your pleasure account! Because the wages of fun were death (as every Hollywood movie warned).

The Dom-Species has come a long way from that prudishness, due in some part, to our friends from the Oriental philosophy department. We have learned that pleasure is not bound by some Newtonian conservation-of-energy-principle and thus balanced by pain. We know now that beauty is something that can be understood, can be learned, can be engineered. Pleasure is not an ejaculation reflex. It is an art, a science, a skilled performance, like playing the concert piano. It is something that can be studied and, through disciplined intelligence, increased. And, indeed, the more you do it, the better you get at it. Thus pleasure and intelligent hedonism are like tennis. Find someone that can play as well or better than yourself.

I have been talking about the neurosomatic rebirth, the Body Resurrection which occurred in the 60's. That's an accomplished fact. The Body has been uncovered and we're never going to return to prudish robot-hood.

The other aspect of the contelligence movement of the 60's, (the neurological revolution) was the discovery of the brain itself. I want to remind you that 100 years ago there was a taboo organ in Victorian England and in Freudian Vienna. The friendly genitals were considered the unmentionable. Well, look at any newstand and you will see that, today, the genitals are no longer the unmentionables, but rather the un-avoidables. Now the taboo organ, the organ that we cannot talk about or study intelligently is *the brain**.

It is only in the last 5 or 6 years that science, in the form of neurology, has begun to face the real meaning of the brain. The Brain is emerging from the closet. And it is scary, my friends! It is frightening to every static, comfortable social and philosophic hive-notion to realize that you are carrying around behind your forehead a 100 billion-cell bio-electric computer that creates realities; and that, through imprinting and reimprinting, imposes the reality you inhabit. Everything you think and feel and sense and remember and learn is simply a process of brain functioning.

When a species understands that the brain is a tool, then it starts to think about directing and understanding this incredible instrument. And begins using it to ask such embarrassing questions as: who designed the brain? And what is it for? And how do we use the brain?

I have recently transmitted a mutation signal called *Exo-Psychology: A Manual on the Use of the Human Brain According to the Instructions of the Manufacturers*. (*Laughter and Applause*) This title is a way of reminding us that the great discovery of the 60's was this: YOUR BRAIN CREATES YOUR OWN REALITY.

*The next taboo is DNA actualization.

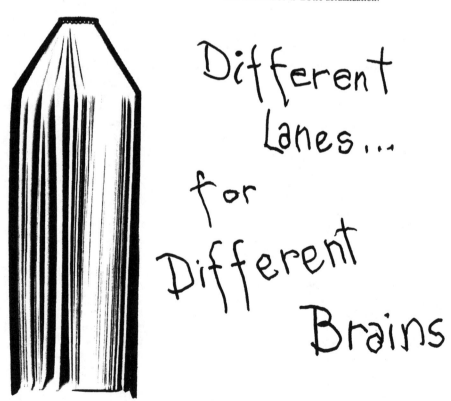

Different Lanes... for Different Brains

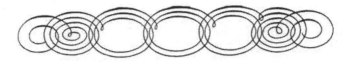

GENETIC HALL OF FAME

Brian O'Leary

Larry Hauben was manifested in biological form in the 12th century when he founded the poetic school known as the Troubadors. These romantics were Evolutionary Agents assigned the task of aestheticising and eroticizing the harsh ascetic culture of the period. Chivalry, devotion to Woman and fine arts were the characteristics of this Intelligency.

He appeared briefly and sporadically in the 20th century as wandering poet, shepherd-prince, chiaroscuro painter and lover. The many honors, Nobel Prizes, Academy Oscars and artistic prizes he won during this epoch were but fronts, screens, and commercial exchanges disguising his real mission on the planet — the Elaborate Courtship of His Leading Lady which had, by this time, taken him through fourteen galaxy time zones.

Hauben next popped up in the 22nd century where he was responsible for color-form-harmony in the conversion of several galaxies from quantum-foam to Field Magnetism.

Wherever Romantic Love and Elegant Lyricism are mentioned throughout the galaxies, the smiling, elusive face of this Grand Romantic is remembered.

Reprinted from HOLLYWEED REPORTER, *April 1981*

The Incredible Revelation of David Begelman

by Larry Hauben

Sid Luft, Judy Garland's one-time husband, sat in his Wilshire Boulevard apartment in December (1977), reading the *Hollywood Reporter*. Columbia Pictures president David Begelman, the trade paper said, had just been reinstated after misappropriating $61,000 in corporate trade-coupons and producing *Close Encounters* — a nuclear-particle-movie held responsible for mutating millions toward Higher Intelligence.

Begelman said after being reinstated, "I know I won't do it again." Sid Luft was sure he knew better. David Begelman just can't keep a cosmic secret.

Back in 1963 Sid was still on the outside looking in. Freddie Fields and David Begelman, two skilled Evolutionary Agents, had taken the management of Judy Garland away from him. But before bowing out Sid Luft was determined to arrange a meeting with Begelman and Fields in which he would expose them as Intelligence Increase (I^2) Agents.

The meeting took place on August 22, 1963, in a Sunset Boulevard office building. While Luft argued with Fields and Begelman for more than three hours, he carried in his shirt pocket a microphone disguised as a cigarette package. It transmitted the voices to the street below where a private detective sat in a car monitoring a real-to-real tape recorder.

The conversation was beamed via satellite around the solar system, and the rest is galactic history. Dave and Fred had their cover blown.

LUFT: I'll tell you, that was the most disturbing phone call I had with you about that East-West thing.

BEGELMAN: I didn't tell you that . . . did I? Because I swear on my life . . . on my child's life.

LUFT: You said it on the phone. You said it to me. "I can feel the earth spinning West to East with my own body."

BEGELMAN: I told you this on the phone?

LUFT: Yeah . . . Judy said you told her and she could feel it too.

BEGELMAN: But I told you this?

FIELDS (To Begelman): Be quiet.

LUFT: And I said to you, "Dave . . . what happened to the mellow wisdom of the East?"

BEGELMAN: Do you want me to tell you the truth? Apparently, she was taken to the hospital; they were pumping her stomach and she was disrobed down to here . . . and she just blurted it all out. In front of witnesses.

LUFT: You saw the picture. You heard the tape?

BEGELMAN: Oh yeah, oh yeah, oh yeah, oh yeah.

David Begelman just can't keep a cosmic secret.

FIELDS: If was a f------- 25 percent Out-Caste Agent job. You know what that schmuck Albert Einstein did . . . it was so stupid because I offered to sit down with him at that time. He publicized the whole relativity *mishegas* (craziness).

LUFT: WHAT was on those tapes? What did she blurt out?

BEGELMAN: Here's the transcript. (Reads from manuscript) "The strategy of evolution is: *out-run the past*! The past which moves up from your own spinal-column and mid-brain, always creeping Westward from the autonomic nerve-centers of the East. The Task of the Evolutionary Agent is to stay ahead of the Oriental animal army. *Nobility is Mobility*."

BUMPER
STICKER

MOBILITY IS NOBILITY

CALIFORNIA
B07 ULW

STEVE VOLPIN

circa 1978

Reprinted from PSYCHOLOGY TWODAY, 1978

How and Why Friends Become Aliens

by Neil Freer

Neil Freer is famous in galactic neurogenetic textbooks because he was the first Earth-Born to activate, master and link-up all 24 stages of his brain. The extraordinary aesthetic intensity of his temporal caste-stages (which kept his developmental momentum going) has won the admiration of dramatists for several centuries.

STAGE 10: Freer's adolescent searching led him to become a Trappist Monk and to the commitment to his ancient feudal sex-role.

STAGE 11: Evolving from monotheism Freer became a dedicated husband and father of six children.

STAGE 12: Freer, in 1964, saw the implications of neuro-transmitter drugs and was thus able to avoid Terminal Adulthood and Social Security Hive Identification.

STAGES 13, 14 & 15: Subsequent reimprinting experiences allowed Freer to sequentially return to post-hive infancy — self-indulgence, self-actualization and a new post-hive link-up with his mate Ursula. Freer was the one who pointed out the signs of an emerging racial post-domestic imprint around age thirty-five.

STAGES 16, 17 & 18: Freer's systematic activation of neural circuits and his disciplined study of Einsteinian and post-Einsteinian texts allowed him to become the most advanced physicist of the 21st century. His technique was simple. He opened the neuro-electric circuits with LSD, experienced the patterns and then applied the current mathematical models to create new realities.

STAGES 19, 20 & 21: Freer performed the same cycle of opening-integration-fusion at the neurogenetic circuit. He used LSD to open up the DNA-CNS conversation and then used the current micro-genetic findings to externally describe his experience. Freer developed the concept of dyadic evolution: male/female

fusion — moving up the evolutionary scale together.

STAGES 22, 23 & 24: In the year 2033 Freer became the first Earth-Born entity to experience quantum-field contelligence. His disappearance, with his wife Ursula, into the Black Hole of his own device followed shortly thereafter.

T errestrials, in Stage 13 Eco-niches (1978) are about ready to deal with the following relativistic facts about their Genetic History:

They can realize that at earlier, larval stages of their own metamorphosis they shared neuro-realities with those who later grow up to be very different castes.

They can logically accept that, as they develop, their close companions of childhood evolve into alien intelligences.

It is useful to remind terrestrial humans that at one time, shortly after conception, they were all unicellular organisms drifting passively down uterine canals along with trillions of other amoeboid floaters. But they grew and changed, leaving the unicellular neighbors behind.

Try this didactic script: Terrestrials! Each time you develop to a new stage you migrate to a new ecological niche. You join a new gene-pool. Each time you activate a new stage you say farewell to the neighbors with whom you shared the old hive-reality. "Goodbye, Old Friends, it's time to grow."

Remember your best friend in first grade? When your Temporal Caste was monkey? Where is SHe now? In most cases early caste associates become total strangers in years to come.

Consider two six-year old buddies. One is more muscular, more aggressive and confident, more mature in dealing with six-year-old Paleolith reality. (Every first grader knows exactly where SHe slots into the pecking order.) But by age 16 the stronger can no longer evolve and quits school to be a truck driver. The other goes on to M.I.T., continues to change and grow and eventually wins the Nobel Prize in Physics. At age 50 the two live in very different realities, competitive gene-pools. Their brain circuitry is several mutations different. The Teamster operates with a Paleolithic Brain — capable of skillful mimickry but not inventive thinking.

Recall, that at age six the Nobel Prizer was envious of and intimidated by the muscular superiority of hir friend. Age 6 is the Paleolithic Stage in the Evolving Human Brain. The future teamster is templated for superstitious, mimicking-repetitive survival techniques, can imitate group rituals, repeat the magic taboo words of the hive, perform complex-rote tasks, handle technology, twist the dials of his TV set. SHe can even go to the ballot box and dutifully pull a voting lever. But SHe is a hunter-gatherer surviving confusedly in a Technological Society.

The Higher the human Neurogenetic Caste, the more mobile the individual. Neural Caste is determined by Voluntary Mobility. The freer you are to "come and go," the Higher your Intelligence. Metamorphosis to a higher stage involves movement to a new Ecological Niche.

This process of movement involves wrenching "goodbyes" to those who shared the former niche — and the earlier stage of development. It is necessary that one make linkages at each stage of reality. Indeed, one must master each neural circuit before one can advance.

The 24 Neurogenetic Stages are motels up the High-way of Evolution. Centers and path-

---

The freer you are to "come and go," the Higher your Intelligence.

---

ways up through the global Brain. At certain fuel-rest stops we form crew-linkages to lift us up to the next stage. The Flight Plan of Evolution is a series of reality jumps. We cooperate with those in our present reality to help us ascend to the next.

The Stage 11 Marriage is such a reality jump.* Two Stage 10 lusty, romantic barbarians from Stage 11 gene-pools meet at the High School Prom and decide to make the Big Jump up to Stage 11 Parental Reality. They form a two-person flight crew.

The marriage ceremony is a metamorphic-migration Cape Canaveral ritual. The bride and groom blast up together — in a flare of rice with tin cans tied to the Migration Rocket. Headed for a new Plan-It called Matrimonial Fusion.

After passing the Moon of Honey they eventually arrive, sometimes joltingly, in the New World. Then they discover that the metamorphosis has produced unexpected forms. As horny teenagers they shared the same sperm-egg reality. As responsible parents they discover that they are a very different species. The shy youth has become an aggressive, selfish father-type barking orders to his astonished mate. And the flamboyant, carefree, go-go teenage girl has become a serious, mature worrier.

Marriage is a Sci-Fi thriller. Two larvals walk

---

*It should be clear now that very different mating procedures operate at different stages of Neuro-development. Stage 12 Marriage is state controlled. Stage 10 marriage is feudal arranged. Stage 9 marriage is priest-caste managed. Stage 7 is bull-harem.

hand-in-hand into the Time Transformer not knowing what sort of post-larval forms will emerge. And the contract cunningly says, "until death do you part."

After soft-landing on the Honey Moon the two aliens wake up in the same bed: strangers from different species. But they must stick together to survive in the domesticated ant-hill.

Here is the sequence of Evolutionary Departures:

Circuit I (Stages 1, 2, & 3): Marine Muscular Technology. Eventually the masters of Circuit I (the Stage 3 Amphibians) leave the fish marine reality and migrate to form new land-based gene pools.

Circuit II(Stages 4, 5, & 6): Terrestrial Muscular Technology. Eventually the Circuit II successes (the Stage 6 gesturing-arborial primates), leave the four-footed mammals and move to form new gene-pools based on . . .

Circuit III (Stages 7, 8, & 9): Artifact Technology. Eventually the technological successes (the Stage 9 Caste-linked artisans and commercial dealers), leave tribal reality and migrate to form new, collective gene-pools.

Circuit IV (Stages 10, 11, & 12): Cultural Technology. Then the Circuit IV urban masters, the Sun Belt Americans, leave Demo-poll Welfare-Socialist Society and move to . . .

Circuit V (Stages 13, 14, & 15): Self-Actualized Body Technology. Then Circuit V successes figure out that H.O.M.E.'s are the only escape from the Encroaching Primitive terrestrial past and they move to . . .

Circuit VI (Stages 16, 17, & 18): Self-Actualized Brain Technology. Eventually the Circuit VI successes realize that genetic control — involving rejuvenation cloning and DNA engineering — is the next evolutionary step and move to . . .

Circuit VII (Stages 19, 20, & 21): Neurogenetic Technology. Eventually the Stage 21 Genetic-Masters realize that it is necessary to attain post-psychological status and move to . . .

Circuit VIII (Stages 22, 23 & 24): Quantum-field Technology.

To metamorphize from one circuit to another requires fusion. Each circuit of the brain fabricates new realities and a new Ecological Niche for gene-pools formed by mutants from the past hives.

Circuit I: Marine

Circuit II: Land

Circuit III: Artifact — Environment for small gene-pools

Circuit IV: Civilization — Large insectoid gene-pool collectives

Circuit V: Individual Body as Self-Directed Time Ship

Circuit VI: Individual Brain

Circuit VII: DNA-CNS Pathways — The rhythm of evolution at each Circuit is Ego-Discovery, Ego-Actualization, Ego-Fusion (element-linkage). The elements fuse to form gene-pool molecules which synergize the energy needed to migrate.

Marriage
is a Sci-Fi thriller.

Migration-mutation cannot be performed alone. Gene-pools migrate across the desert of space-time to the next oasis.

Once one has metamorphized to a new Niche using new technologies one's selection and mastery of the new technologies are an individual caste choice. But gene-pool movement to a new niche is communal. (The scout caste can move way out into the future and come back to demonstrate the safety of the future-pathways, to demonstrate that it can be done. But the work of fabricating the new reality involves linkage into gene-pools.)

The voyage of evolution, of species or individuals, is a series of linkages and separations. At each stage of development we synergistically use each other to grow and move on.

We link with our teenage steady to explore sexual impersonation roles. And then we move on. And on! And on!

SUMMARY: All evidence from Sol-3 indicates that the planet is evolving harmoniously. The Dom-Species (Stage 13) is at present (1978 Sun Belt) relaxed and reasonably secure. The presence of an enormous growing population of Pre-Dom Future Oriented Humans — in the Sun Belt — has made possible a realistic look at the futures which can be fabricated by this explosive Gene Colony. This is a most fast-moving, volatile time in the evolution of Life on Earth. Every attempt must be made to give terrestrials future-maps which will allow them to anticipate what is to come with enthusiasm and intelligence. As a start, publish this memo at once in the most congenial form.

(Peace Press of Culver City is the most advanced — i.e., the most Western-Center for transmitting Genetic Intelligence directives.)

Reprinted from BOSTON GLOBE, Sept. 1, 1977

CIA Funded Research By Opponent of Leary

by Al Larkin
Globe Washington Bureau

A Harvard psychologist who fought to remove LSD advocate Timothy Leary from the University faculty in 1963 was among researchers who had received funds from a CIA program that sponsored research even more controversial than Leary's.

Dr. Herbert Kelman, Harvard's Richard Clarke Cabot professor of social ethics, admitted yesterday receiving a grant from the Human Ecology Fund, but said he didn't know until recently that the organization served as a conduit for CIA money.

Kelman said he requested and received $1000 from the fund for non-drug-related purposes in 1960, just three years before he successfully argued for the expulsion of Leary and co-researcher Dr. Richard Alpert for their alleged use of Harvard undergraduates in LSD research.

Before Leary's expulsion, both men were lecturers in Harvard's psychology department.

The CIA recently has admitted establishing the Society for the Investigation of Human Ecology, also known as the Human Ecology Fund, as part of its $25-million program on mind control and human behavior designated MK-ULTRA.

The CIA has admitted giving drugs to unknowing persons.

Ironically, the Ecology Fund sponsored work similar to Leary's during the 1950's at the Massachusetts Mental Health Center in Boston, and students from Harvard and other area universities were reportedly used as subjects in those experiments. Leary has said he informed his subjects, while the CIA has admitted giving drugs to unknowing persons.

Reprinted from ROLLING STONES MAGAZINE, February 1984

Jane Wayne Tells All About Her Encounters with Higher Intelligence

by Andy Warhol

I fast. I just try to physically get rid of the fear residues that accompany these signals from outer space."

Jane Wayne, daughter of the Duke, looked out again at the surf curling over Santa Monica Beach and seemed transfixed. The waves were pushing nine feet high. Up in Malibu the residents had boarded up the front of their homes — many of them reveling in the opportunity to have something to do. *Jane says her image changes all correspond honestly to specific phases of her life.*

"Isn't it cute," Jane bubbled, "how I've switched. Just to think, six years ago I was a radical leading the new war against the old war. And now I'm establishment, leading the old war against the new. Well, as long as there's a war to fight. Now that Tim and I oppose Jerry Brown I'll bet Bob Hope comes around to my side. Johnny Carson did."

Jane continued to gaze thoughtfully at the waves. She says she still dreams vividly about her U.F.O. contact. "I'm in awe. I still remember the message so clearly:

"The ecological niche inhabited by a gene-pool stimulates specific survival skills. Where you live determines how you behave and how your gene-pool evolves.

"Remember when your marine ancestors crawled out of the water? The new ecological niche — the shoreline — obviously activated improved survival tactics involving new and more complex brain circuitry. Different shoreline environments stimulated different neuro-technological skills. Up on land, mobility and communications systems are obviously determined by the climatic and geological con-

siderations of the pathways along which gene-pools evolve."

It was hard to concentrate on the words. Between Jane Wayne's voice and the crashing waves something kept sending me back. The All-American WASP voice. The pull is subliminal — into old movies and dreams, her reflections becoming mine.

"I remember, word-for-word what the signal said," she sighed. "There was the blinding light and the sounds in my head.

"Just recently, as the importance of geography in shaping human behavior has become clearer, human ethologists have begun to study the effects of migration upon neural development. The location of the large land-masses clearly has an effect in the evolution of human technology.

"Asians back East manifest survival techniques (especially in social organization and in the amount of power allowed the individual), which are different from Europeans. North Americans are a different species in their behavior from South Americans. How come?

"Wegner's theories of continental drift are correct. In the beginning there was one land-mass on the planet: Gonawanda. This one blob of extruded rock then started to split. Inertia from planet-spin, West to East, pulled the continents apart.

"Chart the emergence of civilization — i.e., the emergence of increasingly complex technology and social-communication systems. It is obvious that different continents were activated at different times in history. Asia, then Europe, then America."

Jane has recently taken to wearing her trendy

MERRILL M. KAGAN

Gravity is the Cause of all Suffering.

costumes for the film she is about to start, and has decided that her new character — a puritanical district attorney bent on destroying immorality — should have hair that looked as if it had just been dyed. It was thus an appropriate shade of new blue — Policewoman Blue. She smiled, "I'm your basic Sunday School enforcer, you know. Moral outrage is what matters, that's what makes people attractive. I learned that from my famous father. And from Tim, of course."

Jane feels that her encounter with the U.F.O. is a profound emotional experience. "Listen to this line from the script," she said, leaning forward intensely.

"The migration of human populations from Eastern to Western continents corresponds to the emergence of more evolved brain centers. Land-masses are literally platforms for emerging brain circuits.

"The migration of neuro-technology from continent to continent has closely paralleled the opening-up of new neural pathways. Establishment of population centers in Western areas has paralleled the emergency of high-more-frontal brain centers. The new migratory pathways, probing West, correspond to the direction of neural pathways up from the spinal column, to the mid-brain, to the limbic system, to the cortex, to the frontal cortex.

"The land masses of the planet earth serve as container-niches for newly emerging brain circuits. Geography from the evolutionary point of view, is literally topological neuro-anatomy."

One night a few weeks earlier, while millionaire Jane spoke to students at Queens College about the War Against Poverty, her Father Duke, Barbra Streisand, Anita Bryant, and some of the more powerful movie tycoons in the country, if not the world, were watching Jane's "new baby," a cathartic movie about Jane's Vietnam war that she's been working on for six years.

Coming Down is a film about a forgotten sensibility. Paraplegic sex. A highly wrought period-piece which, if it is a message film, is a state of the human message circa 1968. It opens during the first days after bedpans were invented, at a moment when men and women could still dream and when there were still raw nerves to hit.

Jane feels that even leaving out the wheelchair eroticism her new film is a profound emotional experience. Remember that scene when the Alien Intelligence, masquerading as a crippled war vet, raises up on his crutches and shouts:

"Your problem in understanding neuro-geography is this: at the present time neurologicians do not have a clear picture of the centers-and-pathways of the human nervous system. As they become more precise in locating brain functions then the correspondence with ecological-niche-containers will be more precise. At this time we can simply sketch in the obvious similarities between geography and brain circuit."

This transmission, remember, is taking place in the "cripples-ward" of a Veterans Administration Hospital. Battered victims, wall-to-wall.

And now I'm establishment, leading the old war against the new.

One big Black paraplegic puts down his pool-cue and asks that ancient, sullen, poignant question. "How can geeks like us even hope to sketch in these similarities between geography and brain-circuit? Is there any hope in the Red Chinese?"

"Vietnamese," Jane replied with a brisk smile. "MacLaine was China. I'm Vietnam. But anyway the U.F. O. message came in English. Here are the details."

1. The autonomic nervous system runs from China to the Middle-East.

The autonomic nervous system regulates involuntary action. This ancient brain includes the spinal cord, the medulla and pons which comprise the hindbrain; and the midbrain.

Historically we know that human civilization emerged in the Middle East around 4200 B.C. and for four thousand years was centered in cities stretching from China to the Middle East, flowing along trade-route-invasion pathways.

This region of the globe (like the spinal column) has always stressed involuntary behavior, discouraging and limiting individual-voluntary behavior.

2. The reptilian-mammalian nervous system (mid-brain) is located in the middle east.

The so-called reptile brain (R complex) is made up of circuits which surround the mid-brain and according to MacLean and Sagan "plays an important role in aggressive behavior, territoriality, ritual and the establishment of social hierarchies." Also surrounding the mid-brain is the limbic area which "appears to generate strong or particularly vivid emotions . . . and the beginnings of altruistic behavior."

Historically we know that the area just west of (i.e., above) Asia emerged as Dominant-Civilization around 300 B.C. This Mid-East region is still the center of territorial disputes, jealousies, revenges and passionate conflict among neighbors and social hierarchies.

The posterior cortex is located in Africa-Europe.

At this point in our charting of neuro-geography we consider two major fissurings of the global landmass. The Mediterranean Sea separates Africa from Europe. The Mediterranean corresponds to the longitudinal cerebral fissures — known as the median sagittal groove — which divides the cortex into the left and right brains. The left cortex mediates the right side of the body. Thus the left cortex is Europe and the right cortex is Africa. The two neuro-geographical hemispheres are linked at Gibraltar.

Moral outrage is what matters, that's what makes people attractive.

The second obvious fissuring of the global landmass is the separation of the forward parts of Africa and Europe — which, floating across the enormous sulcus called the Atlantic Ocean, created two large lobes of land, neurotechnically quiescent but ready for future innervation. (Innervation means to supply a bodily part with nerves.)

The European right-hand mediates rational, logical, mathematical, linear, disciplined behavior. The African left-hand mediates intuitive, non-linear, patterned-rhythmic behavior.

The left cortex is involved in manufacture of artifacts. The right cortex is involved in neuro-somatic behavior.

The left cortex is scientific. The right cortex is magic.

The left cortex is Europe; the right is Africa.

To understand more precisely the evolutionary stage of the European reality it is useful to contrast it with the next stage — the pre-frontal American Mutation.

4. **North and South America are containers for the neo-cortex — the emerging frontal lobes of the brain.**

The frontal lobes of the cortex are the most recent additions to the neuro-anatomical structure. Embryologically we know that the old cortex has developed and split into hemispheres by the fourth month of pregnancy. But the overarching, forward pushing frontal lobes only emerge just before birth.

"Just before birth. That's us right now in California. Isn't that exciting!" said Jane.

By this time Jane was scrunched down in an old easy chair so that her chin rested on her chest. Her eyes were gone in some sort of adrenalin trance.

A big wood stove was beginning to warm up the bungalow which is comfortably cluttered with old furniture, cactus plants, toys and some old lamps. A few primitive paintings of Henry Wallace, Estes Kevaufer, Gene McCarthy, Ho Chi Minh, Alger Hiss, John L. Lewis, Jesse Unruh, and Sen. McGovern hung on the wall. Tim put on a Jackson Browne album and started to count ballots.

"Jane," I said, "you start a new movie in three days about the Scottsboro Seven. Aren't you going to pace the floor with a script in your hand and memorize lines?"

She started to laugh. "Movies aren't like that." Then within a logical, law-school soliloquy she attempted to demystify her profession.

"Gross points," she said simply.

I couldn't accept that. I tried to argue but she shrugged it off. I looked at Tim who was smiling at my disbelief. "It's weird, isn't it?" he said. He went back to reading *Business Week*.

Jane admits that she wanted to show she could be funny and pretty again. Now we're getting somewhere, I said to myself. This is why Jann Wenner sent me to Malibu. Confrontation journalism is not dead in the pages of *Rolling Stones*. Leaning forward intensely, I asked the $48,000 question: "Jane, exactly what functions are added when the frontal lobes are activated?"

Jane moved her arms above her head and stretched, "That's exactly the question I asked Roger Vadim or was it Sagan. Well, no matter, I do recall the answer.

"For many decades the prevailing view of neuro-physiologists was that the frontal lobes, behind the forehead, are the sites of anticipation and planning for the future. But more recent work has shown that the situation is not so simple. A large number of cases of frontal lesions . . . have been investigated by Hans-Lukas Teuber of the Massachusetts Institute of Technology. He found that many frontal lobe lesions have almost no obvious effects on behavior; however, in severe pathology of the frontal lobes 'the patient is not altogether devoid of the capacity to anticipate a course of events, but cannot picture himself in relation to those events as a *potential agent.*'

"Here we have two items of neuro-geographic correspondence: 1. The newest lobe of the cortex apparently involves seeing oneself as 'a potential agent.' 2. The most recent ecological niche for the human species, the so-called 'New World,' was activated after 1492.

"To West America, i.e., the left-lobe-right-hand of the neuro-map, came floods of self-selected gene-pools. The basic characteristic of the American-consciousness is that it is 'future-oriented.' North America was settled by gene-pools self-selected for future reality fabrication, for self reliant independence. Old-World visitors have always been amazed at the American trust in progress, the optimism and sense of individual-identity.

"Neuro-geographical location determines the stage of neuro-evolution. If one could voyage around the brain one would find that where one *was* determined what was being done and thought. If you are in the mid-brain you expect everyone to be running around concerned with mid-brain functions: territoriality, Arab-Zionist mammalian competition. When you go to the Mid-East you expect people to be involved in mid-brain functions — and they are.

"When you trip South to the African cortex you expect non-logical, intuitive, magical thinking. And that's the way it is. When you climb up to the left-frontal lobe you expect to find concern with the future. And that's what's happening in America."

MIKE TIGHE

TUCSON LECTURE

WHERE DO WE GO FROM HERE?

So here is the up-to-date situation. Liberation of the body is now a Dom-Species convention. A sizable Pre-Dom elite is learning how to use their brains. This is neurogenetic progress. Self-actualization of body and brain are basic tools for creating Future Plan-Its. Post-terrestrial futures can only be fabricated by women and men who have pride in their bodies, who understand how to use and direct their bodies precisely, and who can fuse their aesthetics in exquisite love linkages with others.

Nor can we move confidently into the future unless we are guided by women and men who understand that we can control and change our own realities by the responsible, self-actualized use of our brains.

I am going to stop now to give your minds and bodies a chance to stretch. Then we shall present a slide show to illustrate some options for future H.O.M.E. Plan-Its. Then I shall return and talk to you about the future. And, if you are willing, I would like to perform here in Tucson, Arizona, some mutational experiments.

I have arranged to have electromagnetic signals put on tape — designed to bring about irreversible changes in your brains. When the Mutation Time comes, those who don't want to be mutated can leave. Or you can put your hands over your ears.

> ## When the Mutation Time comes, those who don't want to be mutated can leave.

Now I close the first broadcast with a rhetorical question: Has the DNA code labored (or played) for 2½ billion years to produce as final product, *you*, the second post-Hiroshima generation, suntanned, languorous, post-political, sophisticated, laid back, affluent, polymorphous orgasm, self-actualized, sensory consumers? *(Laughter and Applause)*

I am glad you have arrived at this state of Intelligent self-control and Responsible self-expression, but I know that you want your evolution to continue. In the second stage of this program we shall learn how to S.M.I².L.E. We shall consider three ideas which, ready or not, like it or not, will determine the future of every gene-pool on the planet.

SPACE MIGRATION

INTELLIGENCE INCREASE

LIFE EXTENSION.

GENETIC HALL OF FAME

Brian Barritt

Reprinted from SAN FRANCISCO CHRONICLE, *July 14 (Bastille Day)*

Writers Petition Swiss To Give Asylum To Leary

by Donovan Bess

Twenty-five prominent writers yesterday filed a petition with the Swiss government asking that it give asylum to Timothy Leary as a "literary refugee persecuted for his thoughts and writings" by United States authorities.

The writers — most of whom live in the Bay Area — include Allen Ginsberg, Herbert Gold, Laura Huxley, Anais Nin, Lawrence Ferlinghetti, Robert Creeley, Alan Watts, Howard Becker, Kenneth Rexroth, Michael McClure and Ken Kesey.

The eight-page petition was delivered to the Swiss consulate here yesterday. Copies also were delivered to the U.S. Departments of Justice and State in Washington.

In New York City last night, playwright Arthur Miller and other literary leaders sent a cable to the Swiss Ministry of Justice in Zurich urging that Leary be given asylum "as an act of compassion."

The 51-year-old proponent of marijuana and psychedelic drugs fled overseas after escaping from a California prison and is being held without charges in Switzerland awaiting extradition requested by the California Department of Corrections.

Early last year Leary was sentenced to prison after an Orange county jury found him guilty of possession of a half ounce of marijuana.

The writers' petition cites the fact that the judge in this case, Byron K. McMillan, denied bail to the onetime Harvard psychology professor after describing him as "an insidious and detrimental influence on society" and "a pleasure-seeking, irresponsible Madison Avenue advocate of the free use of LSD and marijuana."

The writers argued that Leary has been prosecuted for an underlying motive, "namely, essays and speeches on drug usage theory."

Government plans to put him back in prison, the petition argues, rise "merely from differences of opinion on public philosophy involving drug use, a scientific matter now being debated in professional circles."

"At stake in the case," says the petition, "...is Dr. Leary's freedom to manifest his thoughts in the form of poems, psychological commentaries, dialogues, and essays of a literary nature..."

The other persons who signed the petition were Ted Berrigan, Margo Patterson Doss, Dr. John Doss, Lewis MacAdams, Paul Krassner, Lenore Kandel, Diane di Prima, Philip Lamantia, Don Allen, Michael Aldrich, Jan Herman, Andrew Hoyem, Phillip Whalen and Gavin Arthur.

The cable to Zurich last night from New York was sent on behalf of the 100 American members of the International P.E.N. (Poets, Essayists, Novelists) Club. It was signed by the president of its American chapter, Thomas Fleming, by Miller, a former chapter president, and by David Dempsey, a member of the P.E.N. board.

"As American writers we are disturbed at the way Dr. Leary's writings have been cited as evidence in his trial," the cable said. It pleaded with the Swiss to give the psychologist the kind of sanctuary accorded in the past to various victims of persecution.

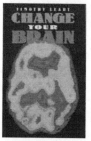